Export-Import and Logistics Management

Export-Import and Logistics Management

Charlie Hill

RANDOM PUBLICATIONS

NEW DELHI - 110 002 (INDIA)

Export-Import and Logistics Management

ISBN 978-93-51113-03-4

Published in 2014 in India by

RANDOM PUBLICATIONS

4376-A/4B, Gali Murari Lal, Ansari Road
New Delhi-110 002
Phone: +9111-43580356, 23289044
E-mail: randomexports@gmail.com; sales@randompublications.com; info@randompublications.com

Type Setting by: Friends Media, Delhi-110089
Printed at Thomson Press (India) Ltd

Preface

The term export means shipping the goods and services out of the port of a country. The seller of such goods and services is referred to as an "exporter" who is based in the country of export whereas the overseas based buyer is referred to as an "importer". In International Trade, "exports" refers to selling goods and services produced in the home country to other markets. Export of commercial quantities of goods normally requires involvement of the customs authorities in both the country of export and the country of import. The advent of small trades over the internet such as through Amazon and eBay have largely bypassed the involvement of Customs in many countries because of the low individual values of these trades. Nonetheless, these small exports are still subject to legal restrictions applied by the country of export. An export's counterpart is an import. The theory of international trade and commercial policy is one of the oldest branches of economic thought. Exporting is a major component of international trade, and the macroeconomic risks and benefits of exporting are regularly discussed and disputed by economists and others. Two views concerning international trade present different perspectives. The first recognizes the benefits of international trade. The second concerns itself with the possibly that certain domestic industries (or labourers, or culture) could be harmed by foreign competition.

An import is a good brought into a jurisdiction, especially across a national border, from an external source. The purchaser of the exotic good is called an importer. An import in the receiving country is an export from the sending country. Importation and exportation are the defining financial transactions of international trade. Direct-import refers to a type of business importation involving a major retailer (e.g. Wal-Mart) and an overseas manufacturer. A retailer typically purchases products designed by local companies that can be manufactured overseas. In a direct-import program, the retailer bypasses the local supplier (colloquial middle-man) and buys the final product directly from the manufacturer, possibly saving in added cost data on the value of imports and their quantities often broken down by detailed lists of products are available in statistical collections on international trade published by the statistical services of intergovernmental organisations, supranational statistical institutes and national statistical institutes. Industrial and consumer goods.

This book gives attention to the knowledge, skills and insight needed to manage imports and exports either in a comprehensive trading company or in a department of a company that depends on sourcing or exporting to achieve its strategic objectives.

I thank all members of my team who have helped in the preparation of the book. My special thanks go to "Random Publications" who have published the book.

—Charlie Hill

Contents

1

Export Management

The term *export* means shipping the goods and services out of the port of a country. The seller of such goods and services is referred to as an "exporter" who is based in the country of export whereas the overseas based buyer is referred to as an "importer". In International Trade, "exports" refers to selling goods and services produced in the home country to other markets.

Export of commercial quantities of goods normally requires involvement of the customs authorities in both the country of export and the country of import. The advent of small trades over the internet such as through Amazon and eBay have largely bypassed the involvement of Customs in many countries because of the low individual values of these trades. Nonetheless, these small exports are still subject to legal restrictions applied by the country of export. An export's counterpart is an import.

Definition

"Foreign demand for goods produced by home country"

In national accounts "exports" consist of transactions in goods and services (sales, barter, gifts or grants) from residents to non-residents. The exact definition of exports includes and excludes specific "borderline" cases. A general delimitation of exports in national accounts is given below:

- An export of a good occurs when there is a change of ownership from a resident to a non-resident; this does not necessarily imply that the good in question physically crosses the frontier. However, in specific cases national accounts impute changes of ownership even though in legal terms no change of ownership takes place (e.g. *cross border financial leasing, cross border deliveries between affiliates of the same enterprise, goods crossing the border for significant processing to order or repair*). Also smuggled goods must be included in the export measurement.

- Export of services consist of all services rendered by residents to non-residents. In national accounts any direct purchases by non-residents in the economic territory of a country are recorded as exports of services; therefore all expenditure by foreign tourists in the economic territory of a country is considered as part of the exports of services of that country. Also international flows of illegal services must be included.

National accountants often need to make adjustments to the basic trade data in order to comply with national accounts concepts; the concepts for basic trade statistics often differ in terms of definition and coverage from the requirements in the national accounts:

- Data on international trade in goods are mostly obtained through declarations to custom services. If a country applies the general trade system, all goods entering or leaving the country are recorded. If the special trade system (e.g. extra-EU trade statistics) is applied goods which are received into customs warehouses are not recorded in external trade statistics unless they subsequently go into free circulation in the country of receipt.
- A special case is the intra-EU trade statistics. Since goods move freely between the member states of the EU without customs controls, statistics on trade in goods between the member states must be obtained through surveys. To reduce the statistical burden on the respondents small scale traders are excluded from the reporting obligation.
- Statistical recording of trade in services is based on declarations by banks to their central banks or by surveys of the main operators. In a globalized economy where services can be rendered via electronic means (*e.g. internet*) the related international flows of services are difficult to identify.
- Basic statistics on international trade normally do not record smuggled goods or international flows of illegal services. A small fraction of the smuggled goods and illegal services may nevertheless be included in official trade statistics through dummy shipments or dummy declarations that serve to conceal the illegal nature of the activities.

History

The theory of international trade and commercial policy is one of the oldest branches of economic thought. Exporting is a major component of international trade, and the macroeconomic risks and benefits of exporting are regularly discussed and disputed by economists and others. Two views concerning international trade present different perspectives. The first recognizes the benefits of international trade. The second concerns itself with the possibly that certain domestic industries (or labourers, or culture) could be harmed by foreign competition.

Process

Methods of export include a product or good or information being mailed, hand-delivered, shipped by air, shipped by vessel, uploaded to an internet site, or downloaded from an internet site. Exports also include the distribution of information that can be sent in the form of an email, an email attachment, a fax or can be shared during a telephone conversation.

National Regulations

United States: The export of defence-related articles and services on the United States Munitions List (USML) is governed by the Department of State under the International Traffic in Arms Regulations (ITAR).

The Bureau of Industry and Security (BIS) is responsible for implementing and enforcing the Code of Federal Regulations Title 15 chapter VII, subchapter C, also known as *Export Administration Regulations* (EAR), in the United States. The BIS regulates the export and reexport of most commercial items. Some commodities require a license in order to export. There are different requirements to export lawfully depending on the product or service being exported.

Depending on the category the 'item' falls under, the company may need to obtain a license prior to exporting. EAR restrictions can vary from country to country. The most restricted destinations are countries under economic embargoes or designated as supporting terrorist activities, including Cuba, North Korea, Sudan, Syria and Iran. Some products have received worldwide restrictions prohibiting exports.

An item is considered an export whether or not it is leaving the United States temporarily, if it is leaving the United State but is not for sale (a gift), or if it is going to a wholly owned U.S. subsidiary in a foreign country. A foreign-origin item exported from the United States, transmitted or transhipped through the United States, or being returned from the United States to its foreign country of origin is considered an export..

Barriers

Trade barriers are generally defined as government laws, regulations, policy, or practices that either protect domestic products from foreign competition or artificially stimulate exports of particular domestic products. While restrictive business practices sometimes have a similar effect, they are not usually regarded as trade barriers. The most common foreign trade barriers are government-imposed measures and policies that restrict, prevent, or impede the international exchange of goods and services. Most trade barriers work on the same principle: the imposition of some sort of cost on trade that raises the price of the traded products. If two or more nations repeatedly use trade barriers against each other, then a trade war results.

Economists generally agree that trade barriers are detrimental and decrease overall economic efficiency, this can be explained by the theory of comparative advantage. In theory, free trade involves the removal of all such barriers, except perhaps those considered necessary for health or national security. In practice, however, even those countries promoting free trade heavily subsidize certain industries, such as agriculture and steel.

Trade barriers are often criticized for the effect they have on the developing world. Because rich-country players call most of the shots and set trade policies, goods such as crops that developing countries are best at producing still face high barriers. Trade barriers such as taxes on food imports or subsidies for farmers in developed economies lead to overproduction and dumping on world markets, thus lowering prices and hurting poor-country farmers. Tariffs also tend to be anti-poor, with low rates for raw commodities and high rates for labour-intensive processed goods. The Commitment to Development Index measures the effect that rich country trade policies actually have on the developing world.

The barriers can take many forms, including the following:

Tariffs

A tariff is either (1) a tax on imports or exports (an international trade tariff), or (2) a list of prices for such things as rail service, bus routes, and electrical usage (electrical tariff, etc.). The meaning in (1) is now the more common meaning. The meaning in (2) is historically earlier. The meaning in (1) developed from a tabular list of tax rates for different import goods.

A tariff is a tax placed on a specific good or set of goods exported from or imported to a country, creating an economic barrier to trade. Usually the tactic is used when a country's domestic output of the good is falling and imports from foreign competitors are rising, particularly if there exist strategic reasons for retaining a domestic production capability. Some failing industries receive a protection with an effect similar to a subsidies in that by placing the tariff on the industry, the industry is less enticed to produce goods in a quicker, cheaper, and more productive fashion. The third reason for a tariff involves addressing the issue of dumping. Dumping involves a country producing highly excessive amounts of goods and *dumping* the goods on another foreign country, producing the effect of prices that are "too low". Too low can refer to either pricing the good from the foreign market at a price lower than charged in the domestic market of the country of origin. The other reference to dumping relates or refers to the producer selling the product at a price in which there is no profit or a loss. The purpose (and expected outcome) of the tariff is to encourage spending on domestic goods and services.

Protective tariffs sometimes protect what are known as infant industries that are in the phase of expansive growth. A tariff is used temporarily to allow the industry to succeed in spite of strong competition. Protective tariffs are considered valid if the resources are more productive in their new use than they would be if the industry had not been started. The infant industry eventually must incorporate itself into a market without the protection of government subsidies.

Tariffs can create tension between countries. Examples include the United States steel tariff of 2002 and when China placed a 14% tariff on imported auto parts. Such tariffs usually lead to filing a complaint with the World Trade Organization (WTO) and, if that fails, could eventually head toward the country placing a tariff against the other nation in spite, to impress pressure to remove the tariff.

Non-tariff Barriers to Trade

Non-tariff barriers to trade (NTBs) are trade barriers that restrict imports but are not in the usual form of a tariff. Some common examples of NTB's are anti-dumping measures and countervailing duties, which, although called non-tariff barriers, have the effect of tariffs once they are enacted.

Their use has risen sharply after the WTO rules led to a very significant reduction in tariff use. Some non-tariff trade barriers are expressly permitted in very limited circumstances, when they are deemed necessary to protect health, safety, sanitation, or depletable natural resources. In other forms, they are criticized as a means to evade free trade rules such as those of the World Trade Organization (WTO), the European Union (EU), or North American Free Trade Agreement (NAFTA) that restrict the use of tariffs.

Some of non-tariff barriers are not directly related to foreign economic regulations but nevertheless have a significant impact on foreign-economic activity and foreign trade between countries.

Trade between countries is referred to trade in goods, services and factors of production. Non-tariff barriers to trade include import quotas, special licenses, unreasonable standards for the quality of goods, bureaucratic delays at customs, export restrictions, limiting the activities of state trading, export subsidies, countervailing duties, technical barriers to trade, sanitary and phyto-sanitary measures, rules of origin, etc. Sometimes in this list they include macroeconomic measures affecting trade.

Six Types of Non-Tariff Barriers to Trade

- Specific Limitations on Trade:
  - Import Licensing requirements
  - Proportion restrictions of foreign to domestic goods (local content requirements)
  - Minimum import price limits
  - Free
  - Embargoes
- Customs and Administrative Entry Procedures:
  - Valuation systems
  - Anti-dumping practices
  - Tariff classifications
  - Documentation requirements
  - Fees
- Standards:
  - Standard disparities
  - Intergovernmental acceptances of testing methods and standards

- — Packaging, labelling, and marking
- — Government Participation in Trade:

- Government procurement policies
- Export subsidies
- Countervailing duties
- Domestic assistance programmes
- Charges on imports:
- Prior import deposit subsidies
- Administrative fees
- Special supplementary duties
- Import credit discrimination
- Variable levies
- Border taxes
- Others:
- Voluntary export restraints
- Orderly marketing agreements

Examples of Non-Tariff Barriers to Trade

Non-tariff barriers to trade can be the following:

- Import bans
- General or product-specific quotas
- Rules of Origin
- Quality conditions imposed by the importing country on the exporting countries
- Sanitary and phytosanitary conditions
- Packaging conditions
- Labelling conditions
- Product standards
- Complex regulatory environment
- Determination of eligibility of an exporting country by the importing country
- Determination of eligibility of an exporting establishment (firm, company) by the importing country.
- Additional trade documents like Certificate of Origin, Certificate of Authenticity etc.

- Occupational safety and health regulation
- Employment law
- Import licenses
- State subsidies, procurement, trading, state ownership
- Export subsidies
- Fixation of a minimum import price
- Product classification
- Quota shares
- Foreign exchange market controls and multiplicity
- Inadequate infrastructure
- "Buy national" policy
- Over-valued currency
- Intellectual property laws (patents, copyrights)
- Restrictive licenses
- Seasonal import regimes
- Corrupt and/or lengthy customs procedures

Types of Non-Tariff Barriers

There are several different variants of division of non-tariff barriers. Some scholars divide between internal taxes, administrative barriers, health and sanitary regulations and government procurement policies. Others divide non-tariff barriers into more categories such as specific limitations on trade, customs and administrative entry procedures, standards, government participation in trade, charges on import, and other categories.

The first category includes methods to directly import restrictions for protection of certain sectors of national industries: licensing and allocation of import quotas, antidumping and countervailing duties, import deposits, so-called voluntary export restraints, countervailing duties, the system of minimum import prices, etc. Under second category follow methods that are not directly aimed at restricting foreign trade and more related to the administrative bureaucracy, whose actions, however, restrict trade, for example: customs procedures, technical standards and norms, sanitary and veterinary standards, requirements for labelling and packaging, bottling, etc. The third category consists of methods that are not directly aimed at restricting the import or promoting the export, but the effects of which often lead to this result.

The non-tariff barriers can include wide variety of restrictions to trade. Here are some example of the popular NTBs.

Licenses

The most common instruments of direct regulation of imports (and sometimes export) are licenses and quotas. Almost all industrialized countries apply these non-tariff methods. The license system requires that a state (through specially authorized office) issues permits for foreign trade transactions of import and export commodities included in the lists of licensed merchandises. Product licensing can take many forms and procedures. The main types of licenses are general license that permits unrestricted importation or exportation of goods included in the lists for a certain period of time; and one-time license for a certain product importer (exporter) to import (or export). One-time license indicates a quantity of goods, its cost, its country of origin (or destination), and in some cases also customs point through which import (or export) of goods should be carried out. The use of licensing systems as an instrument for foreign trade regulation is based on a number of international level standards agreements. In particular, these agreements include some provisions of the General Agreement on Tariffs and Trade and the Agreement on Import Licensing Procedures, concluded under the GATT (GATT).

Quotas

Licensing of foreign trade is closely related to quantitative restrictions – quotas - on imports and exports of certain goods. A quota is a limitation in value or in physical terms, imposed on import and export of certain goods for a certain period of time. This category includes global quotas in respect to specific countries, seasonal quotas, and so-called "voluntary" export restraints. Quantitative controls on foreign trade transactions carried out through one-time license.

Quantitative restriction on imports and exports is a direct administrative form of government regulation of foreign trade. Licenses and quotas limit the independence of enterprises with a regard to entering foreign markets, narrowing the range of countries, which may be entered into transaction for certain commodities, regulate the number and range of goods permitted for import and export. However, the system of licensing and quota imports and exports, establishing firm control over foreign trade in certain goods, in many cases turns out to be more flexible and effective than economic instruments of foreign trade regulation. This can be explained by the fact, that licensing and quota systems are an important instrument of trade regulation of the vast majority of the world. The consequence of this trade barrier is normally reflected in the consumers' loss because of higher prices and limited selection of goods as well as in the companies that employ the imported materials in the production process, increasing their costs. An import quota can be unilateral, levied by the country without negotiations with exporting country, and bilateral or multilateral, when it is imposed after negotiations and agreement with exporting country. An export quota is a restricted amount of goods that can leave the country. There are different reasons for imposing of export quota by the country, which can be the guarantee of the supply of the products that are in shortage in the domestic market, manipulation of the prices on the international level, and the control of goods strategically important for the country. In some cases, the importing countries request exporting countries to impose voluntary export restraints.

Agreement on a "Voluntary" Export Restraint

In the past decade, a widespread practice of concluding agreements on the "voluntary" export restrictions and the establishment of import minimum prices imposed by leading Western nations upon weaker in economical or political sense exporters. The specifics of these types of restrictions is the establishment of unconventional techniques when the trade barriers of importing country, are introduced at the border of the exporting and not importing country. Thus, the agreement on "voluntary" export restraints is imposed on the exporter under the threat of sanctions to limit the export of certain goods in the importing country. Similarly, the establishment of minimum import prices should be strictly observed by the exporting firms in contracts with the importers of the country that has set such prices. In the case of reduction of export prices below the minimum level, the importing country imposes anti-dumping duty, which could lead to withdrawal from the market. "Voluntary" export agreements affect trade in textiles, footwear, dairy products, consumer electronics, cars, machine tools, etc.

Problems arise when the quotas are distributed between countries because it is necessary to ensure that products from one country are not diverted in violation of quotas set out in second country. Import quotas are not necessarily designed to protect domestic producers. For example, Japan, maintains quotas on many agricultural products it does not produce. Quotas on imports is a leverage when negotiating the sales of Japanese exports, as well as avoiding excessive dependence on any other country in respect of necessary food, supplies of which may decrease in case of bad weather or political conditions.

Export quotas can be set in order to provide domestic consumers with sufficient stocks of goods at low prices, to prevent the depletion of natural resources, as well as to increase export prices by restricting supply to foreign markets. Such restrictions (through agreements on various types of goods) allow producing countries to use quotas for such commodities as coffee and oil; as the result, prices for these products increased in importing countries.

A quota can be a tariff rate quota, global quota, discriminating quota, and export quota.

Standards

Standards take a special place among non-tariff barriers. Countries usually impose standards on classification, labelling and testing of products in order to be able to sell domestic products, but also to block sales of products of foreign manufacture. These standards are sometimes entered under the pretext of protecting the safety and health of local populations.

Administrative and Bureaucratic Delays at the Entrance

Among the methods of non-tariff regulation should be mentioned administrative and bureaucratic delays at the entrance, which increase uncertainty and the cost of maintaining inventory.

Import Deposits

Another example of foreign trade regulations is import deposits. Import deposits is a form of deposit, which the importer must pay the bank for a definite period of time (non-interest bearing deposit) in an amount equal to all or part of the cost of imported goods.

At the national level, administrative regulation of capital movements is carried out mainly within a framework of bilateral agreements, which include a clear definition of the legal regime, the procedure for the admission of investments and investors. It is determined by mode (fair and equitable, national, most-favoured-nation), order of nationalization and compensation, transfer profits and capital repatriation and dispute resolution.

Foreign Exchange Restrictions and Foreign Exchange Controls

Foreign exchange restrictions and foreign exchange controls occupy a special place among the non-tariff regulatory instruments of foreign economic activity. Foreign exchange restrictions constitute the regulation of transactions of residents and nonresidents with currency and other currency values. Also an important part of the mechanism of control of foreign economic activity is the establishment of the national currency against foreign currencies.

The Transition from Tariffs to Non-tariff Barriers

One of the reasons why industrialized countries have moved from tariffs to NTBs is the fact that developed countries have sources of income other than tariffs. Historically, in the formation of nation-states, governments had to get funding. They received it through the introduction of tariffs. This explains the fact that most developing countries still rely on tariffs as a way to finance their spending. Developed countries can afford not to depend on tariffs, at the same time developing NTBs as a possible way of international trade regulation. The second reason for the transition to NTBs is that these tariffs can be used to support weak industries or compensation of industries, which have been affected negatively by the reduction of tariffs. The third reason for the popularity of NTBs is the ability of interest groups to influence the process in the absence of opportunities to obtain government support for the tariffs.

Non-tariff Barriers Today

With the exception of export subsidies and quotas, NTBs are most similar to the tariffs. Tariffs for goods production were reduced during the eight rounds of negotiations in the WTO and the General Agreement on Tariffs and Trade (GATT). After lowering of tariffs, the principle of protectionism demanded the introduction of new NTBs such as technical barriers to trade (TBT). According to statements made at United Nations Conference on Trade and Development (UNCTAD, 2005), the use of NTBs, based on the amount and control of price levels has decreased significantly from 45% in 1994 to 15% in 2004, while use of other NTBs increased from 55% in 1994 to 85% in 2004.

Increasing consumer demand for safe and environment friendly products also have had their impact on increasing popularity of TBT. Many NTBs are governed by WTO agreements, which originated in the Uruguay Round (the TBT Agreement, SPS Measures Agreement, the Agreement on Textiles and Clothing), as well as GATT articles. NTBs in the field of services have become as important as in the field of usual trade.

Most of the NTB can be defined as protectionist measures, unless they are related to difficulties in the market, such as externalities and information asymmetries between consumers and producers of goods. An example of this is safety standards and labelling requirements.

The need to protect sensitive to import industries, as well as a wide range of trade restrictions, available to the governments of industrialized countries, forcing them to resort to use the NTB, and putting serious obstacles to international trade and world economic growth. Thus, NTBs can be referred as a new of protection which has replaced tariffs as an old form of protection.

Strategic

International agreements limit trade in, and the transfer of, certain types of goods and information e.g. goods associated with weapons of mass destruction, advanced telecommunications, arms and torture, and also some art and archaeological artefacts. Examples include Nuclear Suppliers Group - limiting trade in nuclear weapons and associated goods (currently only 45 countries participate), The Australia Group - limiting trade in chemical & biological weapons and associated goods (currently only 39 countries), Missile Technology Control Regime - limiting trade in the means of delivering weapons of mass destruction (currently only 34 countries) and The Wassenaar Arrangement - limiting trade in conventional arms and technological developments (currently only 40 countries).

Economic Analysis

Neoclassical economic theorists tend to view tariffs as distortions to the free market. Typical analyses find that tariffs tend to benefit domestic producers and government at the expense of consumers, and that the net welfare effects of a tariff on the importing country are negative. Normative judgements often follow from these findings, namely that it may be disadvantageous for a country to artificially shield an industry from world markets and that it might be better to allow a collapse to take place. Opposition to all tariff Organization aims to reduce tariffs and to avoid countries discriminating between differing countries when applying tariffs.

When incorporating free international trade into the model we use a supply curve denoted as Pw. This curve makes the assumption that the international supply of the good or service is perfectly elastic and that the world can produce at a near infinite q S amount of the good, but had a demand of D. The difference between S and D, SD was filled by importing from abroad. After the imposition of tariff, domestic price rises from Pw to Pt but foreign export prices fall from Pw to Pt* due to the difference in tax incidence on the consumers (at home) and producers (abroad).

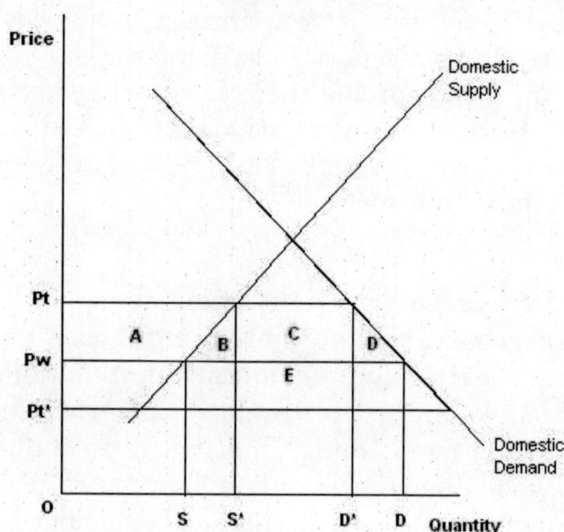

Figure: *The diagram to the right shows the costs and benefits of imposing a tariff on a good in the domestic economy, Home.*

At the new price level at Home, Pt, which is higher than the previous Pw, more of the good is produced at Home – it now makes S* of the good. Due to the higher price, only D* of the good is demanded by Home. The difference between S* and D*, StD* is filled by importing from abroad. Thus, imposition of tariffs reduce the quantity of imports from SD to S*D*.

Domestic producers enjoy a gain in their surplus. Producer surplus, defined as the difference between what the producers were willing to receive by selling a good and the actual price of the good, expands from the region below Pw to the region below Pt. Therefore, the domestic producers gain an amount shown by the area A.

Domestic consumers face a higher price, reducing their welfare. Consumer surplus is the area between the price line and the demand curve. Therefore, the consumer surplus shrinks from the area above Pw to the area above Pt, i.e. it shrinks by the areas A, B, C and D.

The government gains from the taxes. It charges an amount PtPt* of tariff for every good imported. Since S*D* goods are imported, the government gains an area of C and E.

The net loss to the society due to the tariff would be given by the total costs of the tariff minus its benefits to the society. Therefore, the net welfare loss due to the tariff is equal to:

Consumer Loss – Government revenue – Producer gain or graphically, this gain is given by the areas shown by:

$$(A + B + C + D) - (C + E) - A$$
$$= B + D - E$$

that is, tariffs are beneficial to the society if the area given by the rectangle E more than offsets the losses shown by triangles B and D. Rectangle E is called the terms of trade gain whereas the two triangles B and D are also called efficiency loss, as this cost is incurred because tariffs reduce the incentives for the society to consume and produce.

The model above is completely accurate only in the extreme case where no consumer belongs to the producers group and the cost of the product is a fraction of their wages. If instead, the opposite extreme is taken by assuming that all consumers come from the producers' group and that their only purchasing power comes from the wages earned in production and the product costs their whole wage, the graph looks radically different. Without tariffs, only those producers/consumers able to produce the product at the world price will have the money to purchase it at that price.

Political Analysis

The tariff has been used as a political tool to establish an independent nation; for example, the United States Tariff Act of 1789, signed specifically on July 4, was called the "Second Declaration of Independence" by newspapers because it was intended to be the economic means to achieve the political goal of a sovereign and independent United States.

In modern times, the political impact of tariffs has been seen in a positive and negative sense. The 2002 United States steel tariff imposed a 30% tariff on a variety of imported steel products for a period of three years. American steel producers supported the tariff, but the move was criticised by the Cato Institute.

Tariffs can occasionally emerge as a political issue prior to an election. In the leadup to the 2007 Australian Federal election, the Australian Labour Party announced it would undertake a review of Australian car tariffs if elected. The Liberal Party made a similar commitment, while independent candidate Nick Xenophon announced his intention to introduce tariff-based legislation as "a matter of urgency".

Unpopular tariffs are known to have ignited social unrest. Example of this are the 1905 Meat riots in Chile that evolved from protests against tariffs applied to the cattle imports from Argentina.

Tariffs Within Technology Strategies

When tariffs are an integral element of a country's technology strategy, the tariffs can be highly effective in helping to increase and maintain the country's economic health. As an integral part of the technology strategy, tariffs are effective in supporting the technology strategy's function of enabling the country to outmaneuver the competition in the acquisition and utilization of technology in order to produce products and provide services that excel at satisfying the customer needs for a competitive advantage in domestic and foreign markets.

In contrast, in economic theory tariffs are viewed as a primary element in international trade with the function of the tariff being to influence the flow of trade by lowering or raising the price of targeted goods to create what amounts to an artificial competitive advantage. When tariffs are viewed and used in this fashion, they are addressing the country's and the competitors' respective economic healths in terms of maximizing or minimizing revenue flow rather than in terms of the ability to generate and maintain a competitive advantage which is the source of the revenue. As a result, the impact of the tariffs on the economic health of the country are at best minimal but often are counter-productive.

A programme within the US intelligence community, Project Socrates, that was tasked with addressing America's declining economic competitiveness, determined that countries like China and India were using tariffs as an integral element of their respective technology strategies to rapidly build their countries into economic superpowers. It was also determined that the US, in its early years, had also used tariffs as an integral part of amounted to technology strategies to transform the country into a superpower.

Subsidies

To subsidize an industry or company refers to, in this instance, a governmental providing supplemental financial support to manipulate the price below market value. Subsidies are generally used for failing industries that need a boost in domestic spending. Subsidizing encourages greater demand for a good or service because of the slashed price. The effect of subsidies deters other countries that are able to produce a specific product or service at a faster, cheaper, and more productive rate. With the lowered price, these efficient producers cannot compete. The life of a subsidy is generally short-lived, but sometimes can be implemented on a more permanent basis.

The agricultural industry is commonly subsidized, both in the United States, and in other countries including Japan and nations located in the European Union (EU).

Critics argue such subsidies cost developing nations $24 billion annually in lost income according to a study by the International Food Policy Research Institute, a D.C. group funded partly by the World Bank. However, other nations are not the only economic 'losers'. Subsidies in the U.S. heavily depend upon taxpayer dollars. In 2000, the U.S. spent an all-time record $32.3 billion for the agricultural industry. The EU spends about $50 billion annually, nearly half its annual budget on its common agricultural policy and rural development.

Exports and Free Trade

The theory of comparative advantage materialized during the first quarter of the 19th century in the writings of 'classical economists'. While David Ricardo is most credited with the development of the theory (in Chapter 7 of his *Principles of Political Economy*, 1817), James Mill and Robert Torrens produced similar ideas. The theory states that all parties maximize benefit in an environment of unrestricted trade, even if absolute advantages in production exist between the parties.

In contrast to Mercantilism, the first systematic body of thought devoted to international trade, emerged during the 17th and 18th centuries in Europe. While most views surfacing from this school of thought differed, a commonly argued key objective of trade was to promote a *"favourable" balance of trade*, referring to a time when the value of domestic goods exported exceeds the value of foreign goods imported.

The "favourable" balance in turn created a *balance of trade surplus*. Mercantilists advocated that government policy directly arrange the flow of commerce to conform to their beliefs. They sought a highly interventionist agenda, using taxes on trade to manipulate the balance of trade or commodity composition of trade in favour of the *home country*.

Export Strategy

Export strategy is to ship commodities to other places or countries for sale or exchange. In economics, an export is any good or commodity, transported from one country to another country in a legitimate fashion, typically for use in trade.

Advantages of Exporting

Ownership advantages are the firm's specific assets, international experience, and the ability to develop either low-cost or differentiated products within the contacts of its value chain. The locational advantages of a particular market are a combination of market potential and investment risk. Internationalization advantages are the benefits of retaining a core competence within the company and threading it though the value chain rather than obtain to license, outsource, or sell it. In relation to the Eclectic paradigm, companies that have low levels of ownership advantages either do not enter foreign markets. If the company and its products are equipped with *ownership advantage* and *internalization advantage*, they enter through low-risk modes such as exporting. Exporting requires significantly lower level of investment than other modes of international expansion, such as FDI. As you might expect, the lower risk of export typically results in a lower rate of return on sales than possible though other modes of international business. In other words, the usual return on export sales may not be tremendous, but neither is the risk. Exporting allows managers to exercise operation control but does not provide them the option to exercise as much marketing control. An exporter usually resides far from the end consumer and often enlists various intermediaries to manage marketing activities. After two straight months of contraction, exports from India rose a whopping 11.64% at $25.83 billion in July 2013 against $23.14 billion in the same month of the previous year.

Disadvantages of Exporting

For Small-and-Medium Enterprises (SME) with less than 250 employees, selling goods and services to foreign markets seems to be more difficult than serving the domestic market. The lack of knowledge for trade regulations, cultural differences, different languages and foreign-exchange situations as well as the strain of resources and staff interact like a block for exporting. Indeed there are some SME's which are exporting, but nearly two-third of them sell in only to one foreign market. The following assumption shows the main disadvantages:

- *Financial management effort:* To minimize the risk of exchange-rate fluctuation and transactions processes of export activity the financial management needs more capacity to cope the major effort
- *Customer demand:* International customers demand more services from their vendor like installation and startup of equipment, maintenance or more delivery services.

- *Communication technologies improvement*: The improvement of communication technologies in recent years enable the customer to interact with more suppliers while receiving more information and cheaper communications cost at the same time like 20 years ago. This leads to more transparency. The vendor is in duty to follow the real-time demand and to submit all transaction details.
- *Management mistakes:* The management might tap in some of the organizational pitfalls, like poor selection of oversea agents or distributors or chaotic global organization.

Ways of Exporting

The company can decide to export directly or indirectly to a foreign country.

Direct Selling in Export Strategy

Direct selling involves sales representatives, distributors, or retailers who are located *outside* the exporter's home country. Direct exports are goods and services that are sold to an independent party outside of the exporter's home country. Mainly the companies are pushed by core competencies and improving their performance of value chain.

Direct Selling Through Distributors

It is considered to be the most popular option to companies, to develop their own international marketing capability. This is achieved by charging personnel from the company to give them greater control over their operations. Direct selling also give the company greater control over the marketing function and the opportunity to earn more profits.

In other cases where network of sales representative, the company can transfer them exclusive rights to sell in a particular geographic region.

A distributor in a foreign country is a merchant who purchases the product from the manufacturer and sells them at profit. Distributors usually carry stock inventory and service the product, and in most cases distributes deals with retailers rather than end users.

Evaluating Distributors:

- The size and capabilities of its sales force.
- Its an analysis of its territory.

- Its current product mix.
- Its facilities and equipment.
- Its marketing polices.
- Its customer profit.
- Its promotional strategy.

Direct Selling through Foreign Retailers and End Users

Exporters can also sell directly to foreign retailers. Usually, products are limited to consumer lines; it can also sell to direct end users. A good way to generate such sales is by printing catalogues or attending trade shows.

Direct Selling over the Internet

Electronic commerce is an important mean to small and big companies all over the world, to trade internationally. We already can see how important E-commerce is for marketing growth among exporters companies in emerging economies, in order to overcome capital and infrastructure barriers.

E-commerce eased engagements, provided faster and cheaper delivery of information, generates quick feedback on new products, improves customer service, accesses a global audience, levels the field of companies, and support electronics data interchange with suppliers and customers.

Indirect Selling

Indirect exports, is simply selling goods to or through an independent domestic intermediary in their own home county. Then intermediaries export the products to customers foreign markets.

Making the Export Decision

Once a company determines it has exportable products, it must still consider other factors, such as the following:

- What does the company want to gain from exporting?
- Is exporting consistent with other company goals?
- What demands will exporting place on the company's key resources - management and personnel, production capacity, and finance - and how will these demands be met?
- Are the expected benefits worth the costs, or would company resources be better used for developing new domestic business?

Export Promotion

In the U.S.: The U.S. Department of Commerce provides U.S. companies the opportunity to promote their products and services free of charge. To do so, the Export Yellow Pages is published online and in print and is delivered to embassies, trade centres, consulates, and associations worldwide.

The California Centres for International Trade Development (CITD's) have 13 offices throughout California, each CITD is hosted by a local community college and provides a variety of free or low-cost programmes & services to assist local companies in doing business abroad. These include one-on-one technical assistance and consulting, market research, training and educational programmes, trade leads and special events.

Internationally

There are several global B2B directories and also country-specific directories, such as Kelly's Directory in the U.S., Tradeget in India, and Alibaba in China.

Challenges

Exporting to foreign countries poses challenges not found in domestic sales. With domestic sales, manufacturers typically sell to wholesalers or direct to retailer or even direct to consumers. When exporting, manufacturers may have to sell to importers who then in turn sell to wholesalers. Extra layer(s) in the chain of distribution squeezes margins and manufacturers may need to offer lower prices to importers than to domestic wholesalers.

Export Credit Agency

An export credit agency (known in trade finance as ECA) or Investment Insurance Agency, is a private or quasi-governmental institution that acts as an intermediary between national governments and exporters to issue export financing. The financing can take the form of credits (financial support) or credit insurance and guarantees (pure cover) or both, depending on the mandate the ECA has been given by its government. ECAs can also offer credit or cover on their own account. This does not differ from normal banking activities. Some agencies are government-sponsored, others private, and others a bit of both.

ECAs currently finance or underwrite about US$430 billion of business activity abroad - about US$55 billion of which goes towards project finance in developing countries - and provide US$14 billion of insurance for new foreign direct investment, dwarfing all other official sources combined (such as the World Bank and Regional Development Banks, bilateral and multilateral aid, etc.). As a result of the claims against developing countries that have resulted from ECA transactions, ECAs hold over 25% of these developing countries' US$2.2 trillion debt.

Export credit agencies use three methods to provide funds to an importing entity:

- Direct Lending: This is the simplest structure whereby the loan is conditioned upon the purchase of goods or services from businesses in the organizing country.
- Financial Intermediary Loans: Here, the export–import bank lends funds to a financial intermediary, such as a commercial bank, that in turn loans the funds to the importing entity.
- Interest Rate Equalization: Under an interest rate equalization, a commercial lender provides a loan to the importing entity at below market interest rates, and in turn receives compensation from the export–import bank for the difference between the below-market rate and the commercial rate.

Officially Supported Export Credits

Credits may be short term (up to two years), medium term (two to five years) or long term (five to ten years). They are usually supplier's credits, extended to the exporter, but they may be buyer's credits, extended to the importer. The risk on these credits, as well as on guarantees and insurance, is borne by the sponsoring government. ECAs limit this risk by being "closed" on risky countries, meaning that they do not accept any risk on these countries. In addition, a committee of government and ECA officials will review large and otherwise riskier than normal transactions.

Tied Aid Credits

Officially supported export credit may be connected to official development assistance (ODA) in two ways. First, they may be mixed with ODA, while still financing the same project (mixed credit). As the export credit is tied to purchases in the issuing country, the whole package qualifies as a tied aid credit, even if the ODA part is untied aid. Second, tied aid credits are not very different from export credits, except in interest, grace period (the time when there is no repayment of the principal) and terms of repayment. Such credits are separated from export credit by an OECD requirement that they have a minimum degree of "softness". "Softness" is measured by a formula that compares the present value of the credit with the present value of the same amount at standardized "commercial" terms. This difference is expressed as a percentage of the credit and called "concessionality level". Thus a grant has a concessionality level of 100%, a commercial credit scores zero per cent. The higher the concessionality level, the more the tied aid credit looks like ODA, the lower, the more it looks like an export credit.

Partially untied credits consist of a tied and an untied part. The latter is usually intended to finance "local cost", investment cost to be made in the importing country. This part may also be in a local currency. Partially untied aid is treated as tied aid.

International Regulation

Both officially supported export credits and tied aid credit and grants are extended on terms controlled by governments. Therefore, there is a constant temptation to use these financial instruments to subsidize commercial exports in order to win a temporary advantage on an export market or to counterbalance such an action from another government (matching). However, the end result of such action is negative for importing countries (usually developing countries), who are rendered unable to choose the best combination of quality and price but consider financing first. It is also negative for tax payers, who foot the bill. It may only to the benefit of exporters whose government have the deepest pockets and the greatest willingness to subsidize, even though the macro-economic benefit of the subsidy is doubtful. In the past, there have been big, government-sheltered companies that were kept alive to a very large extent by export credits and tied aid credits. To avoid these traps, it was considered useful to standardize export credit conditions and to monitor matching and tied aid credits.

This situation has led first to an informal agreement in 1976 among some OECD countries, known as "The Consensus". This was succeeded in 1978 by a gentlemen's agreement facilitated by the OECD's now defunct Trade Directorate, which established a Working Party on Officially Supported Export Credits. This gentleman's agreement, officially known as the Arrangement on Guidelines for Officially Supported Export Credits, is known as "The Arrangement". Although negotiations are facilitated by the OECD, not all OECD member countries are participants and membership is possible for non-OECD countries. The Arrangement is supplemented by so-called "Sector Understandings" with rules tailored to specific sectors of industry, namely ships, nuclear power plants, civil aircraft, and climate change mitigation and water projects.

Since 1999, country risk categories have been harmonized by the Arrangement and minimum premium rates have been allocated to the various risk categories. This is intended to ensure that competition takes place via pricing and the quality of the goods exported, and not in terms of how much support a state provides for its exporters. The Arrangement does not extend to exports of agricultural commodities or military equipment. A recent decision at the World Trade Organization (WTO) indicates that the use of officially supported export credits in agriculture is bound by WTO members' commitments with respect to subsidised agricultural exports.

At EU level, the European Commission, in particular the Directorate General for Trade, plays a role in the harmonization of Export Credit Agencies and the co-ordination of policy statements and negotiation positions. This is based on council decisions 73/391/EEC and 76/641/EEC. These decisions provide for prior consultations among member states on long term export credits. Member states may ask each other if they are considering to finance a specific transaction with official export credit support. EU members may not subsidize intra-EU export credits. The application of the OECD arrangement in providing export credit is mandatory in EU countries under Art. 1 of Regulation (EU) No. 1233/2011.

The Berne Union, or officially, the International Union of Credit & Investment Insurers, is an international organisation for the export credit and investment insurance industry. The Berne Union and Prague Club combined have more than 70 member companies spanning the globe. Its membership includes both commercial and state-sponsored insurers.

Support and Criticism

Some observers view state-sponsored export credits as nothing more than export subsidies by a different name. As such, the activities of ECAs are considered by some to be a type of corporate welfare. Others argue that ECAs create debt in poor countries motivated not by development goals but in order to support rich countries' industry. In addition, ECAs may soak up aid money as debt relief programmes predominantly relieve poor countries from debt owed to donor countries' ECAs. ECAs are also criticised for insuring companies against political actions which aim to protect workers' rights, other human rights or the natural environment in the countries where the investment is being made.

Advocates of ECAs assert that export credits allow impoverished importers to purchase needed goods that would otherwise be unaffordable; export credits are components of a broader strategy of trade policies; and government involvement can achieve results that the private sector cannot, such as applying greater pressure on a recalcitrant borrower.

These arguments for and against export credits are not new, having been studied at length in academic literature.

List of Export Credit Agencies

Multilateral export credit agencies:

- Multilateral Development Banks - (MDBs)
  - Africa - African Development Bank AfdB
  - Africa - African Export-Import Bank (Afreximbank)
  - Andean Countries - Corporación Andina de Fomento ("CAF")
  - Arab League - Arab Fund for Economic and Social Development
  - Asia - Asian Development Bank
  - Central and Eastern Europe - European Bank for Reconstruction and Development ("EBRD")
  - Islamic Corporation for the Insurance of Investment and Export Credit ("ICIEC") (part of the Islamic Development Bank)
  - Islamic Development Bank (IsDB)
  - Latin America - Inter-American Development Bank ("IADB")
  - Nordic Investment Bank ("NIB")
  - Nordic Development Fund ("NDF")
  - OPEC Fund for International Development ("OFfID")
- Multilateral Financial Institutions
  - Central and Eastern Europe - European Union (EU)
  - Central and Eastern Europe - European Investment Bank ("EIB")
  - Multilateral Investment Guarantee Agency (part of World Bank)

Trade Credit Insurance

Trade credit insurance, business credit insurance, export credit insurance, or credit insurance is an insurance policy and a risk management product offered by private insurance companies and governmental export credit agencies to business entities wishing to protect their accounts receivable from loss due to credit risks such as protracted default, insolvency or bankruptcy. This insurance product is a type of property & casualty insurance, and should not be confused with such products as credit life or credit disability insurance, which individuals obtain to protect against the risk of loss of income needed to pay debts. Trade Credit Insurance can include a component of political risk insurance which is offered by the same insurers to insure the risk of non-payment by foreign buyers due to currency issues, political unrest, expropriation etc.

This points to the major role trade credit insurance plays in facilitating international trade. Trade credit is offered by vendors to their customers as an alternative to prepayment or cash on delivery terms, providing time for the customer to generate income from sales to pay for the product or service. This requires the vendor to assume non-payment risk. In a local or domestic situation as well as in an export transaction, the risk increases when laws, customs communications and customer's reputation are not fully understood. In addition to increased risk of non-payment, international trade presents the problem of the time between product shipment and its availability for sale. The account receivable is like a loan and represents capital invested, and often borrowed, by the vendor. But this is not a secure asset until it is paid. If the customer's debt is credit insured the large, risky asset becomes more secure, like an insured building. This asset may then be viewed as collateral by lending institutions and a loan based upon it used to defray the expenses of the transaction and to produce more product. Trade credit insurance is, therefore, a trade finance tool.

Trade credit insurance is purchased by business entities to insure their accounts receivable from loss due to the insolvency of the debtors. The product is not available to individuals. The cost (premium) for this is usually charged monthly, and are calculated as a percentage of sales for that month or as a percentage of all outstanding receivables.

Trade credit insurance usually covers a portfolio of buyers and pays an agreed percentage of an invoice or receivable that remains unpaid as a result of protracted default, insolvency or bankruptcy.

Policy holders must apply a credit limit on each of their buyers for the sales to that buyer to be insured. The premium rate reflects the average credit risk of the insured portfolio of buyers. In addition, credit insurance can also cover single transactions or trade with only one buyer.

Trade credit insurance was born at the end of nineteenth century, but it was mostly developed in Western Europe between the First and Second World Wars. Several companies were founded in many countries; some of them also managed the political risks of export on behalf of their state.

Following the privatisation of the short-term side of the UK's Export Credits Guarantee Department in 1991, a concentration of the trade credit insurance market took place and three groups now account for over 85% of the global credit insurance market. These main players focused on Western Europe, but rapidly expanded towards Eastern Europe, Asia and the Americas:

- Euler Hermes, merger of the two credit insurance companies of the Allianz Group. Euler Hermes is the world's number one credit insurance provider.
- Atradius, a merger between NCM and Gerling Kreditversicherung. Later renamed Atradius after it was demerged from the Gerling insurance group.
- Coface. Formerly a French government sponsored institution established in 1946, this company is now part of the Natixis group.

Many variations of trade credit insurance have evolved ranging from coverage that can be cancelled or reduced at an insurers discretion, to coverage that cannot be cancelled or reduced by the insurer during the policy period. Other programmes may allow the policy holder to act as the underwriter.

While trade credit insurance is often mostly known for protecting foreign or export accounts receivable, there has always been a large segment of the market that uses Trade Credit Insurance for domestic accounts receivable protection as well. Domestic trade credit insurance provides companies with the protection they need as their customer base consolidates creating larger receivables to fewer customers. This further creates a larger exposure and greater risk if a customer does not pay their accounts. The addition of new insurers in this area have increased the availability of domestic cover for companies.

Many businesses found that their insurers withdrew trade credit insurance during the late-2000s financial crisis, foreseeing large losses if they continued to underwrite sales to failing businesses. This led to accusations that the insurers were deepening and prolonging the recession, as businesses could not afford the risk of making sales without the insurance, and therefore contracted in size or had to close. Insurers countered these criticisms by claiming that they were not the cause of the crisis, but were responding to economic reality and ringing the alarm bells.

In 2009, the UK government set up a short-term £5 billion Trade Credit Top-up emergency fund. However, this was considered a failure, as the take-up was very low.

Export-oriented Industrialization

Export-oriented industrialization (EOI) sometimes called export substitution industrialization (ESI), export led industrialization (ELI) or export-led growth is a trade and economic policy aiming to speed up the industrialization process of a country by exporting goods for which the nation has a comparative advantage. Export-led growth implies opening domestic markets to foreign competition in exchange for market access in other countries.

However this may not be true of all domestic markets, as governments may aim to protect specific nascent industries so they grow and are able to exploit their future comparative advantage and in practise the converse can occur. For example, many East Asian countries had strong barriers on imports from the 1960s to the 1980s. Reduced tariff barriers, a floating exchange rate (a devaluation of national currency is often employed to facilitate exports), and government support for exporting sectors are all an example of policies adopted to promote EOI and, ultimately, economic development. Export-oriented industrialization was particularly characteristic of the development of the national economies of the Asian Tigers: Hong Kong, South Korea, Taiwan, and Singapore in the post-World War II period.

Export-led growth is an economic strategy used by some developing countries. This strategy seeks to find a niche in the world economy for a certain type of export. Industries producing this export may receive governmental subsidies and better access to the local markets. By implementing this strategy, countries hope to gain enough hard currency to import commodities manufactured more cheaply somewhere else.

Origins

From the Great Depression to the years after World War II, under-developed and developing countries started to have a hard time economically. During this time, many foreign markets were closed and the danger of trading and shipping in war-time waters drove many of these countries to look for another solution to development. The initial solution to this dilemma was called import substitution industrialization. Both Latin American and Asian countries used this strategy at first. However, during the 1950s and 1960s the Asian countries, like Taiwan and South Korea, started focusing their development outward, resulting in an export-led growth strategy. Many of the Latin American countries continued with import substitution industrialization, just expanding its scope. Some have pointed out that because of the success of the Asian countries, especially Taiwan and South Korea, export-led growth should be considered the best strategy to promote development.

Importance

Export-led growth is important for mainly two reasons. The first is that export-led growth can create profit, allowing a country to balance their finances, as well as surpass their debts as long as the facilities and materials for the export exist. The second, much more debatable reason is that increased export growth can trigger greater productivity, thus creating more exports in an upward spiral cycle.

The importance of this concept can be shown in the model below from J.S.L McCombie and A.P. Thirwall's *Economic Growth and the Balance-of-Payments Constraint.*

y_B is the balance of payments constraint, meaning the relationship between expenditures and profits

y_A is the actual growth capacity of a country, which can never be more than the current capacity

y_C is the current capacity of growth, or how well the country is producing at that moment

(i) $y_B=y_A=y_C$: balance-of-payments equilibrium and full employments

(ii) $y_B=y_A<y_C$: balance-of-payments equilibrium and growing unemployment

(iii) $y_B<y_A=y_C$: increasing balance-of-payments deficit and full employment

(iv) $y_B<y_A<y_C$: increasing balance-of-payments deficit and growing unemployment

(v) $y_B>y_A=y_C$: increasing balance-of-payments surplus and full employment

(vi) $y_B>y_A<y_C$: increasing balance-of-payments surplus and growing unemployment (McCombie 423)

Countries with unemployment and balance-of-payments problems look to export-led growth because of the possibility of moving to either situation (i) or situation (v).

Types of Exports

There are essentially two types of exports used in this context: manufactured goods and raw materials. Manufactured goods are the exports most commonly used to achieve export-led growth. However, many times these industries are competing against industrialized countries' industries, which often have better technology, better educated workers, and more capital to start with. Therefore, this strategy must be well thought out and planned. A country must find a certain export that they can manufacture well, in competition with industrialized industries.

Raw materials are another export option. However, this strategy is risky compared to manufactured goods. If the terms of trade shift unfavourably, a country must export more and more of the raw materials to import the same amount of commodities, making the trade profits very difficult to come by.

Limitations

Despite its support in mainstream economic circles, its success has been increasingly challenged over recent years due a growing number of examples in which it has not yielded the expected results. EOI increases market sensitivity to exogenous factors, and is partially responsible for the damage done by the 1998 economic crisis to the economies of countries who used export-oriented industrialization. It is also criticized for its lack of product diversity as economies pursue their comparative advantage, which makes the economies potentially unstable if demand for their specialization falls; this is something which occurred during the financial crisis of 2007–2010 and subsequent global recession. Similarly, localized disasters can cause worldwide shortages of the products that countries specialize in. For example, in 2010, flooding in Thailand led to a shortage of hard drives.

Other criticisms include that export oriented industrialization has limited success if the economy is experiencing a decline in its terms of trade, where prices for its exports are rising at a slower rate than that of its imports. This is true of many economies aiming to exploit their comparative advantage in primary commodities as they have a long term trend of declining prices, noted in the Singer-Prebisch thesis though there are criticisms of this thesis as practical contradictions have occurred.

Primary commodity dependency also links to the weakness of excessive specialization as primary commodities have incredible price volatility, given the inelastic nature of their demand, leading to a disproportionately large change in price given a change in demand for them. The problem is that EOI presupposes that a government contains the relevant market knowledge to judge whether or not an industry to be given development subsidies which will prove a good investment in the future. The ability of a government to do this may be limited as it will not have occurred through the natural interaction of market forces of supply and demand. Also to exploit a potential comparative advantage requires a significant amount of investment which governments can only supply a limited amount of. In many LEDCs, it is necessary for multinational corporations to provide the foreign direct investment, knowledge, skills and training needed to develop an industry and exploit the future comparative advantage.

Scholars have shown that governments in East Asia, however, did have the ability and the resources to identify and exploit comparative advantages. EOI has therefore been supported as a development strategy for poor countries because of its success in the Four Asian Tigers. However, this claim has been challenged by the evidence of very specific historical conditions in East Asia that were not present elsewhere, and which allowed for the success of EOI in these nations. Japanese producers, for example, were given preferential access to US and European markets after the Second World War. This, in turn, made it possible for countries like South Korea and Taiwan to later become incorporated into Japan's overseas marketing networks as Japanese trading conglomerates were seeking to offload the lower end of their manufacturing value chain to other countries. By virtue of this connection to Japanese commercial networks, South Korean firms had "access to export markets that virtually no other country—except Taiwan—enjoyed." Without these advantages, it is doubtful that EOI could be as successful in other countries as it was in East Asia.

Export Performance

Export performance is the relative success or failure of the efforts of a firm or nation to sell domestically-produced goods and services in other nations.

Export performance can be described in objective terms such as sales, profits, or marketing measures or by subjective measures such as distributor or customer satisfaction.

Export-led Growth

Export-led growth is an economic strategy used by some developing countries. This strategy seeks to find a niche in the world economy for a certain type of export. Industries producing this export may receive governmental subsidies and better access to the local markets. By implementing this strategy, countries hope to gain enough hard currency to import commodities manufactured more cheaply somewhere else.

2

Import Management

An import is a good brought into a jurisdiction, especially across a national border, from an external source. The purchaser of the exotic good is called an *importer*. An import in the receiving country is an export from the sending country. Importation and exportation are the defining financial transactions of international trade.

In international trade, the importation and exportation of goods are limited by import quotas and mandates from the customs authority. The importing and exporting jurisdictions may impose a tariff (tax) on the goods. In addition, the importation and exportation of goods are subject to trade agreements between the importing and exporting jurisdictions.

Definition

"Imports" consist of transactions in goods and services (sales, barter, gifts or grants) from non-residents to residents. The exact definition of imports in national accounts includes and excludes specific "borderline" cases. A general delimitation of imports in national accounts is given below:

- An import of a good occurs when there is a change of ownership from a non-resident to a resident; this does not necessarily imply that the good in question physically crosses the frontier.

  However, in specific cases national accounts impute changes of ownership even though in legal terms no change of ownership takes place (e.g. *cross border financial leasing, cross border deliveries between affiliates of the same enterprise, goods crossing the border for significant processing to order or repair*).

Also smuggled goods must be included in the import measurement.

- Imports of services consist of all services rendered by non-residents to residents. In national accounts any direct purchases by residents outside the economic territory of a country are recorded as imports of services; therefore all expenditure by tourists in the economic territory of another country are considered as part of the imports of services. Also international flows of illegal services must be included.

Basic trade statistics often differ in terms of definition and coverage from the requirements in the national accounts:

- Data on international trade in goods are mostly obtained through declarations to custom services. If a country applies the general trade system, all goods entering the country are recorded as imports. If the special trade system (e.g. extra-EU trade statistics) is applied goods which are received into customs warehouses are not recorded in external trade statistics unless they subsequently go into free circulation of the importing country.
- A special case is the intra-EU trade statistics. Since goods move freely between the member states of the EU without customs controls, statistics on trade in goods between the member states must be obtained through surveys. To reduce the statistical burden on the respondents small scale traders are excluded from the reporting obligation.
- Statistical recording of trade in services is based on declarations by banks to their central banks or by surveys of the main operators. In a globalized economy where services can be rendered via electronic means (*e.g. internet*) the related international flows of services are difficult to identify.
- Basic statistics on international trade normally do not record smuggled goods or international flows of illegal services. A small fraction of the smuggled goods and illegal services may nevertheless be included in official trade statistics through dummy shipments or dummy declarations that serve to conceal the illegal nature of the activities.

Balance of Trade

Balance of trade represents a difference in value for import and export for a country. A country has demand for an import when domestic quantity demanded exceeds domestic quantity supplied, or when the price of the good (or service) on the world market is less than the price on the domestic market.

The balance of trade, usually denoted NX, is the difference between the value of the goods (and services) a country exports and the value of the goods the country imports:

$$NX = X - I \text{, or equivalently } I = X - NX$$

A trade deficit occurs when imports are large relative to exports. Imports are impacted principally by a country's income and its productive resources. For example, the US imports oil from Canada even though the US has oil and Canada uses oil. However, consumers in the US are willing to pay more for the marginal barrel of oil than Canadian consumers are, because there is more oil demanded in the US than there is oil produced.

In macroeconomic theory, the value of imports I can be modelled as a function of the domestic absorption A and the real exchange rateσ. These are the two largest factors of imports and they both affect imports positively:

$$I = I(A, \sigma)$$

Types of Import

There are two basic types of import:

1. Industrial and consumer goods
2. Intermediate goods and services

Companies import goods and services to supply to the domestic market at a cheaper price and better quality than competing goods manufactured in the domestic market. Companies import products that are not available in the local market.

There are three broad types of importers:

1. Looking for any product around the world to import and sell.
2. Looking for foreign sourcing to get their products at the cheapest price.
3. Using foreign sourcing as part of their global supply chain.

Direct-import refers to a type of business importation involving a major retailer (e.g. Wal-Mart) and an overseas manufacturer. A retailer typically purchases products designed by local companies that can be manufactured overseas. In a direct-import programme, the retailer bypasses the local supplier (colloquial *middle-man*) and buys the final product directly from the manufacturer, possibly saving in added cost data on the value of imports and their quantities often broken down by detailed lists of products are available in statistical collections on international trade published by the statistical services of intergovernmental organisations (e.g. UNSTAT, FAOSTAT, OECD), supranational statistical institutes (e.g. Eurostat) and national statistical institutes. Industrial and consumer goods.

Import Quota

An import quota is a limit on the quantity of a good that can be produced abroad and sold domestically. It is a type of protectionist trade restriction that sets a physical limit on the quantity of a good that can be imported into a country in a given period of time. If a quota is put on a good, less of it is imported. Quotas, like other trade restrictions, are used to benefit the producers of a good in a domestic economy at the expense of all consumers of the good in that economy.

Goals

The primary goal of import quotas is to reduce imports and increase domestic production of a good, service, or activity, thus "protect" domestic production by restricting foreign competition. As the quantity of importing the good is restricted, the price of the imported good increases, thus encourages consumers to purchase more domestic products. In general, a quota is simply a legal quantity restriction placed on a good imported that is imposed by the domestic government.

Effects

Because the import quota prevents domestic consumers from buying an imported good, the supply of the good is no longer perfectly elastic at the world price. Instead, as long as the price of the good is above the world price, the license holders import as much as they are permitted, and the total supply of the good equals the domestic supply plus the quota amount. The price of the good adjusts to balance supply (domestic plus imported) and demand. The quota causes the price of the good to rise above the world price. The imported quantity demanded falls and the domestic quantity supplied rises. Thus, the import quota reduces the imports.

Because the quota raises the domestic price above the world price, domestic sellers are better off, and domestic buyers are worse off. In addition, the license holders are better off because they make a profit from buying at the world price and selling at the higher domestic price. Thus, import quotas decrease consumer surplus while increasing producer surplus and license-holder surplus.

While import quotas and other foreign trade policies can be beneficial to the aggregate domestic economy they tend to be most beneficial, and thus most commonly promoted by, domestic firms facing competition from foreign imports. Domestic firms benefit with higher sales, greater profits, and more income to resource owners. However, by increasing domestic prices and restricting accessing to imports, foreign trade policies also tend to be harmful to domestic consumers.

Other Effects

Domestic Employment: Decreasing imports and increasing domestic production also increases domestic employment.

Low Foreign Wages: Restricting imports produced by foreign workers who receive lower wages "levels the competitive playing field" compared to domestic goods produced by higher paid domestic workers.

Infant Industry: If foreign imports compete with a relatively young domestic industry that is neither mature enough nor large enough to benefit from economies of scale, then import quotas protect the "infant industry" while it matures and develops.

Unfair Trade: The foreign imports might be sold at lower prices in the domestic economy because foreign producers engage in unfair trade practices, such as "dumping" imports at prices below production cost. Import quotas seek to prevent such activity.

National Security: Import quotas can also discourage imports and encourage domestic production of goods that policy makers declare publically to be critical to the security of the national economy.

Corruption: Import quotas can lead to administrative corruption in countries with import quotas as the importers chosen to meet the quota are the ones who can provide the most favours to the customs officers.

Smuggling: If the import quota succeeds in sufficiently raising the price of domestic goods that compete with imports, entrepreneurs will try to circumvent the quota. Smugglers bring in illegal goods (i.e., goods supplies in excess of the quota). Other entrepreneurs may try to incorporate the goods subject to the quota into import goods not subject to the quota. These market responses may limit governments' freedom of action in setting import quotas.

Types

Quotas are established by legislation and Presidential proclamations issued pursuant to specific legislation and provided for in the Harmonized Tariff Schedule of the United States (HTSUS). United States import quotas may be divided into two types: absolute quota and tariff-rate quota. Once a specific quota has been reached in a particular category, goods may still be entered, but at a considerably higher rate of duty.

Absolute Quotas

Absolute quotas limit the quantity of certain goods that may enter the commerce during a specific period. Once the quantity permitted under an absolute quota is filled, no further entries or withdrawals from warehouse for consumption of merchandise subject to the quota are permitted for the remainder of the quota period. Importers may hold shipments in excess of a specified absolute quota limit until the opening of the next quota period by entering the goods into a foreign trade zone or bonded warehouse. The goods may also be exported or destroyed under [Customs and Border Protection] (CBP) supervision.

Tariff-rate Quotas

Tariff rate quotas permit a specified quantity of imported merchandise to be entered at a reduced rate of duty during the quota period. There is no limitation on the amount of merchandise that may be imported into the United States, however quantities entered in excess of the quota limit during that period are subject to a higher duty rate. If the importer has not taken possession of the goods, and elects not to pay the higher rate of duty, they may enter the goods into a foreign trade zone or bonded warehouse until the opening of the next quota period, or export or destroy the goods under CBP supervision.

Once CBP determines the date and time a quota is filled, field officers are authorized to make the required duty rate adjustments on the portion of the merchandise not entitled to quota preference.

Under the North American Free Trade Agreement (NAFTA), there are trade-preference levels (TPL), which are administered like tariff-rate quotas. The U.S. Customs Service administers the majority of import quotas. The Commissioner of Customs controls the importation of quota merchandise, but has no authority to change or modify any quota. The Department of Commerce, in conjunction with the Office of the United States Trade Representative, determines and fixes quota limits. Quota merchandise is subject to the usual Customs procedures applicable to other imports. No import licenses are currently required for quotas administered by the Commissioner of Customs.

Import Quotas vs Tariffs

Both tariffs and import quotas reduce quantity of imports, raise domestic price of good, decrease welfare of domestic consumers, increase welfare of domestic producers, and cause deadweight loss. However, a quota can potentially cause an even larger deadweight loss, depending on the mechanism used to allocate the import licenses. The difference between these tariff and import quota is that tariff raises revenue for the government, whereas import quota generates surplus for firms that get the license to import.

For a firm that gets a license to import, profit per unit equals domestic price (at which imported good is sold) minus world price (at which good is bought) (minus any other costs). Total profit equals profit per unit times quantity sold.

Government may charge fees for import license. If the government sets the import license fee equal to difference between domestic price and world price, the import quota works exactly like a tariff. The entire profit of the firm with an import license is paid to the government. Thus government revenue is the same under such an import quota and a tariff. Also, consumer surplus and producer surplus are the same under such an import quota and a tariff.

So why do countries use import quotas instead of always using a tariff?

When an import quota is used, it allows a country to be sure of the amount of the good imported from the foreign country. When there is a tariff, if the supply curve of the foreign country is unknown, the quantity of the good imported may not be predictable.

If world supply in the home country is upward-sloping and less elastic than domestic demand (as may be the case when the home country is the United States) then the incidence of the tariff may fall on producers, and the price paid domestically may not rise by much. Then if the tariff is supposed to make price of the good rise to allow domestic producers to sell at a higher price, the tariff may not have much of the desired effect. A quota may do more to raise price. However in competitive markets there is always some tariff that raises the price as high as the quota does.

Direct Imports

Direct Imports are products imported directly into a country and not through the manufacturer's authorized agent/distributor. Since there is no factory-authorized middleman involved in the import of these products, the added costs are lower and the customer pays less. In addition, many items that are in short supply or are not imported at all by the manufacturer's authorized distributors can be procured as direct imports. There is no difference in the actual products. In most cases, they are manufactured in the same place by the same people and with the same materials. Occasionally, manufacturers will give them a different name.

It is perfectly legal to directly import and sell such products. The only caveat is that since they are not procured from a local factory-authorized middleman, the manufacturer's warranty may not be applicable. This type of business is fairly recent and follows the trends of the global economy.

In rapidly growing developing economies like India where the demand for international consumer products is growing much faster than in-country supply from authorized distributors, direct imports become the only way for consumers to procure a large set of products (especially long tail). In many cases, even if a particular product is available from an authorized middle-man, a direct import may cost much less since in-country middlemen use their exclusive territorial rights to price products much higher than in the country of origin. Perversely, in countries where such product and price arbitrage is the most obvious, the import process is typically very onerous and not easily navigated by the average consumer leaving the field open to predatory pricing from in-country middlemen.

Disintermediation by Technology

To help bridge this gap, a new breed of E-commerce companies acting as direct import facilitators have developed sophisticated E-commerce and Supply Chain technology to create a cross-border supply chain that allows consumers to shop online for international products and have them delivered duty paid to their doorstep. The entire procurement, international shipping and import process is handled turnkey by the e-commerce providers and the consumer transaction is a simple online purchase.

This is a significant example of how Internet technology is a powerful force for disintermediation in commerce. To illustrate, a typical B2C supply chain involving imports is composed of five entities (in order):

1. Foreign Supplier/Manufacturer
2. In-country Importer
3. In-country Distributor
4. In-country Retailer (online or offline)
5. In-country Buyer

With the advent of online direct imports that leverage the Internet, the supply chain is reduced to three entities:

1. Foreign Supplier/Manufacturer
2. Online Direct Import Facilitator
3. In-country Buyer

As always, the removal of intermediaries in a supply chain i.e. "cutting out the middleman" results in high market transparency and efficient pricing.

International Trade

International trade is the exchange of capital, goods, and services across international borders or territories. In most countries, such trade represents a significant share of gross domestic product (GDP). While international trade has been present throughout much of history, its economic, social, and political importance has been on the rise in recent centuries. Industrialization, advanced in technology transportation, globalization, multinational corporations, and outsourcing are all having a major impact on the international trade system. Increasing international trade is crucial to the continuance of globalization. Without international trade, nations would be limited to the goods and services produced within their own borders.

International trade is, in principle, not different from domestic trade as the motivation and the behaviour of parties involved in a trade do not change fundamentally regardless of whether trade is across a border or not. The main difference is that international trade is typically more costly than domestic trade. The reason is that a border typically imposes additional costs such as tariffs, time costs due to border delays and costs associated with country differences such as language, the legal system or culture. Another difference between domestic and international trade is that factors of production such as capital and labour are typically more mobile within a country than across countries. Thus international trade is mostly restricted to trade in goods and services, and only to a lesser extent to trade in capital, labour or other factors of production. Trade in goods and services can serve as a substitute for trade in factors of production.

Instead of importing a factor of production, a country can import goods that make intensive use of that factor of production and thus embody it. An example is the import of labour-intensive goods by the United States from China. Instead of importing Chinese labour, the United States imports goods that were produced with Chinese labour. One report in 2010 suggested that international trade was increased when a country hosted a network of immigrants, but the trade effect was weakened when the immigrants became assimilated into their new country.

International trade is also a branch of economics, which, together with international finance, forms the larger branch of international economics. Trading is a value added function of the economic process of a product finding its market, where specific risks are to be borne by the trader, affecting the assets being traded which will be mitigated by performing specific functions.

Models

The following are noted models of international trade.

Adam Smith's Model

Adam Smith displays trade taking place on the basis of countries exercising absolute advantage over one another.

Ricardian Model

The Ricardian model focuses on comparative advantage, which arises due to differences in technology or natural resources. The Ricardian model does not directly consider factor endowments, such as the relative amounts of labour and capital within a country.

The Ricardian model is based on the following assumptions:

- Labour is the only primary input to production
- The relative ratios of labour at which the production of one good can be traded off for another differ between countries and governments

Heckscher–Ohlin Model

In the early 1900s a theory of international trade was developed by two Swedish economists, Eli Heckscher and Bertil Ohlin. This theory has subsequently been known as the Heckscher–Ohlin model

(H–O model). The results of the H–O model are that countries will produce and export goods that require resources (factors) which are relatively abundant and import goods that require resources which are in relative short supply.

In the Heckscher–Ohlin model the pattern of international trade is determined by differences in factor endowments. It predicts that countries will export those goods that make intensive use of locally abundant factors and will import goods that make intensive use of factors that are locally scarce. Empirical problems with the H–O model, such as the Leontief paradox, were noted in empirical tests by Wassily Leontief who found that the United States tended to export labour-intensive goods despite having an abundance of capital.

The H–O model makes the following core assumptions:

- Labour and capital flow freely between sectors
- The amount of labour and capital in two countries differ (difference in endowments)
- Technology is the same among countries (a long-term assumption)
- Tastes are the same

Applicability

In 1953, Wassily Leontief published a study in which he tested the validity of the Heckscher-Ohlin theory. The study showed that the United States was more abundant in capital compared to other countries, therefore the United States would export capital-intensive goods and import labour-intensive goods. Leontief found out that the United States' exports were less capital intensive than its imports.

After the appearance of Leontief's paradox, many researchers tried to save the Heckscher-Ohlin theory, either by new methods of measurement, or by new interpretations. Leamer emphasized that Leontief did not interpret H-O theory properly and claimed that with a right interpretation, the paradox did not occur. Brecher and Choudri found that, if Leamer was right, the American workers' consumption per head should be lower than the workers' world average consumption. Many textbook writers, including Krugman and Obstfeld and Bowen, Hollander and Viane, are negative about the validity of H-O model. After examining the long history of empirical research, Bowen, Hollander and Viane concluded: "Recent tests of the factor abundance theory [H-O theory and its developed form into many-commodity and many-factor case] that directly examine the H-O-V equations also indicate the rejection of the theory." In the specific factors model, labour mobility among industries is possible while capital is assumed to be immobile in the short run. Thus, this model can be interpreted as a short-run version of the Heckscher-Ohlin model. The "specific factors" name refers to the assumption that in the short run, specific factors of production such as physical capital are not easily transferable between industries. The theory suggests that if there is an increase in the price of a good, the owners of the factor of production specific to that good will profit in real terms.

Additionally, owners of opposing specific factors of production (i.e., labour and capital) are likely to have opposing agendas when lobbying for controls over immigration of labour. Conversely, both owners of capital and labour profit in real terms from an increase in the capital endowment. This model is ideal for understanding income distribution but awkward for discussing the pattern of trade.

New Trade Theory

New Trade Theory tries to explain empirical elements of trade that comparative advantage-based models above have difficulty with. These include the fact that most trade is between countries with similar factor endowment and productivity levels, and the large amount of multinational production (i.e., foreign direct investment) that exists. New Trade theories are often based on assumptions such as monopolistic competition and increasing returns to scale. One result of these theories is the home-market effect, which asserts that, if an industry tends to cluster in one location because of returns to scale and if that industry faces high transportation costs, the industry will be located in the country with most of its demand, in order to minimize cost.

Although new trade theory can explain the growing trend of trade volumes of intermediate goods, Krugman's explanation depends too much on the strict assumption that all firms are symmetrical, meaning that they all have the same production coefficients. Shiozawa, based on much more general model, succeeded in giving a new explanation on why the traded volume increases for intermediate goods when the transport cost decreases.

Gravity Model

The Gravity model of trade presents a more empirical analysis of trading patterns. The gravity model, in its basic form, predicts trade based on the distance between countries and the interaction of the countries' economic sizes. The model mimics the Newtonian law of gravity which also considers distance and physical size between two objects. The model has been proven to be empirically strong through econometric analysis.

Ricardian Theory of International Trade (Modern Development)

The Ricardian theory of comparative advantage became a basic constituent of neoclassical trade theory. Any undergraduate course in trade theory includes a presentation of Ricardo's example of a two-commodity, two-country model. A common representation of this model is made using an Edgeworth Box. This model has been expanded to many-country and many-commodity cases. Major general results were obtained by McKenzie and Jones, including his famous formula. It is a theorem about the possible trade pattern for N-country N-commodity cases.

Contemporary Theories

Ricardo's idea was even expanded to the case of continuum of goods by Dornbusch, Fischer, and Samuelson This formulation is employed for example by Matsuyama and others. These theories use a special property that is applicable only for the two-country case.

Neo-Ricardian Trade Theory

Inspired by Piero Sraffa, a new strand of trade theory emerged and was named neo-Ricardian trade theory. The main contributors include Ian Steedman (1941–) and Stanley Metcalfe (1946–). They have criticized neoclassical international trade theory, namely the Heckscher-Ohlin model on the basis that the notion of capital as primary factor has no method of measuring it before the determination of profit rate (thus trapped in a logical vicious circle). This was a second round of the Cambridge capital controversy, this time in the field of international trade. The merit of neo-Ricardian trade theory is that input goods are explicitly included. This is in accordance with Sraffa's idea that any commodity is a product made by means of commodities. The limitation of their theory is that the analysis is restricted to small-country cases.

Traded Intermediate Goods

Ricardian trade theory ordinarily assumes that the labour is the unique input. This is a great deficiency as trade theory, for intermediate goods occupy the major part of the world international trade. Yeats found that 30% of world trade in manufacturing involves intermediate inputs. Bardhan and Jafee found that intermediate inputs occupy 37 to 38% of U.S. imports for the years 1992 and 1997, whereas the percentage of intra-firm trade grew from 43% in 1992 to 52% in 1997. McKenzie and Jones emphasized the necessity to expand the Ricardian theory to the cases of traded inputs. In a famous comment McKenzie (1954, p. 179) pointed that "A moment's consideration will convince one that Lancashire would be unlikely to produce cotton cloth if the cotton had to be grown in England." Paul Samuelson coined a term *Sraffa bonus* to name the gains from trade of inputs.

Ricardo-Sraffa Trade Theory

Economist John S. Chipman observed in his survey that McKenzie stumbled upon the questions of intermediate products and postulated that "introduction of trade in intermediate product necessitates a fundamental alteration in classical analysis". It took many years until Shiozawa succeeded in removing this deficiency. The Ricardian trade theory was now constructed in a form to include intermediate input trade for the most general case of many countries and many goods. Chipman called this the Ricardo-Sraffa trade theory. Based on an idea of Takahiro Fujimoto, who is a specialist in automobile industry and a philosopher of the international competitiveness, Fujimoto and Shiozawa developed a discussion in which how the factories of the same multi-national firms compete between them across borders. International *intra-firm competition* reflects a really new aspect of international competition in the age of so-called *global competition*.

International Production Fragmentation Trade Theory

Fragmentation and International Trade Theory widens the scope for "application of Ricardian comparative advantage". In his chapter entitled *Li & Fung, Ltd.: An agent of global production* (2001), Cheng used Li & Fong Ltd as a case study in the international production fragmentation trade theory through which producers in different countries are allocated a specialized slice or segment of the value chain of the global production. Allocations are determined based on on "technical feasibility" and the ability to keep the lowest final price possible for each product. An example of fragmentation theory in international trade is Li and Fung's garment sector network with yarn purchased in South Korea, woven and dyed in Taiwan, the fabric cut in Bangladesh, pieces assembled in Thailand and the final product sold in the United States and Europe to major brands. In 1995 Li & Fung Ltd purchased Inchcape Buying Services, an established British trading company and widely expanded production in Asia. Li & Fung supplies dozens of major retailers, including Wal-Mart Stores, Inc., branded as Walmart.

Largest Countries by Total International Trade

Rank	Country	International Trade of Goods (Billions of USD)	Date ofinformation
-	World	36,688.0	2012 est.
-	European Union	4,469.3	2012 est.
1	United States	3,882.7	2012 est.
2	China	3,867.1	2012 est.
3	Germany	2,575.5	2012 est.
4	Japan	1,684.7	2012 est.
5	Netherlands	1,247.8	2012 est.
6	France	1,243.8	2012 est.
7	United Kingdom	1,164.9	2012 est.
8	South Korea	1,067.5	2012 est.
9	Italy	988.1	2012 est.
10	Hong Kong	952.0	2012 est.
11	Canada	917.3	2012 est.
12	Belgium	884.6	2012 est.
13	Russia	864.7	2012 est.
14	Singapore	788.1	2012 est.
15	India	782.6	2012 est.

RankCountry		International Trade of Services (Billions of USD)	Date ofinformation
-	World	8,452.6	2012 est.
-	European Union	1,465.8	2012 est.
1	United States	1,019.7	2012 est.
2	Germany	539.7	2012 est.
3	China	471.0	2012 est.
4	United Kingdom	453.9	2012 est.
5	France	379.2	2012 est.
6	Japan	313.4	2012 est.
7	India	272.8	2012 est.
8	Singapore	250.1	2012 est.
9	Spain	229.3	2012 est.
10	South Korea	214.2	2012 est.

Top traded commodities (exports)

Rank	Commodity	Value in US$('000)	Date ofinformation
1	Mineral fuels, oils, distillation products, etc.	$2,183,079,941	2012
2	Electrical, electronic equipment	$1,833,534,414	2012
3	Machinery, nuclear reactors, boilers, etc.	$1,763,371,813	2012
4	Vehicles other than railway	$1,076,830,856	2012
5	Plastics and articles thereof	$470,226,676	2012
6	Optical, photo, technical, medical, etc. apparatus	$465,101,524	2012
7	Pharmaceutical products	$443,596,577	2012
8	Iron and steel	$379,113,147	2012
9	Organic chemicals	$377,462,088	2012
10	Pearls, precious stones, metals, coins, etc.	$348,155,369	2012

Elasticity

Elasticity is the measurement of how changing one economic variable affects others. For example:

- "If I lower the price of my product, how much more will I sell?"
- "If I raise the price of one good, how will that affect sales of this other good?"
- "If we learn that a resource is becoming scarce, will people show scramble to acquire it?"

An *elastic* variable is one which responds disproportionately to changes in other variables. Similarly, an *inelastic* variable is one which changes less than proportionately in response to changes in other variables.

Elasticity can be quantified as the ratio of the percentage change in one variable to the percentage change in another variable, when the latter variable has a causal influence on the former. It is a tool for measuring the responsiveness of a variable, or of the function that determines it, to changes in causative variables in a unitless way. Frequently used elasticities include price elasticity of demand, price elasticity of supply, income elasticity of demand, elasticity of substitution between factors of production and elasticity of intertemporal substitution.

Elasticity is one of the most important concepts in neoclassical economic theory. It is useful in understanding the incidence of indirect taxation, marginal concepts as they relate to the theory of the firm, and distribution of wealth and different types of goods as they relate to the theory of consumer choice. Elasticity is also crucially important in any discussion of welfare distribution, in particular consumer surplus, producer surplus, or government surplus.

In empirical work an elasticity is the estimated coefficient in a linear regression equation where both the dependent variable and the independent variable are in natural logs. Elasticity is a popular tool among empiricists because it is independent of units and thus simplifies data analysis. A major study of the price elasticity of supply and the price elasticity of demand for US products was undertaken by Hendrik S. Houthakker and Lester D. Taylor.

Mathematical Definition

The definition of elasticity is based on the mathematical notion of point elasticity. In general, the "x-elasticity of y", also called the "elasticity of y with respect to x", is:

$$E_{y,x} = \left|\frac{\partial \ln y}{\partial \ln x}\right| = \left|\frac{\partial y}{\partial x}\cdot\frac{x}{y}\right| \approx \left|\frac{\%\Delta y}{\%\Delta x}\right|$$

The approximation becomes exact in the limit as the changes become infinitesimal in size. The absolute value operator is for simplicity – generally, depending on context, the sign of the elasticity is understood as being always positive or always negative. However, sometimes the elasticity is defined without the absolute value operator, when the sign may be either positive or negative or may change signs. A context where this use of a signed elasticity is necessary for clarity is the cross-price elasticity of demand — the responsiveness of the demand for one product to changes in the price of another product; since the products may be either substitutes or complements, this elasticity could be positive or negative.

In situations in which an elasticity is known to be non-negative or non-positive, the limiting cases of the elasticity occur when there is no response at all (the *totally inelastic* case with an elasticity of 0) and, at the other extreme, when an infinitesimal change in the causal variable results in an infinite change in the responding variable (the *infinitely elastic* case in which the elasticity equals infinity).

Specific Elasticities

Price elasticity of Demand: Price elasticity of demand measures the percentage change in quantity demanded caused by a percent change in price. As such, it measures the extent of movement along the demand curve. This elasticity is almost always negative and is usually expressed in terms of absolute value (i.e. as positive numbers) since the negative can be assumed. In these terms, then, if the elasticity is greater than 1 demand is said to be elastic; between zero and one demand is inelastic and if it equals one, demand is unit-elastic. A perfectly elastic demand curve is horizontal (with an elasticity of infinity) whereas a perfectly inelastic demand curve is vertical (with an elasticity of 0).

Income Elasticity of Demand: Income elasticity of demand measures the percentage change in demand caused by a percent change in income. A change in income causes the demand curve to shift reflecting the change in demand. IED is a measurement of how far the curve shifts horizontally along the X-axis. Income elasticity can be used to classify goods as normal or inferior. With a normal good demand varies in the same direction as income. With an inferior good demand and income move in opposite directions.

Cross Price Elasticity of Demand: Cross price elasticity of demand measures the percentage change in demand for a particular good caused by a percent change in the price of another good. Goods can be complements, substitutes or unrelated. A change in the price of a related good causes the demand curve to shift reflecting a change in demand for the original good. Cross price elasticity is a measurement of how far, and in which direction, the curve shifts horizontally along the x-axis. A positive cross-price elasticity means that the goods are substitute goods.

Cross Elasticity of Demand Between Firms: Cross elasticity of demand for firms, sometimes referred to as conjectural variation, is a measure of the interdependence between firms. It captures the extent to which one firm reacts to changes in strategic variables (price, quantity, location, advertising, etc.) made by other firms.

Elasticity of Intertemporal Substitution

Combined Effects: It is possible to consider the combined effects of two or more determinant of demand. The steps are as follows: PED = $(\Delta Q/\Delta P) \times P/Q$. Convert this to the predictive equation: $\Delta Q/Q = PED(\Delta P/P)$ if you wish to find the combined effect of changes in two or more determinants of demand you simply add the separate effects: $\Delta Q/Q = PED(\Delta P/P) + YED(\Delta Y/Y)$[12]

Remember you are still only considering the effect in demand of a change in two of the variables. All other variables must be held constant. Note also that graphically this problem would involve a shift of the curve and a movement along the shifted curve.

Elasticities of Supply

The price elasticity of supply measures how the amount of a good firms wish to supply changes in response to a change in price. In a manner analogous to the price elasticity of demand, it captures the extent of movement along the supply curve. If the price elasticity of supply is zero the supply of a good supplied is "inelastic" and the quantity supplied is fixed.

Price Elasticity of Supply

Price elasticity of supply (PES or E_s) is a measure used in economics to show the responsiveness, or elasticity, of the quantity supplied of a good or service to a change in its price or cost. The elasticity is represented in numerical form, and is defined as the percentage change in the quantity supplied divided by the percentage change in price. When the coefficient is less than one, the said good can be described as *inelastic*; when the coefficient is greater than one, the supply can be described as *elastic*. An elasticity of zero indicates that quantity supplied does not respond to a price change: it is "fixed" in supply. Such goods often have no labour component or are not produced, limiting the short run prospects of expansion. If the coefficient is exactly one, the good is said to be *unitary elastic*.

The quantity of goods supplied can, in the short term, be different from the amount produced, as manufacturers will have stocks which they can build up or run down.

Determinants

Availability of Raw Materials: For example, availability may cap the amount of gold that can be produced in a country regardless of price. Likewise, the price of Van Gogh paintings is unlikely to affect their supply.

Length and Complexity of Production: Much depends on the complexity of the production process. Textile production is relatively simple. The labour is largely unskilled and production facilities are little more than buildings – no special structures are needed. Thus the PES for textiles is elastic. On the other hand, the PES for specific types of motor vehicles is relatively inelastic. Auto manufacture is a multi-stage process that requires specialized equipment, skilled labour, a large suppliers network and large R&D costs.

Mobility of Factors: If the factors of production are easily available and if a producer producing one good can switch their resources and put it towards the creation of a product in demand, then it can be said that the PES is relatively elastic. The inverse applies to this, to make it relatively inelastic.

Time to Respond: The more time a producer has to respond to price changes the more elastic the supply. Supply is normally more elastic in the long run than in the short run for produced goods, since it is generally assumed that in the long run all factors of production can be utilised to increase supply, whereas in the short run only labour can be increased, and even then, changes may be prohibitively costly. For example, a cotton farmer cannot immediately (i.e. in the short run) respond to an increase in the price of soybeans because of the time it would take to procure the necessary land.

Excess Capacity: A producer who has unused capacity can (and will) quickly respond to price changes in his market assuming that variable factors are readily available.

Inventories: A producer who has a supply of goods or available storage capacity can quickly increase supply to market.

Various research methods are used to calculate price elasticities in real life, including analysis of historic sales data, both public and private, and use of present-day surveys of customers' preferences to build up test markets capable of modelling such changes. Alternatively, conjoint analysis (a ranking of users' preferences which can then be statistically analysed) may be used.

Graphical Representation

It is important to note that elasticity and slope are, in the most part, unrelated. Thus, when supply is represented linearly, regardless of the slope of the supply line, the coefficient of elasticity of any linear supply curve that passes through the origin is 1 (unit elastic). The coefficient of elasticity of any linear supply curve that cuts the y-axis is greater than 1 (elastic), and the coefficient of elasticity of any linear supply curve that cuts the x-axis is less than 1 (inelastic). Likewise, for any given supply curve, it is likely that PES will vary along the curve.

Returns to Scale

Returns to scale and economies of scale are related terms that describe what happens as the scale of production increases in the long run, when all input levels including physical capital usage are variable (chosen by the firm). They are different terms and should not be used interchangeably. The term returns to scale arises in the context of a firm's production function. It explains the behaviour of rate of increase in the output/production to the subsequent increase in the inputs i.e. the factors of production in the long run. In the long run all factors of production are variable and subject to change due to a given increase in size/scale. The laws of Returns to scale is a set of three inter-related and chronological laws (stages): Law of Increasing Returns to Scale, Law of Constant Returns to Scale, and Law of Diminishing returns to Scale. If output increases by that same proportional change then there are constant returns to scale (CRS). If output increases by less than that proportional change, there are decreasing returns to scale (DRS). If output increases by more than that proportional change, there are increasing returns to scale (IRS). In mainstream microeconomics, the returns to scale faced by a firm are purely technologically imposed and are not influenced by economic decisions or by market conditions (i.e., conclusions about returns to scale are derived from the specific mathematical structure of the production function *in isolation*).

A firm's production function could exhibit different types of returns to scale in different ranges of output. Typically, there could be increasing returns at relatively low output levels, decreasing returns at relatively high output levels, and constant returns at one output level between those ranges.

Example

When all inputs increase by a factor of 2, new values for output will be:

- Twice the previous output if there are constant returns to scale (CRS)
- Less than twice the previous output if there are decreasing returns to scale (DRS)
- More than twice the previous output if there are increasing returns to scale (IRS)

Assuming that the factor costs are constant (that is, that the firm is a perfect competitor in all input markets), a firm experiencing constant returns will have constant long-run average costs, a firm experiencing decreasing returns will have increasing long-run average costs, and a firm experiencing increasing returns will have decreasing long-run average costs. However, this relationship breaks down if the firm does not face perfectly competitive factor markets (i.e., in this context, the price one pays for a good does depend on the amount purchased). For example, if there are increasing returns to scale in some range of output levels, but the firm is so big in one or more input markets that increasing its purchases of an input drives up the input's per-unit cost, then the firm could have diseconomies of scale in that range of output levels. Conversely, if the firm is able to get bulk discounts of an input, then it could have economies of scale in some range of output levels even if it has decreasing returns in production in that output range.

Network Effect

Network externalities resemble economies of scale, but they are not considered such because they are a function of the number of users of a good or service in an industry, not of the production efficiency within a business. Economies of scale external to the firm (or industry-wide scale economies) are only considered examples of network externalities if they are driven by demand.

Formal Definitions

Formally, a production function $F(K,L)$ is defined to have:

- Constant returns to scale if (for any constant a greater than 0) $F(aK,aL) = aF(K,L)$
- Increasing returns to scale if (for any constant a greater than 1) $F(aK,aL) > aF(K,L)$,
- Decreasing returns to scale if (for any constant a greater than 1) $F(aK,aL) < aF(K,L)$

where K and L are factors of production—capital and labour, respectively.

Formal Example

The Cobb-Douglas functional form has constant returns to scale when the sum of the exponents adds up to one. The function is:

$$F(K,L) = AK^b L^{1-b}$$

where $A > 0$ and $0 < b < 1$. Thus

$$F(aK,aL) = A(aK)^b (aL)^{1-b} = Aa^b a^{1-b} K^b L^{1-b} = aAK^b L^{1-b} = aF(K,L).$$

But if the Cobb-Douglas production function has its general form

$$F(K,L) = AK^b L^c$$

with $0 < c < 1$, then there are increasing returns if $b + c > 1$ but decreasing returns if $b + c < 1$, since

$$F(aK,aL) = A(aK)^b (aL)^c = Aa^b a^c K^b L^c = a^{b+c} AK^b L^c = a^{b+c} F(K,L),$$

which is greater than or less than $aF(K,L)$ as $b+c$ is greater or less than one.

Elasticities of Scale

Elasticity of scale or output elasticities measure the percentage change in output induced by a percent change in inputs. A production function or process is said to exhibit constant returns to scale if a percentage change in inputs results in an equal percentage in outputs (an elasticity equal to 1). It exhibits increasing returns to scale if a percentage change in inputs results in greater percentage change in output (an elasticity greater than 1). The definition of decreasing returns to scale is analogous.

Applications

The concept of elasticity has an extraordinarily wide range of applications in economics. In particular, an understanding of elasticity is fundamental in understanding the response of supply and demand in a market.

Some common uses of elasticity include:

- Effect of changing price on firm revenue.
- Analysis of incidence of the tax burden and other government policies. Income elasticity of demand can be used as an indicator of industry health, future consumption patterns and as a guide to firms investment decisions. Effect of international trade and terms of trade effects. Analysis of consumption and saving behaviour.
- Analysis of advertising on consumer demand for particular goods.

Variants

In some cases the discrete (non-infinitesimal) arc elasticity is used instead. In other cases, such as modified duration in bond trading, a percentage change in output is divided by a unit (not percentage) change in input, yielding a semi-elasticity instead.

Supply Chain

A supply chain is a system of organizations, people, activities, information, and resources involved in moving a product or service from supplier to customer. Supply chain activities transform natural resources, raw materials, and components into a finished product that is delivered to the end customer. In sophisticated supply chain systems, used products may re-enter the supply chain at any point where residual value is recyclable. Supply chains link value chains.

The Council of Supply Chain Management Professionals defines supply chain management as follows: "Supply Chain Management encompasses the planning and management of all activities involved in sourcing and procurement, conversion, and all logistics management activities. Importantly, it also includes coordination and collaboration with channel partners, which can be suppliers, intermediaries, third-party service providers, and customers. In essence, supply chain management integrates supply and demand management within and across companies. Supply Chain Management is an integrating function with primary responsibility for linking major business functions and business processes within and across companies into a cohesive and high-performing business model. It includes all of the logistics management activities noted above, as well as manufacturing operations, and it drives coordination of processes and activities with and across marketing, sales, product design, finance and information technology."

A typical supply chain begins with the ecological, biological, and political regulation of natural resources, followed by the human extraction of raw material, and includes several production links (e.g., component construction, assembly, and merging) before moving on to several layers of storage facilities of ever-decreasing size and increasingly remote geographical locations, and finally reaching the consumer.

Many of the exchanges encountered in the supply chain are therefore between different companies that seek to maximize their revenue within their sphere of interest, but may have little or no knowledge or interest in the remaining players in the supply chain. More recently, the loosely coupled, self-organizing network of businesses that cooperates to provide product and service offerings has been called the *Extended Enterprise*.

Guaranteeing acceptable conditions in a global supply chain can be a complex challenge. As part of their efforts to demonstrate ethical practices, many large companies and global brands are integrating codes of conduct and guidelines into their corporate cultures and management systems. Through these, corporations are making demands on their suppliers (facilities, farms, subcontracted services such as cleaning, canteen, security etc.) and verifying, through social audits, that they are complying with the required standard.

Supply Chain Modelling

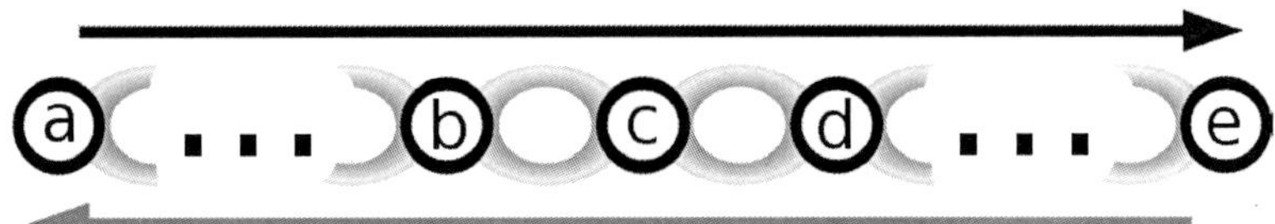

Figure: A diagram of a supply chain. The black arrow represents the flow of materials and information, and the gray arrow represents the flow of information and backhauls. The elements are (a) the initial supplier (vendor or plant), (b) a supplier, (c) a manufacturer (production), (d) a customer, and (e) the final customer.

There are a variety of supply chain models, which address both the upstream and downstream sides. The SCOR (Supply-Chain Operations Reference) model, developed by the management consulting firm PRTM, now part of PricewaterhouseCoopers LLP (PwC) has been endorsed by the Supply-Chain Council (SCC) and has become the cross-industry de facto standard diagnostic tool for supply chain management. SCOR measures total supply chain performance. It is a process reference model for supply-chain management, spanning from the supplier's supplier to the customer's customer. It includes delivery and order fulfillment performance, production flexibility, warranty and returns processing costs, inventory and asset turns, and other factors in evaluating the overall effective performance of a supply chain.

The Global Supply Chain Forum has introduced another supply chain model. This framework is built on eight key business processes that are both cross-functional and cross-firm in nature. Each process is managed by a cross-functional team including representatives from logistics, production, purchasing, finance, marketing, and research and development. While each process interfaces with key customers and suppliers, the processes of customer relationship management and supplier relationship management form the critical linkages in the supply chain.

The American Productivity and Quality Centre (APQC) Process Classification Framework (PCF) SM is a high-level, industry-neutral enterprise process model that allows organizations to see their business processes from a cross-industry viewpoint. The PCF was developed by APQC and its member vbgbbvbas an open standard to facilitate improvement through process management and benchmarking, regardless of industry, size, or geography. The PCF organizes operating and management processes into 12 enterprise-level categories, including process groups, and over 1,000 processes and associated activities.

Supply Chain Management

In the 1980s, the term supply chain management (SCM) was developed to express the need to integrate the key business processes, from end user through original suppliers. Original suppliers are those that provide products, services, and information that add value for customers and other stakeholders. The basic idea behind SCM is that companies and corporations involve themselves in a supply chain by exchanging information about market fluctuations and production capabilities. Keith Oliver, a consultant at Booz Allen Hamilton, is credited with the term's invention after using it in an interview for the *Financial Times* in 1982.

If all relevant information is accessible to any relevant company, every company in the supply chain has the ability to help optimize the entire supply chain rather than to sub-optimize based on a local interest. This will lead to better-planned overall production and distribution, which can cut costs and give a more attractive final product, leading to better sales and better overall results for the companies involved.

Incorporating SCM successfully leads to a new kind of competition on the global market, where competition is no longer of the company-versus-company form but rather takes on a supply-chain-versus-supply-chain form.

The primary objective of SCM is to fulfill customer demands through the most efficient use of resources, including distribution capacity, inventory, and labour. In theory, a supply chain seeks to match demand with supply and do so with the minimal inventory. Various aspects of optimizing the supply chain include liaising with suppliers to eliminate bottlenecks; sourcing strategically to strike a balance between lowest material cost and transportation, implementing just-in-time techniques to optimize manufacturing flow; maintaining the right mix and location of factories and warehouses to serve customer markets; and using location allocation, vehicle routing analysis, dynamic programming, and traditional logistics optimization to maximize the efficiency of distribution. There is often confusion over the terms "supply chain" and "logistics". It is now generally accepted that "logistics" applies to activities within one company or organization involving product distribution, whereas "supply chain" additionally encompasses manufacturing and procurement, and therefore has a much broader focus as it involves multiple enterprises (including suppliers, manufacturers, and retailers) working together to meet a customer need for a product or service.

Starting in the 1990s, several companies chose to outsource the logistics aspect of supply chain management by partnering with a third-party logistics provider (3PL). Companies also outsource production to contract manufacturers. Technology companies have risen to meet the demand to help manage these complex systems. There are four common supply chain models. Besides the three mentioned above, there is the Supply Chain Best Practices Framework.

Supply Chain Resilience

In recent studies, resilience is regarded as the next phase in the evolution of traditional, place-centric enterprise structures to highly virtualized, customer-centric structures that enable people to work anytime, anywhere.

Resilient supply networks should align its strategy and operations to adapt to risk that affects its capacities. There are 4 levels of supply chain resilience. First is reactive supply chain management. Second is internal supply chain integration with planned buffers. Then comes collaboration across extended supply chain networks. Finally is a dynamic supply chain adaptation and flexibility.

It is not about responding to a one-time crisis, or just having a flexible supply chain. It is about continuously anticipating and adjusting to discontinuities that can permanently impair the value preposition of a core business with special focus on delivering ultimate customer centricity. Strategic resilience, therefore, requires continuous innovation with respect to product structures, processes, but also corporate behaviour.

Social Responsibility in Supply Chains

Incidents like the 2013 Savar building collapse with more than 1,100 victims have led to widespread discussions about corporate social responsibility across global supply chains. Wieland and Handfield (2013) suggest that companies need to audit products and suppliers and that supplier auditing needs to go beyond direct relationships with first-tier suppliers. They also demonstrate that visibility needs to be improved if supply cannot be directly controlled and that smart and electronic technologies play a key role to improve visibility. Finally, they highlight that collaboration with local partners, across the industry and with universities is crucial to successfully managing social responsibility in supply chains.

Regulation

Supply chain security has become particularly important in recent years. As a result, supply chains are often subject to global and local regulations. In the United States, several major regulations emerged in 2010 that have had a lasting impact on how global supply chains operate. These new regulations include the Importer Security Filing (ISF) and additional provisions of the Certified Cargo Screening Programme.

Development and Design

With increasing globalization and easier access to alternative products in today's markets, the importance of product design to generating demand is more significant than ever. In addition, as supply, and therefore competition, among companies for the limited market demand increases and as pricing and other marketing elements become less distinguishing factors, product design likewise plays a different role by providing attractive features to generate demand. In this context, demand generation is used to define how attractive a product design is in terms of creating demand. In other words, it is the ability of a product's design to generate demand by satisfying customer expectations. But product design affects not only demand generation but also manufacturing processes, cost, quality, and lead time. The product design affects the associated supply chain and its requirements directly, including manufacturing, transportation, quality, quantity, production schedule, material selection, production technologies, production policies, regulations, and laws. Broadly, the success of the supply chain depends on the product design and the capabilities of the supply chain, but the reverse is also true: the success of the product depends on the supply chain that produces it.

Since the product design dictates multiple requirements on the supply chain, as mentioned previously, then once a product design is completed, it drives the structure of the supply chain, limiting the flexibility of engineers to generate and evaluate different (and potentially more cost-effective) supply chain alternatives.

Logistics Automation

Logistics automation is the application of computer software and/ or automated machinery to improve the efficiency of logistics operations. Typically this refers to operations within a warehouse or distribution centre, with broader tasks undertaken by supply chain management systems and enterprise resource planning systems.

Logistics automation systems can powerfully complement the facilities provided by these higher level computer systems. The focus on an individual node within a wider logistics network allows systems to be highly tailored to the requirements of that node.

Components

Logistics automation systems comprise a variety of hardware and software components:

- Fixed machinery
  - o Automated cranes (also called automated storage and retrieval systems): provide the ability to input and store a container of goods for later retrieval. Typically cranes serve a rack of locations, allowing many levels of stock to be stacked vertically, and allowing far high storage densities and better space utilization than alternatives.
  - o Conveyors: automated conveyors allow the input of containers in one area of the warehouse, and either through hard coded rules or data input allow destination selection. The container will later appear at the selected destination.
  - o Sortation, or sorting systems: similar to conveyors but typically have higher capacity and can divert containers more quickly. Typically used to distribute high volumes of small cartons to a large set of locations.
  - o Industrial Robots: four to six axis industrial robots, e.g. palleting robots, are used for palleting, depalleting, packaging, commissioning and order picking.
  - o Typically all of these will automatically identify and track containers based upon barcodes, or increasingly, RFID tags
  - o AS/RS — Automated Storage and Retrieval Systems. Vertical Carousels based on the paternoster system or with space optimization, these can be thought of as large scale vending machines, giving the same easy access to physical objects as we have become accustomed to with respect to data.

- Motion check weighers may be used to reject cases or individual products by checking them for underweight conditions and rejecting the item. They are often used in kitting conveyor lines to ensure all pieces belonging in the kit are present. Large wholesalers and retail club stores insist on receiving the exact amount of product in each package as specified.
- Mobile technology
  - o Radio data terminals: these are hand held or truck mounted terminals which connect by wireless to logistics automation software and provide instructions to operators moving throughout the warehouse. Many also have in-built bar code scanners to allow identification of containers. Bar codes allow the automatic capture of data without use of the computer keyboard, which is slow and error prone.
- Software
  - o Integration software: this provides overall control of the automation machinery and for instance allows cranes to be connected to conveyors for seamless stock movements.
  - o Operational control software: provides low-level decision making, such as where to store incoming containers, and where to retrieve them when requested.
  - o Business Control software: provides higher level functionality, such as identification of incoming deliveries / stock and scheduling order fulfillment, assignment of stock to outgoing trailers.

Benefits of Logistics Automation

A typical warehouse or distribution centre will receive stock of a variety of products from suppliers and store these until the receipt of orders from customers, whether individual buyers (e.g. mail order), retail branches (e.g. chain stores), or other companies (e.g. wholesalers). A logistics automation system may provide the following:

- Automated goods in processes: Incoming goods can be marked with barcodes and the automation system notified of the expected stock. On arrival, the goods can be scanned and thereby identified, and taken via conveyors, sortation systems, and automated cranes into an automatically assigned storage location.
- Automated Goods Retrieval for Orders: On receipt of orders, the automation system is able to immediately locate goods and retrieve them to a pickface location.

- Automated dispatch processing: Combining knowledge of all orders placed at the warehouse the automation system can assign picked goods into despatch units and then into outbound loads. Sortation systems and conveyors can then move these onto the outgoing trailers.
- If needed, repackaging to ensure proper protection for further distribution or to change the package format for specific retailers/customers.

A complete warehouse automation system can drastically reduce the workforce required to run a facility, with human input required only for a few tasks, such as picking units of product from a bulk packed case. Even here, assistance can be provided with equipment such as pick-to-light units. Smaller systems may only be required to handle part of the process. Examples include automated storage and retrieval systems, which simply use cranes to store and retrieve identified cases or pallets, typically into a high-bay storage system which would be unfeasible to access using fork-lift trucks or any other means.

Export-Import and Exchange Rates

An exchange rate (also known as a foreign-exchange rate, forex rate, FX rate or Agio) between two currencies is the rate at which one currency will be exchanged for another. It is also regarded as the value of one country's currency in terms of another currency. For example, an interbank exchange rate of 91 Japanese yen (JPY, ¥) to the United States dollar (US$) means that ¥91 will be exchanged for each US$1 or that US$1 will be exchanged for each ¥91. Exchange rates are determined in the foreign exchange market, which is open to a wide range of different types of buyers and sellers where currency trading is continuous: 24 hours a day except weekends, i.e. trading from 20:15 GMT on Sunday until 22:00 GMT Friday. The spot exchange rate refers to the current exchange rate. The forward exchange rate refers to an exchange rate that is quoted and traded today but for delivery and payment on a specific future date.

In the retail currency exchange market, a different buying rate and selling rate will be quoted by money dealers. Most trades are to or from the local currency. The buying rate is the rate at which money dealers will buy foreign currency, and the selling rate is the rate at which they will sell the currency. The quoted rates will incorporate an allowance for a dealer's margin (or profit) in trading, or else the margin may be recovered in the form of a "commission" or in some other way. Different rates may also be quoted for cash (usually notes only), a documentary form (such as traveller's cheques) or electronically (such as a credit card purchase). The higher rate on documentary transactions is due to the additional time and cost of clearing the document, while the cash is available for resale immediately. Some dealers on the other hand prefer documentary transactions because of the security concerns with cash.

Retail Exchange Market

People may need to exchange currencies in a number of situations. For example, people intending to travel to another country may buy foreign currency in a bank in their home country, where they may buy foreign currency cash, traveller's cheques or a travel-card. From a local money changer they can only buy foreign cash. At the destination, the traveller can buy local currency at the airport, either from a dealer or through an ATM. They can also buy local currency at their hotel, a local money changer, through an ATM, or at a bank branch. When they purchase goods in a store and they do not have local currency, they can use a credit card, which will convert to the purchaser's home currency at its prevailing exchange rate. If they have traveller's cheques or a travel card in the local currency, no currency exchange is necessary. Then, if a traveller has any foreign currency left over on their return home, they may want to sell it, which they may do at their local bank or money changer. The exchange rate as well as fees and charges can vary significantly on each of these transactions, and the exchange rate can vary from one day to the next.

There are variations in the quoted buying and selling rates for a currency between foreign exchange dealers and forms of exchange, and these variations can be significant. For example, consumer exchange rates used by Visa and MasterCard offer the most favourable exchange rates available, according to a Currency Exchange Study conducted by CardHub.com. This studied consumer banks in the U.S., and Travelex, showed that the credit card networks save travellers about 8% relative to banks and roughly 15% relative to airport companies.

Quotations

A currency pair is the quotation of the relative value of a currency unit against the unit of another currency in the foreign exchange market. The quotation EUR/USD 1.2500 means that 1 Euro is exchanged for 1.2500 US dollars. Here, EUR is called the "base currency" or "unit currency", while USD is called the "term currency" or "price currency".

There is a market convention that determines which is the base currency and which is the term currency. In most parts of the world, the order is: EUR – GBP – AUD – NZD – USD – others. Accordingly, a conversion from EUR to AUD, EUR is the base currency, AUD is the term currency and the exchange rate indicates how many Australian dollars would be paid or received for 1 Euro. Cyprus and Malta which were quoted as the base to the USD and others were recently removed from this list when they joined the Eurozone.

In some areas of Europe and in the non-professional market in the UK, EUR and GBP are reversed so that GBP is quoted as the base currency to the euro. In order to determine which is the base currency where both currencies are not listed (i.e. both are "other"), market convention is to use the base currency which gives an exchange rate greater than 1.000. This avoids rounding issues and exchange rates being quoted to more than 4 decimal places. There are some exceptions to this rule e.g. the Japanese often quote their currency as the base to other currencies.

Quotes using a country's home currency as the price currency (e.g., EUR 0.735342 = USD 1.00 in the Eurozone) are known as direct quotation or price quotation (from that country's perspective) and are used by most countries.

Quotes using a country's home currency as the unit currency (e.g., USD 1.35991 = EUR 1.00 in the Eurozone) are known as indirect quotation or quantity quotation and are used in British newspapers and are also common in Australia, New Zealand and the Eurozone.

Using direct quotation, if the home currency is strengthening (i.e., appreciating, or becoming more valuable) then the exchange rate number decreases. Conversely if the foreign currency is strengthening, the exchange rate number increases and the home currency is depreciating.

Market convention from the early 1980s to 2006 was that most currency pairs were quoted to 4 decimal places for spot transactions and up to 6 decimal places for forward outrights or swaps. (The fourth decimal place is usually referred to as a "pip"). An exception to this was exchange rates with a value of less than 1.000 which were usually quoted to 5 or 6 decimal places. Although there is no fixed rule, exchange rates with a value greater than around 20 were usually quoted to 3 decimal places and currencies with a value greater than 80 were quoted to 2 decimal places. Currencies over 5000 were usually quoted with no decimal places (e.g. the former Turkish Lira). e.g.

(GBPOMR : 0.765432 - : 1.4436 - EURJPY : 165.29). In other words, quotes are given with 5 digits. Where rates are below 1, quotes frequently include 5 decimal places.

In 2005 Barclays Capital broke with convention by offering spot exchange rates with 5 or 6 decimal places on their electronic dealing platform. The contraction of spreads (the difference between the bid and offer rates) arguably necessitated finer pricing and gave the banks the ability to try and win transaction on multibank trading platforms where all banks may otherwise have been quoting the same price. A number of other banks have now followed this system.

Exchange Rate Regime

Each country, through varying mechanisms, manages the value of its currency. As part of this function, it determines the exchange rate regime that will apply to its currency. For example, the currency may be free-floating, pegged or fixed, or a hybrid. If a currency is free-floating, its exchange rate is allowed to vary against that of other currencies and is determined by the market forces of supply and demand. Exchange rates for such currencies are likely to change almost constantly as quoted on financial markets, mainly by banks, around the world.

A movable or adjustable peg system is a system of fixed exchange rates, but with a provision for the revaluation (usually devaluation) of a currency. For example, between 1994 and 2005, the Chinese yuan renminbi (RMB) was pegged to the United States dollar at RMB 8.2768 to $1. China was not the only country to do this; from the end of World War II until 1967, Western European countries all maintained fixed exchange rates with the US dollar based on the Bretton Woods system. [1] But that system had to be abandoned in favour of floating, market-based regimes due to market pressures and speculations in the 1970s.

Still, some governments strive to keep their currency within a narrow range. As a result, currencies become over-valued or under-valued, leading to excessive trade deficits or surpluses.

Fluctuations in Exchange Rates

A market-based exchange rate will change whenever the values of either of the two component currencies change. A currency will tend to become more valuable whenever demand for it is greater than the available supply. It will become less valuable whenever demand is less than available supply (this does not mean people no longer want money, it just means they prefer holding their wealth in some other form, possibly another currency).

Increased demand for a currency can be due to either an increased transaction demand for money or an increased speculative demand for money. The transaction demand is highly correlated to a country's level of business activity, gross domestic product (GDP), and employment levels. The more people that are unemployed, the less the public as a whole will spend on goods and services. Central banks typically have little difficulty adjusting the available money supply to accommodate changes in the demand for money due to business transactions.

Speculative demand is much harder for central banks to accommodate, which they influence by adjusting interest rates. A speculator may buy a currency if the return (that is the interest rate) is high enough. In general, the higher a country's interest rates, the greater will be the demand for that currency. It has been argued that such speculation can undermine real economic growth, in particular since large currency speculators may deliberately create downward pressure on a currency by shorting in order to force that central bank to buy their own currency to keep it stable. (When that happens, the speculator can buy the currency back after it depreciates, close out their position, and thereby take a profit.)

For carrier companies shipping goods from one nation to another, exchange rates can often impact them severely. Therefore, most carriers have a CAF charge to account for these fluctuations.

Purchasing Power of Currency

The real exchange rate (RER) is the purchasing power of a currency relative to another at current exchange rates and prices. It is the ratio of the number of units of a given country's currency necessary to buy a market basket of goods in the other country, after acquiring the other country's currency in the foreign exchange market, to the number of units of the given country's currency that would be necessary to buy that market basket directly in the given country .

Thus the real exchange rate is the exchange rate times the relative prices of a market basket of goods in the two countries. For example, the purchasing power of the US dollar relative to that of the euro is the dollar price of a euro (dollars per euro) times the euro price of one unit of the market basket (euros/goods unit) divided by the dollar price of the market basket (dollars per goods unit), and hence is dimensionless. This is the exchange rate (expressed as dollars per euro) times the relative price of the two currencies in terms of their ability to purchase units of the market basket (euros per goods unit divided by dollars per goods unit).

If all goods were freely tradable, and foreign and domestic residents purchased identical baskets of goods, purchasing power parity (PPP) would hold for the exchange rate and GDP deflators (price levels) of the two countries, and the real exchange rate would always equal 1.

The rate of change of this real exchange rate over time equals the rate of appreciation of the euro (the positive or negative percentage rate of change of the dollars-per-euro exchange rate) plus the inflation rate of the euro minus the inflation rate of the dollar.

Bilateral vs. Effective Exchange Rate

Bilateral exchange rate involves a currency pair, while an effective exchange rate is a weighted average of a basket of foreign currencies, and it can be viewed as an overall measure of the country's external competitiveness. A nominal effective exchange rate (NEER) is weighted with the inverse of the asymptotic trade weights. A real effective exchange rate (REER) adjusts NEER by appropriate foreign price level and deflates by the home country price level. Compared to NEER, a GDP weighted effective exchange rate might be more appropriate considering the global investment phenomenon.

Uncovered Interest Rate Parity

Uncovered interest rate parity (UIRP) states that an appreciation or depreciation of one currency against another currency might be neutralized by a change in the interest rate differential. If US interest rates increase while Japanese interest rates remain unchanged then the US dollar should depreciate against the Japanese yen by an amount that prevents arbitrage (in reality the opposite, appreciation, quite frequently happens in the short-term, as explained below). The future exchange rate is reflected into the forward exchange rate stated today. In our example, the forward exchange rate of the dollar is said to be at a discount because it buys fewer Japanese yen in the forward rate than it does in the spot rate. The yen is said to be at a premium.

UIRP showed no proof of working after the 1990s. Contrary to the theory, currencies with high interest rates characteristically appreciated rather than depreciated on the reward of the containment of inflation and a higher-yielding currency.

Balance of Payments Model

The balance of payments model holds that foreign exchange rates are at an equilibrium level if they produce a stable current account balance. A nation with a trade deficit will experience a reduction in its foreign exchange reserves, which ultimately lowers (depreciates) the value of its currency. A cheaper (undervalued) currency renders the nation's goods (exports) more affordable in the global market while making imports more expensive. After an intermediate period, imports will be forced down and exports to rise, thus stabilizing the trade balance and bring the currency towards equilibrium.

Like purchasing power parity, the balance of payments model focuses largely on trade-able goods and services, ignoring the increasing role of global capital flows. In other words, money is not only chasing goods and services, but to a larger extent, financial assets such as stocks and bonds. Their flows go into the capital account item of the balance of payments, thus balancing the deficit in the current account. The increase in capital flows has given rise to the asset market model.

Asset Market Model

The increasing volume of trading of financial assets (stocks and bonds) has required a rethink of its impact on exchange rates. Economic variables such as economic growth, inflation and productivity are no longer the only drivers of currency movements. The proportion of foreign exchange transactions stemming from cross border-trading of financial assets has dwarfed the extent of currency transactions generated from trading in goods and services.

The asset market approach views currencies as asset prices traded in an efficient financial market. Consequently, currencies are increasingly demonstrating a strong correlation with other markets, particularly equities.

Like the stock exchange, money can be made (or lost) on trading by investors and speculators in the foreign exchange market. Currencies can be traded at spot and foreign exchange options markets. The spot market represents current exchange rates, whereas options are derivatives of exchange rates.

Manipulation of Exchange Rates

A country may gain an advantage in international trade if it manipulates the market for its currency to artificially keep its value low, typically by the national central bank engaging in open market operations. It has been argued by US legislators that the People's

Republic of China has been acting in that way over a long period of time. In 2010, other nations, including Japan and Brazil, attempted to devalue their currency in the hopes of reducing the cost of exports and thus bolstering their ailing economies. A low (undervalued) exchange rate lowers the price of a country's goods for consumers in other countries but raises the price of goods, especially imported goods, for consumers in the manipulating country.

Trade Facilitation

Trade facilitation looks at how procedures and controls governing the movement of goods across national borders can be improved to reduce associated cost burdens and maximise efficiency while safeguarding legitimate regulatory objectives. Business costs may be a direct function of collecting information and submitting declarations or an indirect consequence of border checks in the form of delays and associated time penalties, forgone business opportunities and reduced competitiveness.

Understanding and use of the term "trade facilitation" varies in the literature and amongst practitioners. "Trade facilitation" is largely used by institutions which seek to improve the regulatory interface between government bodies and traders at national borders. The WTO, in an online training package, once defined trade facilitation as: "The simplification and harmonisation of international trade procedures" where trade procedures are the "activities, practices and formalities involved in collecting, presenting, communicating and processing data required for the movement of goods in international trade".

In defining the term, many trade facilitation proponents will also make reference to trade finance and the procedures applicable for making payments (e.g. via a commercial banks). For example UN/CEFACT defines trade facilitation as "the simplification, standardization and harmonisation of procedures and associated information flows required to move goods from seller to buyer and to make payment".

Occasionally, the term trade facilitation is extended to address a wider agenda in economic development and trade to include: the improvement of transport infrastructure, the removal of government corruption, the modernization of customs administration, the removal of other non-tariff trade barriers, as well as export marketing and promotion.

Examples of Regulatory Activity in International Trade

Fiscal: Collection of customs duties, excise duties and other indirect taxes; payment mechanisms

Safety and security: Security and anti smuggling controls; dangerous goods; vehicle checks; immigration and visa formalities

Environment and health: Phytosanitary, veterinary and hygiene controls; health and safety measures; CITES controls; ships' waste

Consumer protection: Product testing; labelling; conformity checks with marketing standards (e.g. fruit and vegetables)

Trade policy: Administration of quota restrictions; export refunds

Topics and Issues in Trade Facilitation

Trade facilitation has its intellectual roots in the fields of logistics and supply chain management. Trade facilitation looks at operational improvements at the interface between business and government and associated transaction costs. Trade facilitation has become a key feature in supply chain security and customs modernisation programmes. Within the context of economic development it has also come to prominence in the Doha Development Round. However, it is an equally prominent feature in unilateral and bilateral initiatives that seek to improve the trade environment and enhance business competitiveness. Reference to trade facilitation is sometimes also made in the context of "better regulation". Some organisations promoting trade facilitation will emphasis the cutting of red tape in international trade as their main objective. Propagated ideas and concepts to reforming trade and customs procedures generally resonate around the following themes:

- Simple rules and procedures
- Avoidance of duplication
- Memoranda of Understanding (MoUs)
- Alignment of procedures and adherence to international conventions
- Trade consultation
- Transparent and operable rules and procedures
- Accommodation of business practices
- Operational flexibility
- Public-service standards and performance measures
- Mechanisms for corrections and appeals

- Fair and consistent enforcement
- Proportionality of legislation and control to risk
- Time-release measures
- Risk management and trader authorisations
- Standardisation of documents and electronic data requirements
- Automation
- International electronic exchange of trade data
- Single Window System

Trade Facilitation and Development

Success in export markets for developed and developing country firms is increasingly affected by the ability of countries to support an environment which promotes efficient and low cost trade services and logistics. Policies related to trade facilitation and economic development reflect the idea that trade can be a powerful engine for accelerating economic growth, job creation, and poverty reduction.

Background

World trade has expanded rapidly over the past decades. This has been driven, in large part, by the changing nature of both production and increased competition in international commerce. Another important factor contributing to the growth in trade has been the periodic rounds of successful multilateral trade negotiations. These talks at the World Trade Organization (WTO) have led to a considerable reduction in tariffs on goods crossing national borders. Today, as the role of traditional trade barriers gradually vanishes, the focus of trade policy has shifted to the remaining non-tariff barriers to trade, including trade facilitation.

Trade facilitation involves a wide range of activities centred on lowering trade transaction costs for firms in global commerce. These costs include the price of moving freight from the factory to final destinations. Firms must manage border clearance procedures and pay trade services fees, among many other steps after goods and services are produced. As such, trade facilitation involves much more than trucking goods across national borders or shipping a package by sea transport.

Cross-country Comparisons and Performance

There is an increasing body of empirical evidence about the impact of trade facilitation on export competitiveness and growth.

Studies reviewed by the Organisation for Economic Co-operation and Development (OECD, 2002) indicate that trade transaction costs amount to up to 15 percent of the value of traded goods globally. A subsequent OECD study (2003) found trade transactions costs to be higher on agricultural and food products, fish, and forest and wood products (since these products are subject to additional border procedures due to sanitary and phytosanitary requirements).

These are products for which many developing countries have an advantage. The same study also reported that small and medium enterprises suffer most from poor trade-related practices and poorer developing countries have a larger share of such enterprises. A number of other studies have illustrated the specifics of why trade facilitation matters and specific sources of trade costs. One study, for example, found that barriers to export performance in Africa are closely related to firm characteristics and policies that raise trade costs. This includes non-transparent customs laws and administration. Much less evidence was found that transport infrastructure, in comparison, had a significant impact on export performance (Clarke, 2005).

World Bank Research

The World Bank is conducting extensive research on the issue of trade facilitation and its effects on trade, economic growth, and development. The main part of the research is carried out under the project Trade Costs and Facilitation. This project is focused on contributing to stronger understanding of the concrete relationships between trade costs, trade facilitation, private sector growth, and export competitiveness in developing countries. A major focus of the work is on exploring the dynamic gains associated with lowering trade transactions costs and identifying the relative importance of related reform measures.

The World Bank's *Doing Business 2007: How to reform* report (2007) documents the wide range of reform needed in developing countries to lower trade costs. The report outlines procedural requirements for importing and exporting a standardized cargo of goods in 155 countries. While the total cost to import (in US$ per container) was $842 on average in high-income countries, it was $1960 in low-income countries. Typical regulations in low-income countries required 13 documents from domestic regulatory agencies as compared to six signatures in high income countries, nine in upper-middle-income and ten in low-middle-income countries. On average it still costs almost two and a half times in expenses, more than twice as many documents and four times as many signatures to trade in a poor country as it does in rich countries.

The *Doing Business* report provides concrete examples of efficiency savings made possible through trade facilitation reforms. Much of these relate to addressing regulatory reform and other steps—that in contrast to hard infrastructure—constitute the major part of why engaging in trade takes longer in developing countries. Progress in reducing costs, however, has been made. For example, Guatemala with the support of the Inter-American Development Bank changed to an electronic system for export authorization in 2000. Within four years the time for authorization of export documents dropped from one day to around three minutes. Tunisia has also introduced an automated system that provides a one-stop trade documentation-processing platform. Due to this innovation the processing time for trade documentation became reduced from 18 to 7 days which probably had led to substantial productivity gains according to the United Nations Economic Commission for Africa.

What are the Gains From Cutting Trade Costs?

There are important gains to lowering trade costs and facilitating trade with some variation across countries and sectors (Francois et al., 2005; OECD, 2003). Several studies have focused on the impact of trade facilitation on the micro-level (OECD, 2005). They observe that in some developing countries inefficient trade regulations, documents and procedures are hindering firms' participation in export markets. The studies find large potential benefits from streamlining trade regulations and hence cutting the costs for exporting.

Analysis by the World Bank suggests that raising global capacity in trade facilitation (port efficiency, customs, regulatory transparency, and information technology used in trade transactions) halfway to the global average would increase world trade by $377 billion (Wilson, et al. 2005). This is an increase of about 9.7 percent in global trade with the majority of the gains due to domestic reform and capacity building. About $107 billion of the total gain comes from the improvement in port efficiency and about $33 billion results from the improvement in customs environment.

The gain from the improvement in regulatory environment is $83 billion. The largest gain ($154 billion) comes from an improvement in information technology infrastructure which is increasingly applied all across the trade value and logistics chain. The important work ahead to lower trade costs however is outside the scope of trade policy, therefore, and squarely centred within domestic reform agendas, including services such as transport, telecommunication, and others that affect trade transactions costs. There is also a key role to be played by private sector-led policy reform according to many of these studies.

Trade Costs and the Multilateral Trading System

Talks are underway on revisions to the WTO rules on trade facilitation in the Doha Development Agenda negotiations. The outlines of a possible agreement includes, among others: (1). New obligations to promote electronic distribution and transmission of government trade regulations on imports and exports; (2). Standardization of certain basic fees for imports; (3). Stronger rules to help ensure freedom of transit for goods crossing national borders.

In the WTO secretariat tabulation of proposals from August 11, 2006 there is consideration of more "ambitious" changes to current obligations, such as establishment of a single window for exporters and importers at customs or accepting copies of documents for import and export in lieu of originals. Since 2002 there have also been talks about explicit ties between a package of technical assistance and development aid as part of any final agreement. Developing countries participated very actively in these negotiations and before the suspension of the Doha Round in late 2006 considerable progress had been achieved (World Bank, 2006).

Changes to the multilateral trade rules noted above can help in advancing transparent and predictable trading procedures for exporters. These rules have not been revised in over 50 years and crafting an achievable and focused next step in the Doha Agenda will be helpful to traders. This is especially true for small and medium-sized firms that lack resources and networks to overcome some of the more complex border rules now in place. Meeting trade facilitation goals in a broader and deeper context, however, will require action well outside and beyond the WTO framework.

More effective delivery of development aid and technical assistance especially in projects to advance regulatory reform and support public agencies that promulgate and administer trade regulations is needed. A better understanding of conditions under which developing countries are ready to receive such assistance so that aid is effectively delivered is required.

The Agenda Ahead

At the most basic level, better data, analysis, and indicators of performance are needed to inform discussions moving forward on how trade costs and facilitation measures affect global commerce. Progress in reaching development goals in trade can only be made with accurate data and analysis to drive policy choice and action.

Taking advantage of the energy behind reaching the Millennium Development Goals (MDGs), building on the datasets in the global monitoring reports which track progress in reaching poverty reduction goals, among other reports, makes significant sense.

In sum, the data gathered to date illustrate the fact that the non-tariff agenda in trade is increasingly important to economic development ahead.

3

Logistics Management: A Resource

Empirical taxonomic approaches, which can reduce complexity or achieve parsimony by breaking the organisation into distinct and internally consistent categories without losing the main information or characteristics that exist within the taxa have become prominent in research on strategic management, marketing management, and operation management but very few published empirical studies have focused on logistics and supply chain management (SCM). Further, even if researchers have employed the taxonomic approach to logistics or SCM, they have used narrow criteria or a few variables to classify firms in taxonomy such as logistics strategy, logistics strategic orientation or logistics technology adoption.

Miller (1996) warned that a too narrowly focus on a tew key elements was dangerous because an organisation would lose its resilience and relevance.

Another critical problem on taxonomic study is clustering dimensions disconnected form theory which may result in the taxa viewed as "data dredging" and not reflecting actual organisational real conditions. Thus, the resource-based view (RBV) of the firm, which contends that the nonimitable resources and capabilities of firms are the key sources of sustained competitive advantage, is one of the most influential theories in taxonomic studies and strongly recommended by logistics/SCM researchers.

In addition, most logistics and SCM empirical studies have concentrated on Western developed countries, displaying a particular bias towards the USA. Non-Western developed countries, such as

Taiwan, have been the focus of very few logistics and SCM studies, even though 60% of the world's desktop PCs or PC's motherboards are made in Taiwan or by Taiwanese company.

In summary, the empirical taxonomic approach and the resource-based view of the firm have become two important theories in other disciplines, but not in the logistics and SCM fields. The present study will combine them, utilising logistics competency factors to classify organisations in the manufacturing industry of Taiwan.

Logistics Competency Approaches: A Resource-based Explanation

The strategic role of logistics has not received attention because logistics is still largely viewed as a separate entity or its activities as operational or tactical functions. However, the logistics competency approach can be regarded as a key strategic resource for acquiring sustained competitive advantage when resources or competencies are valuable, scarce and difficult to imitate.

A resource is valuable because it can exploit opportunities and threats in a firm's environment and thereby enhance efficiency and effectiveness. Likewise, logistics competency approaches are valuable because they can help organisations gain the benefit of both value-added maximisation and cost minimisation.

Logistics relative capability approaches are, nevertheless, scarce because they involve a set of physical assets, knowledge, technology, organisational routines, and people skills, which need time to develop and integrate and are difficult to buy from the market. Additionally, logistics relative capability may include the need to effectively manage the relationship with suppliers, logistics service providers, and customers, and however, suitable and appropriate, supply chain partnerships may be difficult to build.

Logistics relative capability approaches are also difficult and costly to imitate because of causal ambiguity. It is difficult to copy something that you do not know exactly what it is! Furthermore, it is difficult to discern the real cause of competitive advantage due to the complex relations existing within logistics partnerships or logistics networks. 'These exist in a complex web of social interactions and may even depend critically on particular individuals'.

Several empirical studies have focused on logistical capability approaches. Bower and Hout (1992) and Daugherty and Pittman (1995) concentrated on fast cycle capabilities and indicated how firms can utilise time-based strategies to acquire competitive advantage. Fawcett et al. (1996, 2000) employed cross-function research (i.e. logistics and manufacturing) and concluded that flexibility, quality, and cost are important capabilities that help firms enhance their performance and manage worldwide resources and markets.

Morash et al. (1996a, 1996b) explored logistics capabilities conducting cross-function research (i.e. production, logistics, marketing, and new product development) and sole-function research (i.e. logistics) on 65 furniture manufacturing firms. The former concluded that excellence solely in one functional area is not the source of competitive advantage.

Rather, boundary-spanning interface capabilities, including demand management and supply management interface capabilities, across functional areas become a source of SCA. In contrast, the latter identified logistics capabilities as demand-oriented and supply-oriented capabilities and concluded that some (i.e. delivery speed, reliability, responsiveness, and low cost distribution) are sources of SCA.

Gilmour (1999) undertook a cross-national study of Australia, Japan, South Korea and Taiwan, exploring and identifying supply chain capabilities, including process, technology, and organisation capabilities. Morash and Clinton (1997) concluded that transportation capabilities may play a lead role in the integration and coordination of supply chain flow.

An examination of logistics capabilities was performed by MSUGLRT (1995) and later extended by Bowersox et al. (1999). MSUGLRT (1995) identified 17 logistics capabilities included in four logistics competencies.

Bowersox et al. (1999) further expanded the 17 logistics capabilities to 25 supply chain capabilities related to 6 supply chain competencies and confirmed that the capabilities were critical to firms' success. Following on from this work, Stank and Lackey (1997) examined capabilities related to competence and found integration and agility to be of particular importance to logistical performance.

Lynch et al. (2000) combined industrial organisation economics and resource-based theory to explore the relationship between logistics capabilities, generic business strategies, and performance. They identified two logistics capabilities: process capabilities and value-added service capabilities, and concluded that logistics capabilities are associated with strategy and need to be combined in order to achieve superior firm performance. Goldsby and Stank (2000) later confirmed the positive relationship between 17 logistics capabilities, and the implementation of environmentally responsible logistics. More recently, Zhao et al. (2001) found customer-focused capabilities directly affect performance. In contrast, information-focused capabilities indirectly affect performance.

Taxonomic Criteria: Four Logistics Competencies

In this study, we will utilise MSUGLRT's (1995) four logistics competencies as the criteria of taxonomy. The four logistics competencies are introduced below:

Positioning Competency

Strategic positioning is defined as "...performing different activities from rivals, or performing similar activities in different ways", and is the essential starting point to logistical excellence. "World class" firms view logistics positioning competency as a differentiator that can lead to competitive advantage.

Integration Competency

Integration may be the most important issue in logistics and SCM because the "...most fundamental shift in logistics thinking is to view functional excellence in terms of performance that enhances overall supply chain integration". Notably, the Dell computer's virtual integration, blurring of traditional boundaries and roles in the value chain, may become a new organisational model in the new information generation. Integration is not a new concept in the field of management or organisational science. For example, Fayol (1949) identified coordination as one of the five critical functions of management and Lawrence and Lorsch (1967) stated that differentiation and integration are the basic principles for understanding organisational structures. However, in the logistics and SCM field, integration is central to logistics and the key to SCM.

Some logistics researchers have viewed integration as a dimension of organisational structure or design whereas others have identified integration as an outcome of organisational structure. In this study, integration is viewed as the outcome of organisational structure and its scope includes intra-firm and other firms supporting the same supply chain. Integration is therefore identified as "...the degree to which logistics tasks and activities within the firm and across the supply chain are managed in a coordinated fashion".

Agility Competency

Agility is a business-wide capability "...to thrive in a competitive environment of continually and unpredictably changing market opportunities". Agility has replaced delivery speed (1990s), quality (1980s), cost (1970s) and become the main competitive priority in the twenty-first century. Creating agile supply chains has become a source of competitive advantage. Most studies have viewed agility as a general management or a strongly biased manufacturing concept, not focused on the concept in the "supply chain as a whole", and also shown a bias towards the USA. Thus, this study focuses on the concept of agility in the logistics and total supply chain in the manufacturing industry in Taiwan.

Measurement Competency

Measurement refers to a firm's performance measurement system which plays an important role in managing the business because it offers the information necessary for decision making and actions. Keebler et al. (1999) indicated that an excellent measurement system should produce three primary benefits: reduced costs, improved service, and the generation of healthy growth. Measurement is not solely a logistics and supply chain problem, but is particularly critical in the logistics and SCM field because of cross-functional and inter-organisational requirement. Recent research has identified performance measurement as one of the top three areas of logistics research needs.

A questionnaire survey was administered to 1,200 of the largest manufacturing firms in Taiwan drawn from the annual report entitled "The Top 5000: the largest corporations in Taiwan" (China Credit Information Service Company, 2000). Questionnaires were sent to the offices of the presidents or chief executive officers of the 1,200 firms targeted.

The revised seven-page survey instrument was mailed to respondents, after a pilot study interviewing academic and practice experts, together with a cover letter explaining the purpose of the study on university letterhead paper. A postage paid return envelope was attached to the questionnaire. After two weeks, follow-up mailings were sent to those respondents who had not returned questionnaires in the first wave of the survey. Eleven questionnaires were returned as non-deliverable. Ten of the 208 returned questionnaires were discarded because respondents had put the same answers on all Likert-scale items. The total response rate was 16.5% (198/1200).

To detect any potential non-response bias, Armstrong and Overton (1977) and Lambert and Harrington (1990) recommend that the last quartile or second wave of respondents' responses is assumed to be most similar to those of non-respondents. The returned second wave questionnaire responses were compared with those of the first wave, by t-test analysis. Results showed there were no significant differences (at $p<0.05$) as regards all Likert-scale items and therefore non-response bias was not a problem.

The 17 items to determine logistics capabilities were mainly based upon MSUGLRTs (1995) work. It developed and defined these capabilities from a base-line survey administered by mail to 3,700 respondents in 11 countries of North America, Europe, and the Pacific Rim, and subsequent in-depth interviews with 111 firms in order to refine the research framework. Seven-point Likert-type scale anchors were used. Respondents were asked to provide a rating of the strategy business unit (SBU) or the firm's logistics competency relative to its major competitors for each item, where 1 represented "Much Worse" and 7 represented "Much Better". In contrast, logistics, market, and financial performance were measured using a 11-item performance scale most frequently utilised by logistics and SCM researchers.

A series of confirmatory factor analyses (CFA) were performed by AMOS to provide evidence of the validity and reliability of the valuables before submitting the data to cluster analysis. Missing data existed but the amount of missing data in respect of each variable was small (less than 6.6%). Accordingly, the regression substitution approach was used for remedying missing data and the sample size was kept at the original size.

Cluster Analysis

To develop the empirical taxonomy of logistics competencies, a two-stage procedure was employed to take advantage of the strengths of hierarchical and nonhierarchical clustering approaches. A hierarchical algorithm was used firstly to define the number of clusters and cluster centroids which then served as the starting points for subsequent nonhierarchical cluster analysis. Constructs used in the cluster analysis were logistics competency factors, including positioning, integration, agility, and measurement.

It was difficult to determine how many clusters were appropriate. Hair et al. (1998) recommend a relatively simple stopping rule, that is, look for large increases in the average within-cluster distance. Because of the large increases in agglomeration coefficient, the Ward's hierarchical clustering results indicated that a two-cluster solution was adequate and the cluster centres became the initial starting point for nonhierarchical cluster analysis.

Validation and Profiling of the Clusters

"Validation may be the most neglected issue in cluster analysis". A second nonhierarchical analysis was performed to confirm consistency by allowing the programme to randomly select the initial starting points for a twocluster solution. The results indicated that 93% (185/198) of firms were assigned to the same clusters, which gave some confidence in the stability of the clustering results.

Criterion-related validity was assessed through an independent-samples t-test with three performance constructs (i.e. external variables), because the external variables in strategy research are often performance measures. The results confirm the measures of performance were significantly different ($p<0.01$) in these two clusters, supporting the criterion-related validity of the taxonomy.

An independent samples t-test was also employed and indicated there were significant differences ($p<0.01$) between clusters of the four logistics competencies. Discriminant analysis was utilised to confirm the correct assigned rate. Ninety-five per cent (188/198) of the firms were assigned to the correct clusters. These results provided evidences of the relative stability and reliability of the clusters identified. To investigate the sources of the differences driving the clustering, a test was performed on respondents' demographic characteristics. The results indicated that firms' size, sales, and industry were not the main influential factors on the two clusters.

Interpreting Cluster Results

Cluster 1 Extensive logistics competency (108 firms; 54.5% of 198 total firms). The main distinguishing feature of this cluster was that respondents' agreement was low on all four logistics competencies.

Cluster 2 Intensive logistics competency (90 firms, 45.5% of 198 total firms). Respondents' agreement was high on all four logistics competencies. Thus, cluster 1 reflected lower business performance on all indexes, including financial, market, and logistics, than cluster 2.

The research findings reveal that the intensive logistics competency cluster (cluster 2) had excellent logistic competencies in all four logistics factors, thus positioning, integration, agility, and measurement, could produce better performance. The findings also demonstrate that the logistic competency cluster is not associated with employees, sales, and industry. The findings suggest that logistics competencies are directly related to logistics, market, and financial performance and should not exist in a vacuum, but should leverage each other to create sustained competitive advantage. The more logistics competencies are combined together, the more difficult it will be for competitors to imitate them. This viewpoint is the central theme of resource-based theory.

Of particular note, the findings also confirm Kohn et al.'s (1990) and McGinnis and Kohn's (1993) research. Therefore, logistics competencies can be regarded as a key strategic resource for acquiring sustained competitive advantage. Logistics or top managers should constantly seek to enhance and refine their firms' four logistics competencies in relation to those of their competitors in order to acquire and maintain long-term superior performance.

Two important study limitations should be noted. First, this study's sample was drawn from the top, largest 1,200 manufacturing firms in Taiwan. Therefore, the conclusions inferred can only be generalised to include the top largest manufacturing firms in Taiwan and must exclude other smaller or less successful and non-manufacturing firms. Second, all participants responded within a particular time frame and were only given a single opportunity to respond. Therefore, it cannot be reliably established whether such data would hold true over time, especially in dynamic business environments. In particular, different firms have distinct strategic goals in the short term, such as customer satisfaction, market share, growth, etc. Moreover, firms may enhance market share by sacrificing short-term profit in order to acquire long-term profit. The performance items in this study could not reflect these varying situations.

The resource-based view (RBV) of the firm is an excellent theory for application in the logistics and supply chain management field, however, 'due to the intangible nature of important firm resources, researchers have used detailed field-based studies, longitudinal case studies, outlier samples, and case surveys...to test RBV hypotheses'. Thus, more qualitative-based methodologies are possible alternatives for exploring firms' special logistics resources and capabilities.

Communication Technologies on Logistics Management

This chapter explores the impacts of enterprises' applying ICT on their logistics management, by conducting surveys on ICT manufacturers and transport logistics companies; 101 Taiwanese firms, 23% from manufacturing and 77% from transport logistics. Results show that applying ICTs has already had an impact and provided significant benefits to this specific industry sector. ICTs have been widely applied in the operations of customer services, transportation management, order processing, warehousing management, and ERP. Customer service management may be the most worthwhile area to apply ICT in the future. Statistical analyses were conducted between manufacturing and logistics industries, and among different sizes of companies. However, there were no significant differences between these industries and companies in most of the questions.

Most of the managers agree with the value of ICT for their business, no matter what positions they are in the whole business process. Some ICT application were significantly related to the success of operations.

This finding can be an important reference for both public and business sectors, and ICT suppliers. The application and development of Information and Communication Technologies (ICT) have already had significant effects on many industries, especially in the field of logistics. Because of it, the style of business operation, up-/downstream partnership and customer relationship are changing.

The application of computers, internet, and information communication systems can be seen in almost every activity in the logistics industry, such as transportation, warehousing, order processing, material management, and procurement.

It is suggested that passing information to all businesses in the supply chains via ICT will improve performances. ICT has been promoted as a means to enhance logistics competitiveness. It is one of the few factors which has been proved to have the capability of increasing logistics competence and decreasing its costs simultaneously. Today, besides enterprises, governments around the world and the global organisations such as OECD, are all devoting their efforts to searching for chances of new development or application of information and communications techniques.

The application of ICT in logistics management is relatively recent, it lets real-time/online information communication and data exchange through the entire operation chains become realistic speaking of time and cost. Most of the people agree that ICT is valuable to logistics management, however, the ways of applications and impacts are not clear. It is also interesting to note that ICT has been available for local manufacturers and transport logistics firms for a number of years. However, there are many questions that concern members in the industry and ICT suppliers that can be explored, such as: What are the popular applied ICT? What kinds of benefits and impacts have been induced? Are there any different experience of applying ICT among different industries and different scales of enterprises? How much difference is there between expectations and results for ICT applicants? The objective of this study is to thoroughly understand and answer the above questions.

The Application of ICT

Information and communication technologies may be defined as "electronic means of capturing, processing, storing, and disseminating information". All these technologies provide new mechanisms for handling existing resources and information. The term "ICT" is used to delineate various Telecommunication and Information technologies, which have been used in the fields of transport since the mid80s. Over the past decade (the 1990s), there was development in prototype technologies, the systems, and their applications in the fields of transport, such as freight resource management, freight and vehicle tracking and tracing, and front or back-office logistics systems. The internet and related ICT recently enabled the cost effective dissemination of information between disparate parties in the supply chains.

Leek et al. (2003) indicated that the usefulness and frequency of usage of mobile phones and e-mails have caused the uptake of new technologies from business to business companies to be very variable. They believe that the usage of internet, intranet, extranet, and audio/ video-conferences will increase in the future. Stefansson (2002) stated that large companies are using EDI technology to communicate with business data but experiencing problems in communication with those small companies. The advent of the Internet opens up new perspectives on small and medium enterprises. The Internet makes electronic business affordable even for the smallest companies. Companies of all sizes can communicate with each other electronically through the public network (Internet), an inside company network (Intranets) or a specified network between company and its business partners (Extranet).

Logistics Management and LIS

According to the definition made by the US Council of Logistics Management (CLM), "Logistics Management is that part of the supply chain processes that plans, implements, and controls the efficient, effective flow and storage of goods, services and related information from the point of origin to the point of consumption in order to meet customers' requirements". This definition includes the flow of goods, services and information in both the manufacturing and service sectors. The major logistics activities include customer services, demand forecasting, inventory management, logistics communications, material handling, order processing, packaging, parts and service support, plant and warehouse site selection, procurement, reverse logistics, traffic and transportation, warehousing and storage.

The information systems satisfying the concept above can be regarded as Logistics Information Systems (LIS). The function of LIS can be defined as "Logistics Information System is an interacting structure of people, equipment, and procedures which together make relevant information available to the logistics managers for the purposes of planning, implementation, and control ".

ICT/IT and Logistics

Development in ICT has made the integration of supply chains become possible, so that the links between suppliers, producers, customers, and third parties are easier to establish. A survey among members of CLM revealed that logistics managers increasingly seem to focus their efforts on the development of information systems and software tools. This is leading to new logistics practices or even a totally new business model. Closs et al. (1997) proved that information technology capabilities can significantly influence overall logistics competence, specifically on quick response, standardization, and flexibility.

Lancioni et al. (2000) has discussed how the Internet is used to manage the major components of supply chains including transportation, purchasing, inventory management, customer service, warehousing, production scheduling, and vendor relations. They pointed out that the Internet will continue to provide logistics managers with business information and enable them to improve the profitability of their supply chains. The development of IT and e-commerce on Internet has been predicted dramatically to affect the ways that business is conducted. With the integration of information and substantiation, new products, services, and marketing processes can be created to change the relationship between manufacturers and customers and to improve customers orientation ability. The successful companies have developed focused e-business solutions for improving customer service elements that are most important in their business.

IT has played a significant role in the process of business reengineering at YCH DistriPark (Singapore). It helps the company confirm to its current status as a regional leader in offering total logistics. In this case, IT has provide important contribution in there major systems development, including warehouse management systems, freight management systems, and the system integration of logistics management and national EDI networks. Ramani et al, (1995) stated that YCH has achieved superior business performance through its strategic and innovation IT application. Pokharel (2005) indicated that the extent to which the use of ICT in Singapore is perceived positively is related to size of company but is unrelated to the type of industry covered and the type of service offered by the logistics companies.

Most previous research stresses ICT's relation with performance. This chapter examines whether the application of ICT has different effects on different compare groups and on different aspects. We also attempt to discover if the expectations for the adoption of ICT and the actual results are related or independent.

Many researchers concluded that ICT is able to strengthen enterprises' advantages and benefits. Therefore, we assume that ICT brings the same effects to different industries and enterprises scale, and that there is relationship between the objectives for the adoption of ICT and its impact on operations. To do so, five hypotheses have been developed as follows. In this study, we sent out a survey by mail to 350 related enterprises chosen randomly from 302 IT manufactories registered on the Taiwan stock market and about 500 registered local transport logistics companies. There were 101 valid returned questionnaires, with a response rate of 28.8%.

Characteristics of the Respondent Companies

Among those respondents, there were 23% from ICT manufacturing, and 77% from transport logistics. 42% of the respondents had employees more than 200, 58% had employees of 200 or less. In the sample, there were 91.3% of the ICT manufacturers whose annual sale values are over ten millions US dollars, however, there are only 36.4% for those response transport logistics companies. Regarding the status of ownership, 75% of the samples are domestic private companies, 12% are domestic companies with foreign investment, 10% are complete foreign-owned private investment companies, and only 1% are government-owned companies.

Main Questions

The main questions in the survey are: What kinds of ICT are employed for logistics operation, what is the primary objective of using ICT, what are the specific areas most interest to use ICT, does feel different after employing ICT, what impacts have been occurred while using ICT, how much percentage of costs and revenues are affected, what barriers or difficulties are concerns of implementing ICT, what kind of changes in operation and management polices after using ICT, any further plans of ICT application, what supports are expected to obtain from government sector.

ICT

We reviewed the possible technology information related to the definition of ICT in logistics to give us a comprehensive understanding about the effectiveness and concerns of this subject. Reviewed technologies in this study include Electronic Data Interchange (EDI), Extensible Mark-up Language (XML), Internet, E-commerce, Electronic Order System (EOS), Automatic Picking System (APS), Bar Coding and Scanning, Data Warehouse, Global Positioning System (GPS), Radio Frequency Identification (RFID), Geographic Information System (GIS), In-Vehicle Sensor, On-board Data Recorder, Mobile Data Communication, Freight and Fleet Management System, Inmarsat, Container & Equipment Control System, Container Storage Planning System, and etc.

Enterprise Type

Since manufacturer and transport logistics companies are the important and close partners of upstream and downstream on the supply chain. The enterprise type will be classified as ICT manufacturing and transport logistics industries. In the sample, the background of those transport logistics respondents includes carriers (sea and air), freight forwarders (sea and air), shipping agents, integrated carriers, terminal operators, warehousing operators, and etc.

Enterprise Size

The scale of a company can be measured by its number of employees or its annual sale value. Since in Taiwan the size of firms is generally categorized as large enterprises (LE) and small and medium enterprises (SME) according to the number of employees, this chapter thus decides using the number of employees as the criterion to classify the samples. The company had employees more than 200 is classified as LE, and had employees of 200 or less is classified as SME.

Benefits and Operation Impacts

The four-point Likert scale was used to justify the levels of benefits and operation impact from large (4), moderate (3), small (2), to no (1). The benefits of application ICT include better communicate with customers, increase revenue, reduce cost and improve service quality. The items of operations impact include: Increase ICT hardware and software cost, reduce empty miles of travel and communication cost, reduce load-waiting and delivery time, reduce cost of staff, provide faster and reliable service to customers, produce more business and thus increase revenues.

Costs and Revenues

It is difficult for respondents to estimate exactly how much the costs and revenues are of applying ICT. What they can provide is information about the percentages of change in costs and revenues, before and after applying ICT. In this chapter, the levels of percentages were divided into five intervals. Descriptive statistics and analysis of variance (ANOVA) were used to describe the sample and to examine the research hypotheses.

Technology Selection and Application Area

The most popular ICT applied in ICT manufacturing is the Internet and its associates; EDI, bar coding and scanning, database warehouse, and electronic order systems. Likewise, the Internet is also the most popular ICT applied in logistics industry; the other popular ICT are in order EDI, e-commerce, bar coding and scanning and data warehouse. In the categories of SME and LE, the top 5 popular ICT are similar to each other, with more difference in the other ICT selections.

Both ICT manufacturers and transport logistics companies agree that to communicate with customers easily and quickly is the most important concern, followed by to improve quality and to increase revenue. Reducing cost is relatively less important compared to other identified objectives. It seems the most important motivation for the companies in this study is to apply ICT is to improve their service. The issues of reducing cost or increasing revenue are not most important when making decisions.

In pooling the samples from manufacturing and transport logistics, the top 5 most popular ICT application areas are customer services, transportation management, order processing, warehousing management, enterprise resource planning (ERP). However, for the respondents from ICT manufacturers, the most popular application areas of ICT are; order processing, warehousing management, ERP, and purchasing/ procurement (Rank 1 to Rank 3). Unlike ICT manufacturers, the most common application areas for the respondents from transport logistics are; transportation management, customer services, and order processing (also Rank I to Rank 3). However, the top 5 chosen application areas for SME and LE are the same, except for order processing.

Benefit of ICT Application

In this survey, respondents were asked to rank the benefits of ICT application on a fourpoint scale; large (4), moderate (3), small (2), and no (I). After applying ICT, both ICT manufacturers and transport logistics companies thought that the levels of benefit they obtained were moderate to large. With regard to different types of business, the average benefits to ICT manufacturers and to transport logistics are 3.52 and 3.42 respectively. The average benefits to large enterprises and to small/medium sized enterprises are 3.48 and 3.42 respectively.

ANOVA analysis was used to examine whether the benefit of ICT applications is significantly different between different types of enterprise. Results show that the t-test value is -0.864 and p-value is 0.390, indicating that there is no significant difference in perceived benefit between ICT manufacturers and transport logistics firms. Therefore, the H1 cannot be rejected. The same test was used to examine if there is a significant difference between the two different sizes of enterprise groups. The t-test value and the p-value here were 0.482 and 0.631, which means the null hypothesis (H,) cannot be rejected. It means there is no significant difference between SME and LE in perceived benefit from ICT applications.

Impact of ICT Applications

The average perceived impact of ICT application given by all respondents is between 2.55 and 3.39. The top three identified categories of impact are

(1) providing taster and reliable service to customers (mean=3.39),

(2) increasing ICT hardware and software costs (mean=3.06), and

(3) producing more business and thus increase revenues (mean=3.01).

It is interesting that the top impact has a direct relationship to enterprise's primary objective of ICT application, namely "better communication with customers".

ANOVA statistics analysis is used to examine whether there is significant different between different types of enterprise on the aspect of impacts. Results show that only the impact of "Increase ICT hardware and software cost" has significant difference between ICT manufacturers and transport logistics firms. On the other hand, in terms of the two different size of enterprise groups (LE and SME), there is no statistical significant difference on all identified impact aspects.

Analyses between Objectives and Operation Impacts

To know more about the relationships between objectives and obtained results, the chapter conducted further statistical analyses between four determined objectives and six specified impacts of ICT application. Statistical analysis results indicate that significant relationships can be proved to exist in 5 aspects highlighted which are "Reduce cost" vs. "Reducing the cost of staff, "Improve quality" vs. "Provide faster and reliable service to customers", "Support business growth and thus increase revenue" vs. "Produce more business and thus increase revenue", "Reduce cost" vs. "Provide faster and reliable service to customers" and "Reduce cost" vs. "Produce more business and thus increase revenue". It means there does exist significant relationships between some objectives and operation impacts of ICT application. Therefore, the Hypothesis 5 can be partially supported.

Cost and Revenue Analyses

69.2% of the respondents suggest that ICT application does help them reduce operation costs, with an overall average cost reduction of 9.9%. The rest of the respondents (30.8%) said that applying ICT has increased their operation costs, with the overall average cost increase being 6.67%. In terms of the impact on revenue, almost all respondents believed that ICT application has increased their operation revenue.

The overall average revenue increase was 9.14%. 78.1 % of the respondents said that applying ICT can increase their revenues within the range of 10%. In terms of the size of enterprise, for respondents experiencing cost reduction, SME is higher than LE in their level of changes (10.5% vs. 9.17%). However, for respondents experiencing cost increase, SME is less than LE in their perceived level of changes (5.75% vs. 7.95%). In terms of experienced impact of cost reduction or increase, the sample analysis shows us that SME can get better returns than LE. Similar findings can be seen in the impact analysis on revenue increase between SME and LE (9.56% vs. 8.67%). With regard to the return of ICT applications it favours small and medium enterprises more than large enterprises.

The Expected Supports from Government

According to the survey, the top 5 difficulties facing ICT manufacturers while implementing ICT are

(1) compatibility of ICT systems between companies,

(2) information security,

(3) timeliness of information,

(4) shortage of professional staff, and
(5) accuracy of information exchange.

Most transport logistics firms had the same difficulties except with a different ranking order. Again there were no statistically significant differences in terms of major difficulties between LE and SME. In the age of rapidly growth of information technology, enterprises will face many new problems. In the survey, respondents said that the assistance they mostly expect from the government is to help them obtain new technology information quickly, to provide a shareable platform, and to provide professional training programs. What are the potential ICT application areas for a company to consider in the future? According to the survey, the top five candidate application areas for ICT manufacturers are customer services/customer relation management/CRM, ERP, order processing, purchase/procurement, and warehouse management.

For transport logistics companies, their choices are transportation management, customer service/CRM, order processing, ERP, and warehouse management. Besides, the choices of purchase/procurement and transportation management, the rest of the choices are similar to each other. This may reflect the diffcrence in business characteristics between the two industries. The choices of future application areas between LE and SME are also similar to each other. Most of the respondents (irrespective of which type of the business or what size of the company) agree that customer service management will be the most worthwhile area to apply ICT in the future. This chapter conducted a survey of ICT manufacturers and transport logistics companies in Taiwan to find out their opinion or experience of ICT applications.

Analysis of the results showed that the most popular information and communication technologies are internet, EDI, bar coding and scanning, e-commerce, and data warehouse.

In terms of the objectives of ICT application, respondents believe that better communicating with their customers, improving service quality, and supporting growth and thus increasing revenues are more important than reducing cost. This suggests that the motivation of ICT application is more driven by service improvement than cost saving. In general, ICT is widely used in the fields of customer services, transportation management, order processing, warehousing management, and ERP. The subjects believed that customer services, customer relation management, and transportation management are still the most interesting application fields in the expected future. The survey showed that most of the respondents believe they have obtained moderate to large levels of benefit and similar levels of impact on their operations.

With regard to returns from ICT applications, it is believed to be better for small and medium enterprises than large enterprises. Our results show that there are no significant differences in perceived benefits and impact levels of ICT application between two different types of businesses, and two different sizes of companies. It recommends that information and communication technologies can provide benefits to business operation. It is specially recommended for small and medium enterprises.

The application and development of ICT has great potential for all kinds of business and operation areas. The logistics industry is believed to be a good area to test ICT applications. The future development of ICT should satisfy diversity requirements. It is believed that the ones who can provide the fastest, the most correct, and the 'most satisfied' services for all parties inside the business chain will have the best chance of success.

It is mainly the medium and small-sized enterprises in Taiwan, which are good at acclimatising, imitating, and learning. As global information technology improves, they should be capable of adopting ICT in their operations. Many ICT-oriented companies in Taiwan are important worldwide suppliers and manufacturers. Besides, a great number of them are asked to adopt ICT by their foreign partners. To survive in the international arena, enterprises in Taiwan hope to use ICT to improve their competence, to strengthen their chances of winning. However, medium and small-sized companies are less able than large enterprises to invest in ICT. Therefore, they generally want aid from the government sector.

The government can establish a shareable common platform. Because medium and small-sized enterprises have a large proportion of product and export value in Taiwan, they contribute greatly to the nation and are the foundation of economic development of the country. In recent years, the Taiwanese government has actively aided local companies in adopting ICT in their operation and management, to upgrade the general industries of the country and to protect their survival. This is a comprehensive study to understand the role of ICT in manufacturing and transport logistics industries in Taiwan, the results of which can help decision makers in devising better policies and programs.

Materials and Logistics Management

This chapter examines the various stages and activities of consumers' management of owned possessions including acquisition, ownership, and disposition. Using a materials management perspective, more frequently found in industrial marketing, the authors develop a consumer model of management of household goods. Stages of the model are illustrated using consumer anecdotes collected as exploratory research. Implications for researchers, practitioners, educators, and policy makers are discussed in terms of how the materials management perspective can be used to help deliver better value in products and services to consumers by understanding the activities in each stage of ownership.

Although some shopping activity is an end in itself, that is, shopping for entertainment or social interaction, consumers usually shop to buy products to own, use, or reuse. Yet, most buyer behaviour theory and research has focused on the pre-acquisition and acquisition stages of goods ownership, ignoring behaviours that occur after purchase. Economic theories of household management do take a post-purchase focus; however, their emphasis is, understandably, on goods consumption and use in the creation of utility for household members.

The focus of this chapter is on that area of household management dealing with the logistics of possession, ownership, and maintenance. Although parts of the conceptual model presented could apply to services as well, it is concerned here only with physical products—thus ownership implies more than just consumption. We explore how concerns about logistics, storage, and disposal can influence other decisions and then demonstrate how awareness of logistical considerations can benefit household decision making, consumer education, and product planning and marketing.

Systems approaches to household management have long recognised the role of possessions as inputs to a system designed to maximize household well-being. While recognising the importance of sequencing of action and management of resources, most systems approaches and models make general reference to such actions, facilitating broad understanding, but turning attention from specific ways to improve efficiency or value. It seems clear that possession management is implied in economic models of the household that talk about planning, controlling, decision making, and goal setting.

However, general open systems models, by necessity, deal with household management at a much broader level, in effect grouping possession management and logistics issues together with other day-to-day household activities such as repair and maintenance of physical plant, value creation, and negotiation. As such, they seem to downplay the specific stages of the process of resource management (e.g., physical movement, storage, and maintenance) and the influence these activities can have on household well-being.

The open systems approach, through its focus on interactions (frequently expressed as inputs and outputs between the household and the environment), tends to draw attention to general issues related to efficient use of resources and creation of value. This perspective is useful and important. However, at some point we need to delve into specific internal household activities to increase understanding.

In their model of household production and consumption, Magrabi et al. (1991) use arrows to represent inputs and outputs of various processes. Although they make reference to technical operations of the household, they focus on creation of "household commodities" rather than movement, and their discussion makes no mention of the impact of what goes on in the arrows (representing the flow of materials in and out of use) on household well-being.

Here, the authors suggest that, by paying attention to these movements, consumers, educators, and marketers can gain additional insights into how to create value for households. When consumers make purchase decisions based on these physical flows, marketers can gain competitive advantage through a more careful analysis of these processes of goods management. Consumer educators can also help households by introducing this framework which identifies additional criteria for making better decisions. By taking a broader view of buyer behaviour, going beyond pre acquisition and acquisition to ownership and disposal activities, it becomes apparent that consumer goods marketers could gain useful insights from industrial marketers.

Industrial marketing scholars and practitioners have increasingly recognised materials and logistics management as an area through which customer service levels and satisfaction can be increased via improved effectiveness (e.g., improved response time and delivery) and through which customers' costs can be reduced via improved efficiency (e.g., just-in-time materials receiving practices).

Similar to other organisations, households are continually acquiring, using, and disposing of inventories of both consumable and durable goods in their "operations." By recognising the household materials management function, marketers may identify new opportunities to better meet customer needs by facilitating the household materials management effort. For example, marketers may recognise ways to provide greater customer value through better package design or shape for ease of transport to or storage at home. Inventory management, therefore, seems to be a theoretically and pragmatically important area of investigation in understanding consumer buyer behaviour.

Additionally, with growing pressure to conserve material resources that are processed into products and to prolong landfill capacity, consumers may be more likely to accumulate or transfer their goods than to simply "trash" them. Relevant trends in new home construction, in fact, suggest the need for better storage spaces; builders tout pantries, walk-in closets, and oversized garages as key features in new homes. (Perhaps we are moving from a throw-away society to a stowaway society!)

When usable items are not kept, consumers are seeking responsible modes of transfer (e.g., donating, passing along, selling) to secondary owners, those who acquire a used good. We do not refer here to secondary users within the household of original ownership, but to members of a subsequent household that has acquired the good. It is the ownership history of the good that determines whether the current owner is a secondary owner. Post-acquisition behaviours are of interest to marketers, consumer educators, and policy makers alike.

By increasing consumer awareness of household logistics, these professionals may help reduce the number of purchasing errors that lead to "premature burial" of usable goods. Therefore, there is increasing reason to improve understanding of all stages of consumer behaviour—from pre-acquisition to disposition of possessions. As the organisation is the unit of interest in industrial buyer behaviour, the household is the unit of interest in consumer buyer behaviour. Here a household is defined as any physical site, managed by a consumer, wherein the individual resides, alone or with others, and runs a "life-support" operation by acquiring, using, storing, transporting, and disposing of goods. The degree of involvement with, and investment of time and money in, the household inventory can vary widely.

At a minimum, householders acquire their supplies of clothing and hygiene products. The extremes are students in residence halls who hold their own clothes, toothpaste, soap, etc. and homeowners who have consumable and durable possessions and also invest in property improvements that are relatively permanent installations:

items attached to the residence in such a way that they are unlikely to be moved to the next residence when the owner moves (e.g., glass fireplace doors, landscaping, or carpeting). Most consumers purchase food and cleaning products. Next, furnishings and artifacts are typically used to personalize the surroundings, even for those who rent. For those who own the residence, purchases also include appliances, lawn and garden equipment, and installed improvements to the property.

A few exceptions to the "householders" are individuals who live in institutions, where almost all items are provided (food, uniforms, etc.). These exceptions include prison inmates, nuns in convents, military personnel living aboard ships or in barracks, and individuals living in nursing homes, hospices, etc.; even these people own some personal items. Beyond these exceptions, the inventory ownership cycle and materials management concept broadly applies, in varying degrees, to all consumers, regardless of individual circumstances or characteristics.

Perspective

This chapter proposes an integrated model of the consumer household's materials and logistics management system. It reviews a recognised organisational logistics framework and then compares it to the proposed consumer inventory ownership cycle and materials management system. Specific stages are defined and explained, and their general relevance is discussed. Examples describing behavioural activities at each stage are provided to illustrate definitions. The authors also explore preliminary evidence that consumers may consider factors from preceding or following stages throughout the materials management cycle. Finally, relevant suggestions for marketers, researchers, and policy makers, as to usefulness of this conceptual framework, form the conclusions section.

In 1976, Nicosia and Mayer noted the need to broaden the study of buyer behaviour beyond pre-acquisition and acquisition to include consumption and disposal activities. Reviewing the state-of-the-art of buyer behaviour research, Jacoby (1976) reiterated this need. Jacoby (1977) with Berning and Dietvorst, in fact, was one of the first to explore "disposition" (disposal). Some researchers have begun to pay more attention to nontraditional modes of acquisition, experiential aspects of usage, and occasion of usage. Also, disposition has received attention because of environmental issues such as waste stream reduction. However, these efforts generally have been non-integrative; that is, the stages of ownership have been treated more or less separately.

The following discussion introduces a framework for such integration. The authors have termed this framework the Inventory Ownership Cycle (IOC). To introduce the concept of consumer materials management, an organisational materials and logistics management model is presented as a starting perspective. This brief description is followed by a presentation of a model of the Inventory Ownership Cycle. The former provides a well researched and understood parallel to the latter.

Industrial Materials and Logistics Management (MLM) Model

In this system, an industrial manufacturer receives raw/processed materials from a source of supply and manages those materials through a process that adds value. The goods are then "disposed of" through a system of-physical distribution.

The main difference between an industrial manufacturer and a household seems to be that the manufacturer is more likely to process and combine raw materials or components into output that has ". . . exchange value with transactions characterized by formal money or in-kind exchange". Whereas a manufacturer buys and stores materials which are then assembled to make a finished product of greater value than the sum of the inputs, a household usually "processes" goods or adds value for the purpose of meeting family goals or increasing well-being.

There are, however, many examples of how consumer goods as inputs can also involve added value for transmission to parties outside the household (e.g., craft materials turned into gift items or eggs for a cake baked for a friend or a bake sale). While experts have addressed household production and the valuation of household production activity, the general intent of most purchasing by most households is consumption, even if items are internally processed into products or services. Conversely, organisations process raw materials into products with the intention of moving them to end users outside of the organisation.

Through adaptation of and expansion on the above industrial model, the consumer ownership/inventory management system model emerged. Both models clearly show products moving into and out of ownership and/or possession. Although the logistics model for organisations tends to focus on entering goods that will be incorporated into products for sale, conceptually it could apply equally to operating supplies that are consumed, capital equipment that could be disposed of eventually, and/or waste stream materials that leave the operation regularly. The consumer adaptation is thus quite similar, with some products staying in the individual's possession longer and others being incorporated, consumed, or disposed of more quickly. To maintain consistency with the industrial model, it seems appropriate to describe consumer goods in terminology parallel to that of industrial goods.

Entering Goods

In industrial terms, these are parts and materials (raw, processed, or partially assembled) incorporated into value-added products that are then sold to customers.

Although most entering goods for consumers are used by themselves or combined for internal use (e.g., food products as components of meals, fabric for a dress), others may be combined to create gifts (e.g., crafts materials to make dolls, dried floral arrangements, handmade furniture). The important similarity from an inventory perspective is that entering goods are materials usually stored at the "operation" to use in the production of something else related to household goals or values, although the holding period may be extremely brief, as with just-in-time inventories.

Installations

In the industrial setting, these are capital improvements that are built into the facility, for example, an elevator or conveyor belt assembly. Consumers, likewise, build in bookshelves and install wallpaper and alarm systems. Generally, in either setting, "disposal" of such goods usually occurs when the entire physical facility is sold, although replacement or upgrade is common in both settings. Decisions about acquiring installations, in both cases, involve considerations about the relative benefits of long-term ownership. The physical facility, while not part of the model, provides the context for activities described in the model.

Accessory Equipment

Accessory equipment is defined as items that are not consumable but are not physically attached to the facility. For the industrial buyer, such items may include fax machines, fork lifts, and office furniture. Similarly, consumers buy furniture, appliances, lawn mowers, etc. Space for storage, use, and maintenance are some of the considerations in accessory equipment purchases. Consumer accessories can be functional, entertaining, value expressive, or have investment value.

Facilitating Goods

These are usually referred to as maintenance, repair, and operating (MRO) "supply" items in the industrial context. Repair, cleaning, and maintenance consumables (e.g., nails, soaps, lubricants, respectively) as well as operating items (e.g., stationery, paper clips) are often strikingly similar to those held in inventory by consumers. Consumer supplies, of course, also include health and beauty aids and pet supplies. They are not held for long periods of time but create routine expenses associated with running the operation or household.

Proposed Inventory Ownership Cycle (IOC)

In simple terms, the IOC depicts a model of stages in consumers' management of physical goods and materials, similar to the key material management stages in a business-to-business logistics system.

The consumer gathers information and makes decisions about acquiring products within categories and selects brands or suppliers (Pre-acquisition Decision Making). Some form of commitment occurs by ordering, purchasing, or otherwise agreeing to accept goods (Acquisition/ Purchase). Goods must then be moved from the supplia's location to the consumer's household (Transportation-Inbound External Movement).

The consumer may use the product immediately or store it for use/reuse (Possession and Ownership). The item may move within the household from one area to another or in and out of storage (Transportation-Internal Movement). If the item is no longer needed, it is transported for "disposal" (Disposition) to another person or organisation. Even "trashed" items are transferred to a disposal company for removal (Transportation-Outbound External Movement) and final permanent storage in a landfill or incineration at a waste-to-energy plant. Exploring the consumer cycle of inventory ownership from start to finish, an attempt was made to identify issues within and among the goods management constructs.

The stages are pre-acquisition (decision making); acquisition (taking title); possession (usage and storage); and disposition (disposal). Internal and external movement flows are indicated by arrows. Acquisition parallels the purchasing activity underlying the physical supply of materials. Possession activities correspond to the production and storage activities.

Although the uses to which materials are put in these stages may differ widely between the two systems, both have some goods which are incorporated (entering goods), some consumable facilitating supplies, accessory goods which are used and/or stored, and permanent installations. Finally, disposition parallels the transfer of goods to sources of demand. While disposition via physical distribution to markets usually implies sale of goods, disposition usually implies giving away or throwing away goods. However, consumers, in fact, increasingly also sell some goods (e.g., at garage sales, by consignment, etc.). Thus, each system disposes of some waste and "disposes" of some goods for use by others.

Anecdotal Investigation of Model Stages

To help clarify model constructs and explore behaviours related to the model, the authors conducted exploratory research consisting of interviews with 130 respondents to learn more about the inventory control and management behaviours in which consumers engage. Respondents' anecdotes are included in the discussion of the model to help illustrate constructs and as examples of behaviours. Similar anecdotal techniques were used successfully by Belk, Wallendorf, and Sherry (1989) to provide a more vivid picture of consumers' behaviours regarding their possessions than could be achieved by quantitative analysis of structured questionnaire items.

Before describing the model, we report the collection methods used to help the reader understand the data sources. After this description, a discussion of the model stages is presented. Respondents were taken from two convenience samples; one consisting of 120 undergraduate students and the other of ten nonstudent adult residents from two midwestern communities. The students were juniors and seniors, ages 20-23, 59 percent female. The non-student respondents consisted of six men and four women, ages 30-65.

Convenience samples were deemed adequate for this exploratory research as initially the authors only looked for evidence of relevance of constructs and possible relationships among model constructs and are not empirically testing relationships. Respondents were recruited from undergradute business classes and adult volunteers who responded to a request to spend 30 minutes answering a few questions. Respondents were given the following instructions:

Think of a possession, something you own, and describe how you buy, use, store, or get rid of that possession. [It can be a special possession or something ordinary that you use or consume frequently.] Where appropriate, describe how you care for the possession.

The instructions to respondents deliberately left the response choice open to each individual (as to which stage of the ownership cycle they would discuss). Bracketed instructions were given verbally and were paraphrased. The methods yielded two sets of anecdotes. Responses from the students were written and involved no additional discussion or probing. The 120 student respondents yielded 79 usable anecdotes. Non-student respondents were encouraged to describe as many anecdotes as came to mind. The ten 30-minute interviews yielded 15 usable anecdotes. Combined responses provided a total of 94 usable anecdotes. Some anecdotes were more elaborate than others and described more than one activity from our model. In such cases, the anecdotes were classified in multiple activities. Fifty anecdotes were classified in one activity, 35 anecdotes were classified in two activities, and nine anecdotes were classified in three, for a total of 147 items for the seven activities.

Content analysis was used to help develop a clearer picture of consumer material management behaviours. Two judges classified the stage(s) of the model in the anecdotes.

Additionally, some respondents provided anecdotes that illustrated how past or future stages of the model influenced behaviour at the stage being discussed; judges classified the direction of inter-stage influence described in the anecdote, if appropriate. Inter-rater agreement was initially 72 percent. For items about which judges disagreed, the judges met and, if agreement could not be reached immediately, the item was dropped. Three of 94 items were dropped, thus bringing final inter-rater agreement to 97 percent. Each activity was mentioned at least once. Storage and acquisition were mentioned most often and transportation and disposition least, suggesting that activities related to transport and disposal of possessions may be less salient to consumers. This would certainly justify more consumer education focused on issues of disposing in a responsible manner. The remainder of this chapter has three main objectives:

(1) to describe more fully the constructs of the model and present an array of behavioural options under each construct,

(2) to explore preliminary evidence describing various behavioural options under the key constructs, and

(3) to suggest how model stages may affect one another in the overall consumer goods management process.

Model Stages

In addition to the reported anecdotes, the authors provide additional examples of each stage and, in some cases, of how behaviour at a stage could be influenced by behaviour at other stages. Both reported anecdotes and observed examples are used for clarification and illustration. Anecdotes supplied by respondents are bolded.

Pre-Acquisition

This stage is the cognitive and affective information processing stage of the pre-purchase process. Problem recognition, search, evaluation of alternatives, preference formation, and intention are mental activities that occur prior to behavioural commitment. Much consumer research focusing on models of problem solving and information processing has already described this stage and because this chapter is mainly concerned with materials management of goods once they are actually owned, little discussion is needed here. However, preacquisition is included in the model because several subsequent stages of behaviour may affect or be affected by pre-acquisition activities.

Pre-acquisition decisions can be described along a continuum of high to low involvement. For example, in decorating the home, a consumer may have engaged in considerable search effort (high involvement situation) to find the right painting to hang over the fireplace mantel.

Such high involvement in pre-acquisition would tend to suggest certain appropriate modes of usage, storage, and disposition for the item. Conversely, if disposition is considered ahead of time, pre-acquisition may be affected. For example, a senior level college student who knows the couch for his/her apartment will be set out with the trash upon graduation may not develop fine criteria or engage in extensive search (low involvement situation). Thus, preacquisition processes and the subsequent stages of acquisition, possession, and disposition behaviours may affect one another.

Two respondents illustrated how their intended use of an article of clothing influenced their buying behaviour during pre-acquisition: "[When] buying a suit for interviewing [I ask] is it fashionable, appropriate, does it fit, will it be ready in time, worth it?" and "When I used to get a dress for the prom I would go to every possible store to look for a dress. Then I wouldn't buy a dress until the last minute because I was worried I might find something I liked better." These comments show the importance of intended usage to search behaviours in the pre-acquisition stage.

Acquisition

Acquisition includes activities of actually purchasing, ordering, or agreeing to accept a product; the process implies a contract between the buyer and seller. In industrial terminology this is referred to as "taking title." Although some items are leased (e.g., furniture) and may have similar aspects to possession, by definition they are not acquired as the ownership title is not transferred. In most cases, acquisition and physical possession are simultaneous because the product is carried out of the store. However, even store purchases may be delivered at a later date (e.g., major appliances and furniture).

Obviously, catalogue and telephone orders never arrive immediately upon ordering, although fast delivery is now more common. While the convenience of direct delivery is a benefit, for some the risk of theft of packages left by the front door may affect choice of seller.

The point is that acquisition (taking title) and physical ownership (taking physical possession) can involve separate activities with transportation between them and should thus be treated as separate constructs. (The topic of transportation is treated separately later in this chapter.)

Most acquisition research in consumer behaviour has focused on purchase via a retailer or ordering through a direct marketer's catalogue, phone solicitation, or an 800 number advertised in the media. It is important to recognise that many acquisition modes do not occur via traditional retailers.

Products may be acquired with or without an actual purchase, and many items enter the home used or second-hand, thus not through conventional marketing channels. However, some modes could occasionally appear in cells other than those shown. For example, as the recipient of a charitable donation acquisition typically involves second-hand clothing or toys. These items, nonetheless, could be received brand new via drives like Toys for Tots, a program that requests donations of only new merchandise.

The manner by which one acquires a good may well affect usage, maintenance, and storage. For example: "Grandmother's engagement ring that I inherited: every time [I wear it] I take the ring off and put it in the same ring box, and put it in the same place. (Then five minutes later I check the ring box to make sure it's there.)" Another example is trophies or medals acquired through accomplishments and frequently displayed prominently in the home.

Intended usage and disposition may also affect selection of an acquisition mode. For example, an item intended for short-term use may more likely be bought "used," for example, a college student's car or a child's bicycle. Social norms, on the other hand, usually consider it taboo to purchase used goods if the acquisition will be "disposed of" as a gift to a friend for a special occasion, such as a wedding. Alternatively, it is considered acceptable to "pass-along" certain possessions, if not disposed of as a "gift," and pass-along disposition behaviour may even influence the original purchase. A 68-year-old woman reports: "[When shopping] I keep in mind things my daughter would like because when I get tired of them I can pass them on to her."

Physical Possession

The physical possession stage occurs once the good is in the hands of the consumer, whether simultaneous with purchase or upon subsequent delivery. Two activities are then possible. The item may either be used immediately or stored for future use. Usage and storage are thus described separately in this section. Assembly and/or maintenance may also be required prior to or after usage or storage and are discussed here. Finally, reuse and restorage are briefly mentioned.

Usage

Usage is considered to occur when the product is contributing to household well-being, whether functional or aesthetic. However, usage can occur simultaneously with storage, as with items that are on display when stored (e.g., fine china in a glass-front cabinet). Usage can occur in several forms. Entering goods (e.g., eggs) and supplies (e.g., light bulbs) are truly "used up" (albeit not destroyed) in the usage process. Durable goods and equipment are used on a long-term basis. Installations become part of the real estate. Goods may have functional or aesthetic, or both, uses. For durable goods, a beautiful dining room set could be both, whereas art's usage is purely aesthetic, and a sewing machine's usage is, generally, purely functional. Installed items may also be functional, aesthetic, or both.

For example, wall paper is mainly aesthetic; a thermostat is mainly functional, and a chandelier could be both. Even consumables may have aesthetic value (e.g., a bowl of fruit). Intended usage may influence acquisition mode. An empty-nest couple reports that while they would never dream of furnishing their home with used appliances, they had shopped primarily at garage sales for small appliances for their new cottage. They reported that, "not only was it economical, but [we] were more comfortable letting renters and visitors use the cottage when equipped with used items, especially small appliances, which [we] felt [were] frequently mishandled by people." The usage situation clearly affected selection in the acquisition mode.

Storage

Storage is the placement of a household item during periods when it is not being used for its primary function. Both consumable and durable goods may be stored, awaiting use or reuse. While consumables (e.g., canned food) are almost always stored out of sight, small durables such as copper pots and pans may be kept out of sight in cabinets by some but treated as accessory furnishings by others (e.g., the gourmet cook whose copper pans are proudly displayed on an overhead rack). Lines are blurred as to primary function in this example; and, thus, it is difficult to say whether the pans are "in use" or stored.

Storage spaces for food include pantries, cupboards, refrigerators, and freezers. Laundry room cabinets store bleach and detergent; linen closets may store tissues and soaps; medicine cabinets receive aspirin and bandages. The charcoal and lighter fluid probably go to the garage. Some items may be used so infrequently that they are stored in the basement or attic. For example, a consumer purchases luggage and stores it in an out-of-the-way location until needed.

Respondents reported a variety of reasons for their storage strategies, including keeping possessions organised, well-maintained, and protected from others in or outside the household: "[I] store clothes by type of clothing, by season, and by material. Sweaters are stored by how well I like them." Also, "I store my pearl necklace and earrings in a soft padded pouch, and put the pouch in a silver lock box." and "[I] keep putting my hair comb in top right drawer after recovery from kids."

There is evidence that practitioners can better serve customers by knowing storage behaviours. Proctor and Gamble did their homework when selling Tide detergent in the newly formed Russian republic. After learning that, in the typical Russian household, detergent is stored in a bathroom where frequent leaks wet the detergent box, they designed a box that would remain intact when wet. If they had not recognised the importance of the storage stage of ownership, they would have been selling a good product in an unusable container.

This example underlines the critical importance of identifying differences in consumers' post-acquisition activities. Storage may also involve off-site locations (akin to businesses using public warehouses) such as safe deposit boxes, storing items in a relative's basement, or renting a storage unit. All of these involve transportation to and from a site. Thus, while retaining title, the consumer may shift the goods in and out of physical possession.

Use of items stored at off-site locations may be infrequent. Heirloom jewellery stored in a bank safe deposit box may be picked up for special occasions. Access to the off-site location could be an issue in selecting one. The owner can enter some rented storage anytime, but must arrange time for access if the item is stored at a friend's home. While doing major remodelling of her home, one individual reports that she has numerous boxes of precious memorabilia and photographs safely stored in a friend's basement. She now has to call ahead for a mutually convenient time to gain access.

Maintenance

Maintenance is defined here as activity that helps restore or retain possession quality and usefulness and facilitates future usage of an item. Frequently maintenance includes proper storage, thus creating possible overlaps between these activities. Two main forms of maintenance include

(1) physical maintenance and

(2) record keeping.

Examples of physical maintenance include washing clothes and dishes, repackaging food as leftovers, repairing appliances, polishing silver, reinforcing seams, applying stain resistant finishes to upholstered furniture, waxing floors, and emptying ashes from grills and fireplaces. The copper pans in an earlier example provide a maintenance dilemma; they need frequent polishing if prominently displayed, less so if stored. How do consumers determine which items merit extra maintenance effort? We found evidence that the role the possession plays in a "performance" oriented activity is important. For example, "Golf clubs. Before playing, I clean the clubs, and make sure each club is in its special place. After playing, [I] put dirty clubs back into bag," or "My figure skates. After I take them off, I clean them well, and put them away carefully." Third respondent reports: "My flute. After I'm finished practicing my flute I always polish each piece and make sure to put it back in its case."

The acquisition mode might also be influential in determining maintenance. An inherited silver tea service may be cherished and kept on display, thus deserving extra effort to polish. In contrast, a skirt acquired at a garage sale may never be repaired once a seam splits. A reported anecdote echoes the tea service example; one respondent reports: "Grandmother's shawl. I take special care to make sure it stays clean and neat. I fold it over a spiced hanger in the middle of the closet to keep it from getting dusty." Although storage (hanging it in the closet) is necessary, for this respondent it is the special source of the shawl that justifies the maintenance described (hanging it in the middle of the closet on a spiced hanger) to ensure preservation and future quality. The second basic form of maintenance is record keeping. Record keeping effort is considered part of maintenance because of time and effort to keep track of inventory much as businesses do. Insurance companies suggest keeping written records, photographs, or videotapes of valuables and household items in case of loss or damage.

This listing is especially important if the consumer is relocating the entire household inventory to a new home. In addition, record keeping of what belongs to whom is required for prenuptial contracts. Wills delineate specific itemization of what will go to whom (disposition) upon the owner's demise. This effort is important if items have high economic or sentimental value.

Copies of warranties and instruction manuals can be filed for problem and use situations. Cataloguing or alphabetizing also could be considered a maintenance activity. Some cooks keep spices in alphabetical order for ease of retrieval. One respondent reports: "After I listen to a CD, I put the case on and put it back in the exact spot. The CDs are separated categorically, and alphabetized." The above examples are clearly systematized storage, however, they are also maintenance because the alphabetization clearly facilitates future use. Another form of record keeping effort is updating the value of items in a collection. This activity will frequently involve hobbies, such as one respondent who reports: "Twice a month I look at, enjoy the beauty of, and check the value of my baseball cards."

The model shows that both storage and usage can recur before disposition. After initial use, many items are stored and used again. This requires movement to and from the storage space. All items that are not totally consumed on initial use go through this process unless disposal occurs. Clothes go back to closets; dishes back to cabinets. Less frequently used items are returned to basement or attic (e.g., holiday decorations). Some items have seasonal use (e.g., porch furniture) and can be stored out-of-season. For dishes and clothes, such movement is so habitual that effort may go virtually unnoticed (unless, like the authors, you dread emptying the dishwasher and folding the laundry!). However, extensive obvious effort is required to more heavy porch furniture to the basement or repack and store delicate holiday ornaments. In some cases, this effort may not be deemed worthwhile. For example, some empty nesters, unless entertaining family for the holidays, may choose not to unpack, use, and repack holiday decorations.

Disposition

Disposition is defined as the process of getting rid of an item by intentionally or unintentionally moving it to the ownership of another person or entity. Taxonomies of disposition were proposed by Jacoby, Berning, and Dietvorst (1977) and by Burke, Conn, and Lutz (1978). Hanson (1980) developed a model of factors affecting choice of disposition modes; a more detailed taxonomy, with rationales for behaviour choices, was described by Harrell and McConocha (199V. The "disposition" options have previously included "keep," which is considered as storage/restorage in this model.

The other options are

(1) sell/swap (which includes many modes like garage selling, auctioning, advertising in a classified ad, setting up a flea market booth, selling via a consignment store);

(2) passing along to a friend, relative, neighbour, coworker, etc. which may not involve reciprocal exchange from the recipient;

(3) donating to a charitable organisation to get a tax deduction;

(4) donating to a charitable organisation without a tax deduction; and

(5) simply trashing.

These different modes of disposition can also affect acquisition, storage, and maintenance. For example, clothing headed for the Salvation Army as a donation may be bagged and stored in the basement rather than kept in an "active use" closet. The owner may accumulate bags until there is a sufficient quantity to travel to the Salvation Army or call for a pickup.

Table: *Intentional Disposition Options and Examples*

Disposition Option	***Examples***
Sell/Swap	Acquaintance, commission shop, flea market, auction, garage sale, classified ad
Pass along	Friend, neighbour, relative, coworker, leave behind in house/apartment
Donate: for tax deduction	Charitable organisation
Donate: not for deduction	Charitable organisation
Throw away	Contract trash pickup, public trash barrel/dumpster, litter/ illegal dump

Another option, not typically included in disposition taxonomies, is "return to store." Consumers sometimes "over purchase," then dispose by returning the items for credit, cash, or exchange. As one respondent reports: "I buy three shirts at a store, I don't try them on [there] and then take them home and [later] return two of them."

Return policies have also been very important in the growth of catalogue shopping, because the customer can choose not to keep the product after receiving it, or even before receiving it. Container deposit laws are, in effect, return policies as well. Yet they differ because the packaging—not the product—is returned. In either case, the cost of return is partially borne by all consumers.

Finally, it is important to recognise that consumers may experience unintended disposition if items are misplaced, lost, stolen, or loaned but not returned. Many people have lost so many pairs of sunglasses or umbrellas that how they acquire, use, and maintain such items may be affected. For example, consumers are probably less likely to shop at expensive stores for umbrellas if they have previously lost several. Similarly, such possessions may not be maintained very carefully if loss is anticipated.

Transportation

Transportation is limited to the areas of inbound and outbound external movement and internal movement within a given location rather than between residence addresses. Transportation of the entire household inventory during relocation to a new address is clearly an emotional experience for the householder and an important topic, but it is not within the scope of this chapter.

External Movement

Transportation is required to bring inbound physical goods to the residence and to move outbound goods upon disposition. In regard to inflow, while routine entering goods and supplies are usually purchased and received simultaneously and thus transported home by the consumer, delivery services provided by the seller are important for larger appliances, furniture, bulky landscaping (e.g., balled-in-burlap saplings and shrubs). For catalogue and phone orders, third-party transportation (e.g., UPS) is common practice. Occasionally, the consumer provides his/her own transportation to pick up the item. Or, if the consumer has access to a van or truck, he or she may opt to pick up the item rather than pay a delivery charge or deal with inconvenient delivery schedules. A consideration for some consumers may be the tradeoff between new or rent-to-own items with free delivery and cheaper used items that may represent a better value, but do not offer delivery.

On the outflow side, transportation has not been as clearly standardized. For consumable goods, waste and packaging materials have traditionally been picked up at the curb by the local waste hauler. Now, communities, under the gun to reduce the waste stream, debate alternative programs with economic inducements for consumers to recycle. For still usable items, charities that provide pickup service may be more likely to receive donations of durable and semi-durable goods that would be a nuisance for the original owner to deliver to the organisation. While many consumers would like to pass furniture to offspring starting a new household, the costs of paying a professional mover may not warrant shipping the furniture.

Garage sales' popularity may be due in large part to the fact that the secondary buyer usually comes to the seller's home and removes the merchandise with little or no transportation effort by the seller. The issue of how to "get rid of it" (i.e., physically move it) may well affect the disposition mode chosen. For example, a couch may have been a good contribution for a needy family; but if there is no pickup service by-the intermediary charitable organisation, the original owner may set it out with the trash. Conversely, if there are special fees from waste haulers for large item pickup, the householder may seek other disposal alternatives, such as passing along to a neighbour or illegal dumping.

There is also movement both into and out of the residence when third-party storage entities are involved. Recognising the related need for transportation, some storage facilities include access to a truck for a day if the household leases a storage unit for a minimum time. Use of non-commercial storage sites, such as a friend's or relative's garage, may involve renting or borrowing a vehicle for transportation and limits the donor's space use. Other examples of combined internal and external movement would be taking clothes to and from the dry cleaner or a VCR to and from the repair shop.

Internal Movement

Moving goods into internal storage before initial use, in and out between reuse occasions, and out after final use has been mentioned in preceding sections. It is mentioned again here because it could play a role in consumers' pre-acquisition criteria, usage, and disposition. Items stashed at the back of a cabinet or in the attic may be forgotten or too much trouble to retrieve and thus not used as frequently. After prolonged storage, they may be deemed disposable when the consumer does locate them.

Finally, items are also moved within visible areas of the residence, for example, rearranging furniture or moving it to different rooms as need or choice dictates different patterns of usage. Typically, when children leave for or graduate from college parents move some or all furnishings from the child's room and redecorate it as a guest room or study. Furnishings that are not too awkward to move and are flexible as to usage facilitate such "rearranging" options for the consumer.

The consumer household materials management IOC framework provides new opportunities for dialogue and study by offering a perspective that considers the effects of rarely studied consumer behaviours such as storage, usage, maintenance, disposition, and transportation of possessions. Consumer educators, researchers, practitioners, and policy makers can all benefit from this perspective; a few examples are discussed.

Consumer Educators

For those who study and teach consumption as a phenomenon (e.g., home economics educators, consumer behaviourists, social workers and counsellors, and government agencies that develop educational brochures), the implications of the post-purchase stages may seem obvious. However, inexperienced householders may not think much beyond the attractiveness or initial price of a product. Recently more than one student has said to us, "I'll be graduating soon and getting my first real place [home] as a professional person. How do I know what to buy for it; how do I compare alternatives?"

Clearly, their choice criteria for durable goods are not well defined, and the IOC can help identify additional criteria. The costs of durable goods can be a large percentage of a young person's income and errors in judgement can also have costs of social embarrassment and self-esteem. As the young person moves to new places, expected maintenance, difficulty in moving, or limited flexibility to fit in different residences can all affect long-term value of the possession.

The IOC can help teachers clarify post-purchase activities for students, helping them understand the importance of purchase criteria beyond price and attractiveness. Social workers who counsel families about budgeting and life management can use the IOC to help illustrate the long-term implications of possession ownership and management. Similarly, government agencies that publish brochures and educational pamphlets may use IOC perspectives to help illustrate the importance of anticipating future goods movement when making important purchases. Also, marketing educators need to be alert to long-term possession management considerations when they teach consumer behaviour because they have the opportunity to make students aware of their future as consumers. A buyer behaviour text by Peter and Olson (1993) alludes to some points about post-acquisition behaviour; however, additional detail could help marketing students clarify the career-related impacts of this knowledge.

Policy Makers

The integrated perspective of the IOC can also provide policy makers with new insights and opportunities. A few possibilities are listed according to the relevant model stage. In regard to the acquisition stage, policy makers should study the effects of underground economy exchanges via alternative acquisition modes and the implications for consumer protection and government tax revenues.

Another area of interest is the study of the public benefit from facilitating alternate modes of acquisition, such as how consumers can be better served by government policies that encourage more choices of acquisition and how charitable acquisitions can be facilitated by more socially responsible consumer disposition strategies.

The model also helps focus on criteria beyond initial attractiveness or price of the product. For example, policy makers help consumers by requiring manufacturers to provide information on appliances to show operating costs and energy efficiency. Much is already known about the storage and reuse stages of the IOC, such as child-proof containers and non-breakable materials.

Currently consumers are requesting medicine container caps that can be opened by those with strength limitations in their hands. Also, more work is needed to improve convenience in use, reuse, and proper storage of items that are potentially dangerous or prone to deterioration or contamination of, and damage to, adjacent products. Therefore, opportunities exist for labelling and design improvements to become policy. Maintenance-related issues provide many opportunities for policy makers. Questions such as responsibility for the costs of downtime, manufacturer liability for defects, and responsibility for maintenance costs all need further exploration. Policy makers can also benefit from exploration of issues as the role of consumer education on product maintenance, for example, the best ways to educate consumers about needed maintenance during pre-acquisition stages.

Also, we need resolution of issues related to the ethics of initially designing products for replacement versus repair.

Finally, policies on disposition could explore the effect of community standards and laws regarding responsibility for the transportation of recyclables and the effect of various policies on environmentally responsible behaviours. Incentives might be created to spur responsible disposal of household hazardous wastes. Charitable donations by consumers may be related to tax deduction policies.

We need clarification of the net effects of such tax issues on the disposition of used goods and the potential costs/benefits to society when policy does influence consumers' selection of disposition options. The concept of integrating behaviours throughout the consumer IOC has the greatest potential for contributing to future research. By taking an integrated approach, researchers studying any stage of consumer ownership will be more likely to consider, and increase knowledge about, previously unexamined correlates of behaviour at various stages. A few examples are listed.

(1) Prior focus on decision making and choice has caused researchers to overlook the effects of materials management concerns on consumer behaviour, including how these concerns may determine choice criteria. The IOC model provides a framework that links choice to other consumer behaviours and helps us recognise that the choices consumers make may be dependent upon previous decisions or other rarely recognised factors that occur after purchase. For example, storage or disposal constraints may influence brand choice and quantity of purchase. In one way, this potentially adds a whole new list of product attributes to traditional multi-attribute approaches to choice. These post-purchase behaviours and influences are little studied, yet may provide valuable information for consumer researchers. In addition, strategies that consumers devise for dealing with possessions during other stages of the model may provide motivation for behaviour at a given stage.

(2) The model links acquisition to subsequent consumer activities and thus provides insights into the effect of acquisition on consumer behaviour. The ways we acquire possessions help define our relationship with them and that relationship, in turn, affects our post-acquisition behaviours related to that good. Special meaning implies special treatment. Thus, when studying post-acquisition consumer behaviour it is important to consider the stage, the behaviour, and what happened at

other stages to fully understand the "relationship" between consumers and their possessions.

(3) This approach provides needed clarification of the model constructs. Several of the model's constructs have not previously been clearly differentiated. Part of the function of this model is to provide a framework that helps to define and differentiate storage, usage, and related maintenance activities. Consumer behaviours related to packaged goods, home furnishings, and keepsakes differ widely; future research can refine this framework and clarify how possession-related behaviours vary.

Practitioners

The examples may currently exist or serve as potential ideas for improvements in the total product offering. Underlying these suggestions is the opportunity for innovation; whether that be a new product or seemingly small improvements in package design, service, etc. By revisiting some "old" innovations, we can show their relevance to various ownership cycle stages. We will also mention some possible opportunities for new products/product features. Some of these may already be in design process in laboratories but not commercially available.

Promotion: Promotion strategies should include information about how all these "features" are consistent with desired lifestyle and consumer convenience, safety, value, etc. Many aspects of usage can be improved, especially in the area of packaging when it allows less mess, more safety, and/or measurable dispensing. Flexibility of usage could be a major benefit in some furniture design. Some designers of children's furniture create cribs that convert to daybeds as the infant becomes a toddler. A fascinating space-age technology recently became available as a consumer good—a portable unit that can function as either a warmer or chiller of food, depending on control settings. Flexibility benefits to campers, picnickers, and others are obvious. One possible product innovation that combines safety and measurable dispensing is an insect repellent in a container that automatically dispenses the proper amount to avoid overexposure to potentially unhealthy ingredients.

The automatic dishwasher is, on the surface, simply a convenient maintenance alternative to hand washing dishes. Perhaps less obvious, but maybe more important, is the storage function. Dishes can be whisked out of sight prior to actual washing. The ability of a dishwasher to deodorize dirty dishes while being stored prior to washing would certainly be an attractive feature for small households. Appliances, like vacuum cleaners, with multiple attachments can be stored more efficiently when the attachments fit onto or into the basic equipment rather than having to be stored separately and possibly misplaced. Self-lock storage units are a great convenience to those with small storage areas on site. Self-storage unit locations off-site were created to assist consumers between residences or with limited space. An opportunity might be storage units that could be dropped off for a limited time on the consumer's property. For example, where does one put a room full of furniture while painting that room if other rooms are already utilised? The opportunity is one for a service provider because ownership of the means of storage is not desirable when usage is only short term.

The microwave oven's fast preparation benefit is equally matched by its ability to eliminate tiresome scrubbing (physical maintenance) of pots and pans, as food is heated directly on the plate, which is then easily rinsed. The self-cleaning oven eliminates what must be one of the worst household maintenance tasks. What if someone invented a self-cleaning toilet, shower, or refrigerator? Record keeping could be improved with user-friendly language manuals of a standardized size (e.g., 8.5" × 11" so that they could be stored in a file folder). Moving and insurance companies have already created fill-in-the-blank inventory booklets to aid consumers' tracking of property. Auto companies could provide value to customers by facilitating record keeping with small on-board computers to record mileage and dates of maintenance activities, such as oil changes, with the touch of a button. This type of feature might also prolong the service of heating/air conditioning or other systems that require regular maintenance.

Reuse can be facilitated by self-sealing food packages and package designs that indicate the product on all sides so that when stored in a cabinet the crackers, cookies, etc., can be identified quickly even in a sideways-shelved box. This perspective suggests an innovative opportunity for manufacturers to print the names of spices on the caps of containers for storage in drawers and on low shelves, for easy identification. Disposal via recycling back to the manufacturer has been embraced by ALCOA who reprocesses aluminum cans. Not a product innovation, this innovation serves as a model that could be emulated by plastics manufacturers who are under attack by environmentalists. (Although many plastics are reprocessable into new forms, recycling activity has been mainly the domain of outside entrepreneurs who create plastic lumber, etc. from discarded milk jugs.) Because coated cardboard is hard to recycle economically, more packaging conversions to recyclable aluminum or plastic could be responsible innovations and might appeal to consumers who consider disposition options when purchasing. Another possible opportunity for packaging material is to create packaging that can be used as mulch or to discourage growth of weeds around plants. Transportation was facilitated by the mere addition of a sturdy plastic strap handle on a large box of powdered laundry detergent. Likewise, reformulation of detergents to concentrated forms benefits the apartment dweller who must move the container to and from coin-operated laundries or a building laundry room. This situation suggests the benefits of packaging detergents and soaps in mesh packets that disintegrate in the washer. Thus, the user transports only the amount needed, with no product or container on the return trip.

These are but a few examples of ways that mindfulness of post-acquisition stages can enhance a marketer's position as a provider of value to the consumer. As marketers and brand managers become more oriented to the whole cycle of inventory ownership, research into specific consumer needs will become richer than ever. These insights should provide extensive opportunity for future product and operations innovations. This chapter has attempted to set the stage for more integrative analysis of the consumer's inventory ownership cycle. The anecdotal evidence provided relates to the specific behaviours of individuals and does not suggest that all consumers behave in the same manner toward an inherited item, alphabetize their compact discs, or keep "passing along" in mind when they shop. Yet any of these anecdotes might spur in-depth research into any given stage of the cycle. For example, study of the role of joint decision making in regard to very specific aspects of maintenance, storage, record keeping, or disposition could provide substantial insight into how household members allocate such decisions and tasks. Conflicts that may arise among household members in acquisition may also arise in post-acquisition activities (e.g., arguments about whose job it is to change the oil in the car, empty the dishwasher, take donations to a charity, etc.). Underlying all of these issues is the concept of ongoing value in ownership to the consumer, and it is strongly suggested through our anecdotal evidence that consumers receive both costs and benefits beyond those derived from the physical functioning of at least some goods. Recognition by researchers, educators, and practitioners of these consumer considerations can lead to increased opportunities for manufacturers and, more importantly, better value for consumers throughout the inventory ownership cycle as well as benefits to society as a whole.

4

Comparison of Logistics Management

An increasing number of North American firms have become aware of the need for establishing a presence in global markets. Coordinated global manufacturing strategies have emerged as a response to both increased competition and the allure of access to global markets. These strategies are sometimes carried out through international alliances, which involve a formal long-term relationship between two firms in different countries. Firms also may choose to internationalize through the establishment of supplier linkages in foreign countries. Foreign buying may initially take place solely on need, but may progress to a proactive inclusion of international sources in pursuit of potential new markets, leading to full integration and coordination of global sourcing requirements to maximize buying leverage.

In general, it is believed that internationalization is part of a natural process of growth that evolves from an interplay between the development of knowledge about foreign markets and operations on one hand, and an increasing commitment of resources to foreign markets on the other. The role of logistics is a critical component of the internationalization process. Nevertheless, several studies have found that many American and European firms continue to deemphasize logistics capabilities in the global context. For instance, logistical inefficiencies in Europe were particularly prevalent in logistics planning, inventory holdings, use of logistics services suppliers, and the price paid for logistics services.

Not only are the transportation and distribution issues complicated by a host of unique regulations in different countries, but the very infrastructure of such environments can be fundamentally different than those found in North America. Before managers enter into global ventures, a clear understanding of the logistical conditions is essential to formulating a logistics strategy and establishing the terms of agreement. While basic logistics decisions usually involve trans-portation mode, carrier choice, and the location and size of inventory stocking points, Bowersox points to a more thorough definition of integrated logistics as "the process of managing all activities required to strategically move and store materials, parts, and finished inventory from suppliers, between enterprise facilities, and to customers."

Cohen and Lee expound on this model to develop an integrated logistics framework consisting of several submodels: material control, production control, finished goods stockpile, and distribution network control, all linked through inventory and scheduling decisions. Whybark further states that a global manufacturing strategy will affect the organisation of logistics activities, the evaluation of material flows, the development of new technical skills, and the maintenance of a strategic perspective.

Using these conceptual frameworks as a basis for exploration, this chapter examines some of the critical differences found in four countries that represent a diverse set of logistical environments. Moreover, the promise of new markets in Eastern Europe, Asia, and the Far East has attracted many American firms to explore the possibility of manufacturing and distribution sites in these areas. Other reasons for the increasing number of ventures in these areas involve material, technological, and strategic considerations.

Some of these countries are striving to increase export-led growth and are eager for development, while other more developed countries are less inclined. This study focuses on four distinct players which represent a diversity of infrastructural conditions found in these regions. Hungary and China are relatively new forces in the global market, and are still striving to shed many of the limitations formerly imposed by their centrally planned economies.

Many American firms are quickly building plants and distribution networks in these areas in an effort to establish a presence. Korea and Japan, on the other hand, have established themselves as global leaders in many industries, yet their markets have proven to be more difficult to enter.

While many American firms have suppliers in these two countries, the logistical and manufacturing conditions are very different from those found in North America. Korea and Japan also are included as a basis for comparing conditions in Hungary and China.

Although caution should be used in making generalizations, the data in this study nevertheless demonstrate some important differences in the logistics infrastructure within each of the different areas. The study first briefly reviews the general political, social, and economic conditions within each country. Second, several measures of productivity, process technology, materials management, and production and distribution control in the different countries are compared. Finally, the implications of establishing alliances or sources in each of these countries are discussed.

Political and Economic Conditions

A discussion of the political and economic conditions within each country is essential in providing a background for analyzing existing logistical infrastructures.

Hungary

Recent social and political changes in Eastern European countries have introduced an urgency into the transition from their centrally planned economies (CPE's) toward market-based economies. The distorting effects of centrally planned economies ultimately proved devastating and have left a trail of deep and worsening economic crises throughout Eastern Europe. Radical privatization reforms encompass fundamental social, political, and economic changes within each country's infrastructure. The problems that must be overcome in order to achieve these reforms are formidable: not only are there structural hurdles to surmount, but opposition to cuts in subsidies and government programs arising from industrial restructuring will no doubt be strong.

Structural problems permeate the social, economic, and political environments of these countries. The socialist ownership structure deprived individuals of the right and motivation to act efficiently. This led to a misallocation of resources that most notably manifested itself as chronic shortages throughout these countries. The bureaucratic structure inherent in the previous governments created a massive managerial elite who are largely unprepared to function in a market-driven, sophisticated economy. The industrial structure, skewed toward heavy industry, is comprised primarily of large, monopolistic firms that are both horizontally and vertically integrated.

The centrally planned and controlled economic structure creates a contrived communication system which, when removed, leaves an informational vacuum with respect to the reallocation of resources. All of these structural problems will need to be addressed in the economic reform process. Hungary, compared with Poland, Romania, Bulgaria, Czechoslovakia, Estonia, Latvia, and Lithuania, is well advanced in its market reform efforts. Prior to the late 1940s, when the communist regime took over, Hungary had sound industrial and agricultural bases.

During the forty-five years of the communist regime, manufacturing managers in Hungary operated under a controlled system of resource allocation and manufactured output distribution. Since 1968, however, Hungary reverted to a modified centrally planned economy in which managers operated partly in a market and partly in a centrally planned environment. During this period, the country experienced "partially liberalizing" prices and alternated between periods of reform (1968-1972 and since 1979) and years of reactions (1973-1978).

Generally speaking, the country has enjoyed a relatively high GNP, although growth has been minimal. Until the late 1980s, Hungary enjoyed a single digit rate of inflation, although recent changes in the market structure have increased inflation rates to 18%. Exports are almost a third of GNP, divided approximately evenly between CMEA Soviet-bloc countries and convertible currency markets. Much of what Hungary and other Eastern European countries produce for Soviet CMEA partners and domestic consumption cannot readily be sold in Western markets for convertible currency because of the poor quality of much of this output. This has led to difficulties in convertible-currency balance of payments on increasing imports from non-CMEA countries, and increasing levels of inflation. As in many Eastern European countries, the Hungarian government is intent on encouraging export-led growth through the creation of a new middle class of small-and medium-sized businesses.

Significant reforms occurred in 1988, including a new Law on Corporate Association, which by permitting joint stock and limited liability companies, established new operating rules for both foreign and domestic firms, and a Foreign Investment Act that allowed 100% foreign ownership of Hungarian businesses, simplified registration procedures, and conversion of soft currency profits into foreign exchange for repatriation.

Nevertheless, existing firms are large and bureaucrat-ridden, and profitability remains an elusive goal. There are few firms in these countries with fewer than 100 employees, a condition which has been described as the "socialist black hole." Unfortunately, a consequence of the centrally planned and authoritative business environment was the evolution of a managerial elite who were deprived of their decision making power. Managerial processes and decisions traditionally motivated by market forces were replaced with an authoritarian system that simply required orders to be executed.

Thus, it is not surprising that the managerial elite in these bureaucratic organisations had little reason or opportunity to retain or develop managerial decision-making skills. The unemployment is low and industry production growth is minimal. In addition, Hungary's $21.7 billion gross hard currency debt continues to grow.

Despite these problems, East European countries enjoy a reasonable standard of living, and are generally well-educated and have a high rate of literacy. Combined with the fact that their wages are competitive on the world market, there exists a real potential for rapid growth and industrialization within their manufacturing sectors. The procedures to found a joint venture, start a new company, or buy into an existing enterprise have been simplified, and Hungary's new stock market has become fully operational. It should be noted that all of the data for the Hungarian firms in this study are from 1987, and therefore do not reflect changes that have occurred since.

China

China, although less developed, has been promoting export-led growth for the last decade, with a lesser degree of success. In this sense, China represents a failed attempt at export-led industrialization. The China of the pre-reform period was one of little industrial competition, and was truly a seller's market. Manufacturing capacities and distribution channels were so inadequate that the market availability of most products was typically low. In this period, many Chinese managers were selected on the basis of their political expertise rather than technical backgrounds. However, the reforms developed under the leadership of Deng Xiaoping in the mid 1980s have attempted to reduce planning and move the enterprise closer to the market, stimulate competition, open up the economy to increased foreign presence, and invest the managerial position with considerably more autonomy and accountability.

While the reforms in China have successfully privatized agricultural sectors, the market socialization of state-owned enterprises in the manufacturing sector have largely failed. Nevertheless, a recent figure quoted by the New York Times reveals that the Chinese economy is growing at a rate of 6 per year, and is enjoying low inflation and increased foreign investment. China's exports and foreign exchange reserves are at a record high. In this sense, the Chinese economy is enjoying more vigorous growth than the economies of the United States, Japan, India, or most other countries.

Foreign investors signed more than 5,000 contracts totaling more than $4.5 billion (a 93 increase over the previous year) with companies such as RJR Nabisco, Gillette, Coca Cola, Procter and Gamble, Heinz, and Avon, which are all manufacturing within China. Xerox, Boeing, and General Electric are all watching their sales grow through exports to China. However, China's economy is still dominated by massive state-owned businesses. The state sector accounts for only about one-third of China's GNP, and 18% of its labour force. For the first time in four decades, China is approaching less than half of its industrial output from state enterprises.

Despite its labour wage advantages, the greatest inadequacy of the Chinese manufacturing base has been its ability to respond to unforeseen changes in market environments and its failure to become a dependable producer of manufactured products. This has severely limited the potential for Chinese enterprises to compete effectively against foreign competition without protection in the domestic Chinese market. The government is nevertheless continuing to institute reforms in many areas to encourage a market economy, including capital creation, housing, pricing for consumer goods, currency valuation, corporate ownership, state subsidies, and foreign investment.

The youth market (over two-thirds of the 1.1 billion Chinese are under the age of 35) favours the private sector, since the majority of available jobs are in this area. Wages also are rising faster than prices, as quoted by the Wall Street Journal: basic pay in the first nine months of 1991 rose almost 14%, bonuses 18%, and allowances 10%, as prices in cities rose 8% to 10%.

South Korea

South Korea's economy attained unprecedented levels of growth in recent years, through a policy of export-led industrialization centred on fostering exports. Korea's industrialization policies have been described as "selective intervention," which focus on achieving dynamic efficiency through detailed, industry-specific government policies promoting potential comparative advantages from every possible source. Through encouraging exports and promoting infant industries such as cement, fertilizer, steel, chemicals, and consumer durables, Korea's expos to date have been both privately profitable and internationally competitive.

The primary variables believed to contribute to export-related growth in Korea include the differential advantages in product uniqueness and price, management's perceptions of the importance of exporting, high rates of return-on-investment, and growth goals. In recent years, these policies have occasionally gone amiss, most notably in the case of heavy engineering in the late 1970s. Also, selective intervention has lost the support of important segments of the Korean public, who prefer democratic government to economically enlightened dictatorship.

Nevertheless, Korea's growth per capita income was well in excess of 7% over the past three decades. In 1960, the Korean economy was dominated by agriculture and mining; exports amounted to about 3% of GNP. Today, the economy is dominated by the manufacturing sector, exports account for more than 30% of GNP, and manufactured products constitute over 90% of this total. Wages remain relatively low, although employee compensation doubled from 1979 to 1984, and the prospects or future growth are excellent. Certain peculiar laws exist within Korea. For instance, Korea denies copyright protection to software, semiconductors, or foreign works.

A common notion, derived from the belief in the primacy of culture in shaping a nation's managerial system, is that Japanese and Korean management styles are essentially identical. This is largely based on the similarity of cultural heritages, which stem from East Asian Buddhist value systems. However, major differences between these two managerial styles exist, notably the absence of lifetime employment, the absence of seniority-based wages, and the enterprise-based union system within Korean firms. In this sense, Korea represents an approach to export-led growth, which is different from Japan's. The importance of culture, in this sense, is diminished by the differences in management.

Japan

Japan is clearly the most advanced country of the four along the path to export-led growth. Its government-initiated efforts began shortly after the Second World War, at which time the Japanese industrial base was essentially in ruins. This export-oriented drive was particularly emphasized through the "Trade or Die" mentally, which became prevalent in many of the newly industrialized countries during the following decades. After a rapid expansion in the 1960s-1990s, exports as a percent of GNP have diminished somewhat, although production growth rate is still strong.

This is partly due to Japan's increasing stature and diminished labour wage advantage. Through excelling in implementing new technologies and perfecting them through incremental process innovations, Japanese industries were able to successfully enter many American markets by offering products having both the best quality and lowest cost, especially in high technology products. Concurrent with this position, Japan has recently become officially classified as a "wealthy industrialized nation." with high disposable income levels, and the accompanying educational levels, academic and cultural backgrounds, and access to information common to these countries.

Despite the perception of strong import restrictions, American consumer products are widely evident. As wages become higher and the labour shortage in Japan becomes more severe, automation is increasingly replacing labour as a means of maintaining price competitiveness. Thus, many Japanese industries are using such offshore manufacturing sources as China and Thailand, and are increasingly eager to develop their own technology-intensive industries and marketing capabilities.

Japanese also are increasingly investing in the United States in order to increase their political clout and prevent further trade restrictions by creating jobs for Americans, ensure access to the American market, to become more responsive to the American market, and hedge against fluctuations in the value of the dollar. Conversely, many American firms are forming strategic alliances with Japanese companies to alleviate the large fixed costs of establishing distributor networks in such markets as shoes, nuclear reactors, pharmaceuticals, automobiles, tires, and glass.

While the data provides a general illustration of the relative economic status of these countries, they provide little information on the manufacturing and logistical environments within. Attributes of firms with respect to their productivity, process technologies, materials management and control, and production and distribution network infrastructure were compared to assess the major differences for firms operating within these countries, concurrent with the integrated logistical models proposed by Cohen and Lee, Bowersox, and Whybark. A description of the sample of firms used precedes this analysis.

The data used for this study are a subset of a manufacturing data base collected by the Global Manufacturing Research Group. This data base constitutes a worldwide survey of manufacturing practices. Hungary, China, Korea, and Japan are four of the countries for which these data are available. The sample includes firms from two manufacturing industries: nonfashion textiles and machine tools. These two industries provide a suitable basis for analysis, in that they represent two diverse points on the process spectrum.

Nonfashion textiles consist of consumer products like towels, sheets, underwear, etc., as well as industrial goods such as netting, plain woven cloth, and cloth wrapping materials. This industry is largely process-intensive in that many processes are integrated, from spinning through dyeing, weaving, cutting, and final sewing of the products. Because such mass-produced products are characterized by little customization or fashion, competition is largely based on price. As a result, there is often little opportunity for the manufacturer to achieve attractive profit margins.

In some of these markets, developed countries are making inroads through intensive automation, often at a lower per unit cost than in the labour-intensive processes of low wage-countries. However, low-wage countries typically rely on the economies of scale inherent in high-volume, low-variety production in order to compete on world markets. Such industries usually rely on a minimally skilled work force in which there are few opportunities for learning or skill formation.

The small machine tool industry consists of firms producing industrial products such as lathes, grinders, milling machines, and metal forming equipment. Most processes are batch-oriented job shops, with some firms offering options to be determined by the customer. In contrast to the textile industry, such processes generally rely on a highly-skilled, cross-trained workforce.

This industry has received substantial government support in Eastern European countries, largely because of links to defence industry ministries. Although such products compete on the basis of quality and product technology, achievements in Eastern Europe still consist largely of updating current technologies and production of relatively standard machine tools. Once again, products in less developed countries often suffer from delays in technological diffusion standardized product mixes, and unreliable quality.

The questionnaire for the study gathered information on general firm data and activities in several areas of manufacturing planning and control. Interviews were carried out by the Korea Productivity Centre and the Sogang University on a random sample of firms in South Korea. The Chinese data were collected by students through the Shanghai Institute of Mechanical Engineering. Data from Japan and Hungary also were collected through onsite interviews by members of the Global Manufacturing Research Group.

Because much of the data exhibited skewness, which implied departures from normally, a distribution free nonparametric test was used to test for significant differences existing between firms in different countries. In particular, the Kruskal-Wallis H statistic, which is equivalent to the sum of squares for treatments in a one-way analysis of variance, was calculated to determine whether the data from firms in each country was significantly different from those in other countries. This statistic was used in comparing all numerical data, but not for categorical data. General data on the number of firms from each country and industry, average sales per firm (in dollars), and average exports as a percentage of total sales. As a whole, sales for Chinese firms in both industries were significantly less than in the other countries. Although Hungarian firms have a seemingly large percentage of their sales going to exports, most of these sales are to Soviet-bloc countries and cannot be readily converted into currency.

The success of Korea's export-oriented policies is again apparent, particularly in the textile industry where on average 40% of total sales are exports. Japanese textile production, on the other hand, is focused largely on the domestic market, although protectionist measures may be partially responsible for this fact. Exports also are greater for Chinese textile firms than for Chinese machine tools, which produce largely for domestic markets (probably due to the low level of technological proficiency in the machine tool industry). In the following sections, various attributes of firm performance in each country are introduced and compared.

Productivity

An overview of some general measures of productivity and growth provide a comparative snapshot of the productive efficiency of firms in these industries. A significant difference in number of employees, sales per employee, and capacity utilisation exists between firms in the four countries. In both textiles and machine tools an obvious difference between the socialist and capitalist firms is the difference in size. The average number of employees in both Hungarian and Chinese firms is significantly larger than Korean and Japanese firms. In socialist economies, the original goal of centralized production and planning was to take advantage of economies of scale. However, these efforts have generally resulted in diseconomies, largely through an inability to take advantage of true capacity.

For instance, many Soviet-bloc plant managers are given quotas to achieve every year. In negotiating these quotas, different ploys are often used by the factory director:

He'll try to hide productive capacity of request greater quantities of inputs than needed just to make certain he has enough on hand...They have no urge to set unrealistically high quotas. It is not in their best interest to have those below them fail. The end result is that entire industries, often with bureaucratic connivance, get more than they need while producing less than they are capable of. Meanwhile, other industries have to halt production for lack of supplies.

Productivity, measured by average sales per employees, are significantly below the levels attained by Korea and Japan. In the case of Hungary, capacity utilisation is also well below normal utilisation levels of 80% to 90%. This state of affairs is such that Hungary and China's principal comparative advantage in the world economy, cheap labour, is rendered ineffective in the face of abysmal productivity and output rates.

Another reason for the productivity gap of large socialist factories has to do with the supply problems that exist in both China and Hungary (an issue discussed later in the study). Factory directors in Eastern Europe and China often try to establish fully integrated operations in order to be as independent of other enterprises as possible. Factories are often equipped to produce items which cannot be done efficiently, rather than depending on a source for the item. Managing such enterprises becomes increasingly complex due to their large size and the wide variety of activities which take place. Such factories lack a central "focus" on a set of critical manufacturing tasks; the result is a general state of chaos, which translates to low levels of productivity.

Process Technologies

Differences between socialist and industrialized manufacturing capability also are apparent in the state of technology in the textile and machine tool industries. Hungary's expenses have testified that the technology gap vis-a-vis the West has probably not narrowed significantly since 1968. Between 1968 and 1983, Hungary imported a large quantity of machinery, yet has not succeeded in enjoying any major benefits from it. The state of technology in Soviet-bloc industries has been compared to a pyramid, with the quality of resources diminishing as one descends to the lower levels. At the base are the ill-equipped enterprises that use labour-intensive techniques and produce at the low levels of quality, while the upper branches enjoy a better standing in relation to Western countries.

The upper level firms are typically in well developed industries such as metallurgy, machine tools, and electric power generation, which are often critical inputs to defence capabilities. For example, the defence industry builds some 10% of all metal-cutting tools in the Soviet Union, including about one-fourth of numerically controlled machine tools. Such new technologies, which result from a deliberate attempt at cooperation between the defence sector and the civilian engineering industry, often receive priority treatment at the expense of consumer-oriented industries.

The ratio of equipment dollars per worker for firms differs, providing evidence of a higher intensity of automation in Japan vs. the other three countries. This higher rate of automation is probably in response to Japan's higher wage rates, particularly in the low-margin labour-intensive textile industry. While many Eastern European firms recognise the importance of intensive development of new technologies, the capacity to respond is restricted to a great extent by ceilings fixed by central authorities. Since capital markets are tricking, many plants can only invest what they can raise by their own efforts.

In terms of the technological knowledge base within these countries, Hungary spends significantly less time on training their employees as measured by the number of training days per year although the higher levels of "training" days in China may in fact include repeated exposure to communist dogma. Korean machine tool employees receive the greatest intensity of on-the-job training, attesting to their rapid technological development. With respect to the percent of firms having engineers making production planning decisions, Hungary is clearly not lacking. This corroborates, pointing out that the majority of Eastern Europeans have a solid educational foundation.

In this respect, it appears that the infrastructural requirements for technology transfers from the West to occur in China and Eastern Europe are well-established. However, this does not obviate the need for a well-grounded technical education in these countries, which is generally lacking. Given the size and quality of the Soviet-bloc science and technology establishment, remarkably few technical innovations of any substance have been produced, partly due to a political and economic system that discourages risk taking. Many Soviet technical projects are limited also because they lack good instrumentation, which in turn is a function of the limited ability of the industrial base to produce it. This lag is often compensated for by importing foreign technologies, which unfortunately does not provide many benefits because of a lack of technical learning. To coin a phrase, just as "science is not technology," technology is not manufacturing.

Materials Management and Control

Another area of critical importance in industrial firms is the management of materials and associated logistics problems. While manufacturing plants in newly industrialized countries and the West have developed planning systems such as Material Requirements Planning (MRP) and execution systems such as Just-in-Time to reduce inventory investments and improve efficiency, such systems are by and large unheard of in Eastern Europe and China. A comparison of a simple measure, the number of annual inventory turns, is indicative of the problems of material management in these countries. A significant difference exists between the number of turns in firms from each of the countries.

In the machine tool industries, Korean and Japanese firms have a high rate of inventory turnover, signifying an ability to smooth the flow of materials through the plant. Hungarian and Chinese machine tool factories have abysmally low inventory turns. Further, a significantly larger portion of inventory in Hungarian and Chinese firms is held in raw materials. This result suggests that a major stumbling block in socialist economies is the procurement of materials. Hungary, for instance, possesses few natural resources other than agricultural land, bauxite deposits, and some lesser coal, oil, and natural gas deposits. (By comparison, China has a vast array of natural resources.)

Consequently, most raw materials in Hungary are imported, and as such, are controlled by authorities. In many cases, ministries specify the supplies a factory receives and on what delivery dates. As a result, deliveries are often too small, of substandard quality, behind schedule, or fictitious. The response of factory directors is thus to hoard materials: They might not even have any direct use for it. But they might be able to trade it for something else. Sadly, surplus goods stand idle or even rot away in one location while at another production is halted because the input is unavailable. Note that the hoarding of raw materials is a rational response to infrastructural problems within the economy. To compensate for these inherent deficiencies, enterprises often employ tolkachi (expediters), whose job is to beg, borrow, or steal supplies that are otherwise unavailable. In addition, the measure of turns for Hungarian textile firms is not much greater than their Japanese and Korean counterparts, and there is not a significant difference in the quantity of finished goods held in inventory.

This can partly be explained by the fact that textiles are consumer goods, which are badly needed and for which a chronic shortage exists. As such, finished goods levels are minimal, and the factories can sell virtually all that is produced. This is especially true in China, where finished goods are in some cases immediately appropriated by government ministries.

In striving to obtain an item or material, Hungarian firms are likely to employ as many sources and suppliers as possible, either through government ministries or through tolkachi. Chinese firms are likely to use hedging (i.e., hoarding) in obtaining a dependable source. On the other hand, Korean and Japanese firms are more likely to procure materials from one or two sources, based on production plan requirements, customer orders, or other factors. Japanese manufacturers, in particular, very rarely change suppliers, expect suppliers to achieve cost reductions as a matter of course. While this has increased the stability of their buyer-supplier relationships, it has made it very difficult for American firms to compete as suppliers within this arena.

Production Control and Distribution Networks

In centrally planned economies, the net result of misallocations associated with centralized planning is ultimately felt by the consumer in the form of chronic shortages. The bureaucracies that arise in planning production inevitably lead to poor market linkages and a failure to meet demand. This can be seen through examination of several different facets of firms' production planning and distribution performance. Whether they explicitly recognise it or not, all manufacturing organisations establish some kind of production plan which establishes the annual production rate for a product group or other broad category. Although the units can vary (either currency or physical units), the production plan is instrumental in determining the approach to be used in coping with sales activity. As such, a key indicator of how responsive a production system is to the market is the number of times the plan is revised, the planning increments used, and the assumptions used in determining the plan. A realistic plan is based on actual demand and is revised more frequently according to changes in sales patterns.

The Hungarian and Chinese firms are significantly less responsive to the market, revising their plans on average three or four times per year, compared to six to ten times per year in Japanese and Korean firms. More importantly, these production plans are more likely to be based on backlog and projected inventory figures as opposed to actual sales data and forecasts. An example of this situation is provided by Desai's description of state-run firms in the Soviet Union. Typically, gross output (val) targets are the main elements of production plans, which specify the number of tons to be produced, pages to be printed, etc.

A telling cartoon in Krokodil depicted a factory manager who produced a single gigantic nail in fulfillment of a target specified in tons rather than as an assortment of nails! Gross output targets have traditionally dominated all other measurement criteria including profit and actual demand, and as such have hindered market responsiveness. This lack of responsiveness to market demand has carried over to the production floor. A significant difference in the percentage of late orders exists, and such orders are likely to be delayed by as long as 9 weeks in Hungarian firms. The most common reasons in Hungary for late orders are transportation problems and unavailable materials. These figures attest to he inability of centrally planned economies to support a logistical infrastructure that keeps materials flowing into factories as required.

Delivery lead times for the Hungarian and Chinese firms are significantly greater (i.e., more then double) those of their Japanese and Korean counterparts. The most common reason in the case of Hungary is again material shortages. In a system in which firms can sell all that they produce and there is no incentive for meeting delivery dates or reducing delivery lead times, this vicious cycle of shortages echoes throughout the value chain, from unprocessed materials all the way to the consumer bread line. In this chapter we have identified several major differences in foreign manufacturing organisations that were evident when comparing performance data from Hungarian, Chinese, Korean, and Japanese firms in the same industries.

One major problem faced by firms in centrally planned economies is their size, which inhibits management's "focus" on a concise set of manufacturing tasks. The complexity of such organisations hinders the ability of factory directors to manage available capacity effectively. A second problem is a lack of technical knowledge that prevents the adoption of new process technologies. Although many managers have a good deal of educational training, much of it is theoretical in nature and is of little help in making capital investment decisions such as retooling and establishing logistics networks. There also is a lack of managerial skills in Hungary and China with respect to planning, production, distribution, and inventories. Because factory directors had only to meet a fixed quota in the past, there is no precedent for matching production and inventory levels with demand.

The only rule of thumb common to these managers is the accumulation of raw material inventories whenever possible, regardless of whether or not they are needed. This hoarding of materials not only represents a wasteful use of resources, but serves to worsen the chronic material shortages and distribution problems that exist in the supply chain. This state of affairs is a virtual Catch-22, as production delays occurring due to material shortages result in longer lead times and late deliveries in other sectors of the economy.

Implications for American Managers

As mentioned earlier, many Western firms seek to establish international alliances or sources overseas. While a number of potential opportunities for strategic advantages and new markets may exist, managers need to be aware of the existing logistics environments. Conditions in Japan and Korea are likely to be more similar to American planning modes, although new entrants into Japanese home markets may have difficulty in overcoming possible biases regarding the quality of American suppliers. In Hungary and China, however, a significant amount of restructuring may be necessary.

The single greatest resource which managers in such countries can benefit from is education in basic management principles. In tandem with this re-education, several infrastructural barriers to effective logistics management will necessarily have to be removed. New production planning mechanisms that effectively measure available capacity will have to be devised.

Large firms will have to be broken down into manageable units, as opposed to the huge monoliths which encompass a variety of disjoint operations. Such smaller units will be more prepared to focus on specific tasks, thereby improving the quality of resulting products. In the process, productive capacity can be utilised more efficiently. Allowing these firms to be able to compete in world markets by taking advantage of lower wage rates initially.

In the long run, technological capabilities can be built up and firms can progress into other types of industries. Increased technical training of the workforce will be a precursor to higher rates of innovation and adoption of new process technologies. In many cases, the building of new distribution and supply networks will be a precursor to the establishment of American joint or sourcing ventures.

The importance of Western direct foreign investment in promoting growth in newly reformed economies cannot be overemphasized. Such ties can encourage the transfer of "hard" and "soft" technologies, for which there is already a solid educational base.

In the process, there will be economic hardships, as the labour market will be flooded as unproductive capacity is eliminated. While internationalization offers enticing new markets and forms of increased price competitiveness, managers must enter into such ventures prepared with a logistics strategy to deal with a variety of new and difficult situations.

Just-in-Time for Logistics Organisation Management

Just-in-time (JIT) in its simplest form refers to a method of inventory control with a focus on waste elimination. The visible performance improvements of some firms adopting JIT led to a great deal of excitement. Implementing JIT at the operational level and creating competitive advantage through JIT became topics of widespread interest.

Yet despite its popularity, clinical analysis of JIT at the organisational level has been sparse. One can ask, for example, exactly how and to what degree does JIT impact the organisational design of the logistics function, the management of logistics, and the performance of the firm. The purpose of this research is to provide logistics managers with a richer understanding of what JIT means to: (1) the management of the logistics function; and (2) the performance of the firm. This is accomplished through an analysis of questionnaire data completed by 200 Council of Logistics Management (CLM) members. The framework of the study, which is presented in the Exhibit, consists of two major thrusts. First, we examine the association of JIT on those facets of organisational structure that are of direct importance to logistics managers. The facets examined include formalization of performance measurement, specialization of the logistics function, decentralization of strategic logistics decision-making, and integration of logistics strategy formulation.

The connection between JIT and the number of logistics layers and the span of control of the senior logistics executive is also studied. The second major thrust of the research is the association of firm performance with JIT implementation. Here we focus on firm performance indicators such as profit, ROI, sales growth, and market share growth. In the section that follows, we discuss six research questions concerning the relationship of JIT with: (I) logistics organisational design; and (2) firm performance. This is followed by the method section describing the study of CLM members. Results of multiple regression modelling are presented, followed by a discussion from a managerial perspective.

Does JIT Associate with Formalization? Formalization encompasses performance control mechanisms and written rules, procedures, and policies. Control mechanisms refer to "after-the-fact" measurement of performance. In this research we study: (1) internal performance measurement (e.g., a firm monitors its own customer service level); (2) comparative or benchmarking performance measurement (e.g., a firm compares its service level to that of the competition); and (3) supplier performance measurement (e.g., a firm measures the service levels of alternative suppliers). JIT should correlate positively with these formal performance control mechanisms.

It has often been noted that JIT manufacturers intensively monitor suppliers on price, quality of goods, on-time delivery, and so on. JIT manufacturers intensively monitor their own performance from internal sources (e.g., their own defect rates and costs) and may be more likely to monitor performance relative to competition (i.e., benchmarked performance). Taking a systems perspective provides additional reasons why measurement should be associated with JIT. For example, JIT requires substantial financial and human investment in improving product quality both before and during production or assembly.

The benefits, however, are felt by diverse functional units. Logistics may benefit from higher product quality because fewer goods are returned or because fewer spare parts for after sales service need to be handled. JIT benefits many functions, but the costs may be borne by a more limited number of entities.

A total system perspective examines multiple functions and their interactions and acts as an arbiter to minimize total system cost. A necessary facilitator of analyzing the total system is intensive measurement of performance. The firm that implements JIT but fails to monitor performance from multiple sources may fail to fully understand the costs and benefits of JIT, both firmwide and within various functions.

Does JIT Associate with Specialization? Specialization refers to the subdivision of labour, and in this research, we concentrate on the specialization of indirect logistics labour.

For instance, the firm that employs at least one full time individual in the area of warehouse facility layout is more specialized than the firm that does not. We expect JIT to relate positively with the level of indirect logistics labour specialization. One rationale for the connection is that investment in specialized skills is required to handle the complex transactions that accompany JIT. For example, specialists may be required to design systems capable of dealing with small lots sales or purchases of variable size. Another explanation focuses on JIT from a total system perspective. Specialization of indirect logistics labour allows the firm to increase the understandability of system components and related interactions.

Thus the more specialized firm, in terms of product storage and flows, may be better positioned to fully leverage JIT implementation into performance improvements. Does JIT Associate with Decentralization? Decentralization refers to the vertical locus of decision-making in the firm. Interest here lies with the locus of decision-making over strategic logistics issues (such as required distribution service levels).

In general, JIT is associated with decentralized structures. For example, using factory labour to spot defects in products or parts/ materials design under a JIT regime (where less existed previously) represents decentralization in one particular domain that domain being product defect identification. A question that remains unresolved is whether decentralization of strategic logistics decision-making is similarly pushed down the organisational chart under a JIT regime. Defect identification in shipment timing or assortment, rather than in product, may also best be accomplished by lower level employees.

Does JIT Associate with Integration? Integration concerns lateral communications within the firm designed to coordinate functional activities. It is installed to counter the functional isolationism that accompanies vertical communication channels. In this research, we examine the extent to which different functions engage in face-to-face collaboration in the formulation of logistics strategy. An increase in JIT should associate with an increase in face-to-face integration of strategy making in general and of logistics strategy in particular.

Shared decision-making across functions by senior managers increases management understandability of the functional interdependence and interactions necessary for the adoption of JIT. Cross-functional shared decision-making in logistics strategy formulation may be particularly important to ensure that logistics competencies support organisational goals. For example, JIT targets service levels that logistics must meet, but JIT also reduces inventory buffers and increases the number of boundary-spanning transactions with suppliers and customers. Does JIT Associate with Layers and Span? Layers and span of control are straightforward concepts: layers refers to the number of levels in a firm and span refers to the number of individuals reporting directly to an individual.

JIT should be associated with fewer layers for the logistics function and a wider span of control for the senior logistics executive. This expectation is derived from the simplification of many operations that accompany JIT. JIT is associated with better product quality, and this leads to fewer returned goods, less scrap and rework material, and less after sales service parts. JIT is also associated with more factory-to-customer direct shipments and more direct internal product flows.

The overall organisational efficiency associated with JIT should translate into fewer layers for the logistics function. Overall simplification should translate into the senior logistics manager being able to directly oversee a greater number of subordinates without unduly increasing the control burden.

Does JIT Associate with Performance? Performance refers to the competitive standing of the firm. In this research, we examine both financial and market performance. To capture the relative standing of the firm and to isolate JIT from other factors that may have a long term impact, we measure performance over the past three years, relative to other firms in the same industry.

JIT should be associated with better financial and market performance. The lower cost structure resulting from JIT implementation may translate into better financial performance relative to the competition.

For example, relative return on investment may improve. JIT should also be correlated with better market performance-that is, as JIT increases, market indicators such as sales growth and market share should also increase. The market, whether comprised of final consumers or industrial customers, should reward the better service and product quality associated with JIT implementation.

Controlling for Size

Size should be controlled for two reasons. First, size predicts organisational structure and may even correlate with JIT. Larger firms are typically more formalized, specialized, decentralized, and integrated. Formalized control and policies arise to overcome wider spans of control and greater layers, specialization increases as firms continually find ways to subdivide labour, decentralization is introduced to reduce senior manager control costs and burdens, and integration increases to offset increased compartmentalization. If size does predict structure and JIT, then it is important to control for size in allocating predictive variance.

Modelling both should allow us to determine whether it is size, JIT, or both that affect logistics organisational structure. Second, it is important to examine whether JIT and size interact in predicting logistics organisational structure and performance. For example, JIT may have a greater impact on face-to-face logistics strategy integration when the size of the firm is large. Small firms may already utilise a minimum level of integration regardless of the level of JIT. While there are precedents for expecting size to relate to logistics organisation, the question of the impact of JIT/size interactions is largely exploratory and worthy of investigation. The CLM provided their manufacturers mailing list. The list was culled to 1,002 names by eliminating non-U.S. residents and by selecting only one member from any given firm. A questionnaire was mailed, followed one month later by telephone callbacks. Nineteen questionnaires were nondeliverable, and 218 were returned by CLM members leading to a 22.2% (i.e., 218/981) response rate.

Eighteen questionnaires were discarded because of too many missing values or because they were completed by the distribution divisions of manufacturing firms. Since the questionnaire was specifically designed to be completed by manufacturers, those completed by distribution organisations were discarded. The analysis that follows is based on 200 responses. Mean annual sales of the sample firms is $1.175 billion and the average number of employees is 3,935. Seventeen percent of the respondents were vice-presidents, followed by directors (36%), and managers (43%). Most selected logistics or distribution as their primary area of functional responsibility (73%).

The industry distribution, based on 2-digit SIC codes, is: food and kindred products (SIC 20), 15.1%; chemicals and allied products (SIC 28), 14.1 %; miscellaneous manufacturing industries (SIC 39), 12.6%; electronic and other electrical equipment and components, except computer equipment (SIC 36), 8.5%; paper and allied products (SIC 26), 6.5%; rubber and miscellaneous plastics products (SIC 30), 5.5%; fabricated metal products except machinery and computer equipment (SIC 34), 5.5%; and measuring, analyzing, and controlling instruments, photographic, medical, and optical goods, watches and clocks (SIC 38), 5.5%. The rest were spread across the remaining SIC groups.

We examined nonresponse bias by comparing early versus late respondents using t-tests. The former were significantly larger in terms of the natural logarithm of the number of employees. ANCOVA models were then used to determine whether these firms differed on any of the other variables after controlling for size. No other differences were found. A literature review was undertaken and a pool of items measuring JIT was selected for inclusion in the questionnaire. Respondents were asked to express their level of agreement with 6 statements describing JIT implementation on 7-point scales with endpoints of "strongly disagree" and "strongly agree." The items are:

(1) total preventative maintenance is used;
(2) reduced machine set-up times are an important goal;
(3) cross-training of direct labour is relied upon;
(4) factory labour is encouraged to spot defects in materials or production/assembly processes;
(5) Pareto charts, fishbone diagrams, and other analytic techniques are used to identify sources of defects in products; and
(6) small amounts of in-process buffer inventory are used.

These items were subjected to an exploratory principal components analysis. Since only the first eigenvalue was greater than one, the scale appears to be unidimensional.

Eight dimensions of organisational structure are in the analysis, three of which concern formalization. Formal performance measurement was measured by asking for ratings on the extent to which performance was monitored on:

(1) functional costs;
(2) customer service;
(3) cost controls by fixing standard costs and analyzing variation;
(4) productivity analysis;
(5) customer satisfaction and follow-up; and
(6) profitability.

Formal benchmarking was measured by asking for ratings on the extent to which performance was compared to industry standards or competitors on:

(1) functional costs;
(2) customer service;
(3) productivity levels;

(4) operations (such as warehousing); and

(5) profitability.

Formal supplier evaluation was measured by asking for ratings on the extent to which alternative suppliers were evaluated on:

(1) distribution service;

(2) product quality;

(3) competitive price;

(4) personnel/ management resources; and

(5) manufacturing capability/capacity.

In all instances 7-point scales with endpoints of "rarely used" and "frequently used" were employed. Specialization was measured by asking whether at least one full-time individual dealt exclusively with each of six indirect labour work areas critical to logistics operations. They are:

(1) warehouse facilities design;

(2) material handling;

(3) distribution equipment procurement;

(4) production scheduling;

(5) warehouse facility location; and

(6) transportation scheduling.

"Yes/no" scales were used and a sum of the number of "yes" responses was taken. Decentralization was measured by asking respondents to rate the organisational level at which each of four decisions were made. The decisions represent strategic ones from the logistics domain. They are:

(1) the number of finished goods field warehouses to operate;

(2) the location of finished goods field warehouses;

(3) distribution service levels; and

(4) channels of distribution to be used.

Seven-point scales were used, each scale point indicating a particular organisational level. For example: 1=above the chief executive (e.g., board of directors or owners); 2=chief executive; 3=divisional manager; and 7=individual below first level supervisor.

Integration was measured by asking for the extent to which decision-making at top levels is characterized by participative, cross-functional committees in which different departments, functions, or divisions get together to decide issues related to logistics strategy formulation. A seven-point scale with endpoints of "rarely used" and "frequently used" was used. Layers for logistics were measured by asking for the number of levels in the logistics function (i.e., the count in the longest chain between direct worker and the senior executive, including both levels). The span of control was measured by asking how many individuals reported directly to the senior logistics executive (excluding secretaries and assistants). Open-ended scales were used in both cases.

Respondents rated the performance of the firm over the past three years on 7-point scales with endpoints of "well below industry average" and "well above industry average." Financial performance was measured by the following four items:

(1) profit growth;

(2) average return on investment;

(3) average profit; and

(4) average return on sales.

Market performance was measured by:

(1) market share growth; and

(2) sales growth.

The measure of performance is perceptual and is not objective such as would be actual return on investment. It was left to the respondent to assess the "industry" base against which to evaluate performance; the number of firms in that competitive base was determined by each respondent independently. Moreover, to avoid cuing, the JIT scale was the last one on the questionnaire. Finally, size was measured by the natural logarithm of annual sales. For each variable, it presents the mean, standard deviation, reliability estimate (where applicable), and number of items in the scale. With one exception, Cronbach a's were used to assess scale reliability for multi-item measures. The exception is the Kuder-Richardson 20 estimate provided for the summed binary measure of specialization. All reliability estimates exceed .70. Multiple regression was used to examine the relationship of JIT with logistics organisation and on performance. Each of the organisational structure and performance variables was modelled separately as a dependent variable.

JIT, size, and the interaction of the two served as predictor variables. Initially, the product of size and JIT was used as the interaction variable, but the interaction was highly correlated with size. To overcome multicollinearity problems, size and JIT were first standardized (i.e., mean zero, variance one), and the interaction was then estimated as the product of the standardized variables. This interaction term was uncorrelated with size and JIT (r<.OS in both instances). In the regression models, the dependent variables thus consist of JIT and size main effects (both of which are unstandardized) and their interaction (which is the product of the variables after standardization).

As seen there, more JIT intensive manufacturers are more formalized regarding internal, benchmarking, and supplier performance measurements. They are more specialized concerning indirect logistics labour. Strategic logistics decision-making is more decentralized and face-to-face, and cross-functional formulation of logistics strategy is more integrated as JIT increases. JIT is associated with the number of layers within the logistics function or with the span of control of the senior logistics executive. It also is associated with better performance over the past three years relative to competitors in the firm's primary industry. This applies to both financial and market performance.

Size predicts most dimensions of organisational structure. Larger firms are more formalized (with the exception of internal performance measurement), specialized, and integrated concerning logistics strategy formulation. The number of layers for the logistics function and the span of control of the senior logistics executives increase as size increases. Size does not predict decentralization of strategic logistics decision-making, nor is it related to performance.

Finally, the interaction of JIT with size is significant in only two models: the model predicting specialization and the one predicting the senior logistics executive span of control. The interactions can be interpreted as follows: the effect of JIT on specialization and on the senior logistics executive span of control is dependent on the size of the firm, that is, the larger the firm, the greater the effect. This research suggested that JIT would have significant implications for the management of logistics within the firm and for firm performance. The findings, based on a survey of 200 CLM members employed by manufacturers, were largely supportive. First, JIT is associated with the formalization of performance measurements. As JIT increases, the firm increasingly monitors performance from internal sources, compares its performance to competitors and industry standards, and scrutinizes the performance of suppliers. Logistics managers in JIT oriented manufacturers have at their disposal a greater volume of cost, service level, productivity, and profitability information. Performance information allows logistics managers to better implement a total system orientation. When the understandability of system components increases through intensive performance measurement, the logistics manager's ability to effectively engage in trade-offs also increases. Moreover, the collection of benchmarking performance information allows the logistics manager to better respond and possibly anticipate market and competitive shifts. By engendering a focus on performance measurement, JIT may allow the firm to better understand its competitive environment. Second, JIT is associated with the extent of indirect logistics labour specialization. JIT manufacturers enjoy a greater reliance on logistics personnel with specialized skills.

For example, JIT manufacturers may be more likely to employ at least one full time employee to handle warehouse location analysis, materials handling, transportation scheduling, and so on. Specialized logistics labour can have a direct impact on performance (through, for example, more efficient usage of transportation assets), as well as provide senior logistics managers with better knowledge of functional operations. Specialization and formalized performance measurement benefits may complement one another: JIT firms may be increasing total system understandability by both operating a superior performance control system and by employing staff with greater skills. It is important to note that the interaction between JIT and size was significant in the model predicting specialization.

One way of looking at this finding is to think of the amount of systems knowledge demanded by managers. As JIT increases, the amount of systems knowledge demanded may increase faster in a large firm compared to a small firm, since it is within the large firm that more complex inventory and scheduling decisions are made. Thus large firms may require more in the way of knowledge-creating specialists as JIT increases than small firms.

Third, under a JIT orientation, decisions concerning strategic logistics issues are pushed (or delegated) down the organisational chart. Decentralization occurs in deciding, for example, the location and number of field warehouses, distribution service level standards, and channels of distribution to be used.

Decentralization fosters greater participation and input by a wider range of individuals. Employees of the logistics function within a JIT firm may feel a greater sense of empowerment and involvement with the firm, which in turn may lead to a greater sense of responsibility and willingness to promote novel solutions to problems facing the firm. Thus JIT may result in a greater number of individuals in the logistics function willingly seeking solutions to problems.

Fourth, JIT is associated with greater involvement by senior executives from different functions in the creation of logistics strategy. JIT firms attempt to ensure that the logistics strategy of the firm complements those of other functions and the firm overall.

Some managers may feel restricted by encroachment from other functions on the design of logistics strategy. But such integration is no doubt more than a one-way street. Logistics managers in a JIT organisation may increasingly be able to influence strategy in other functions such as marketing and production to ensure that strategies in these functional areas complement logistics strategy and capabilities.

Moreover, cross-functional involvement (or integration) in formulation of logistics strategy increases managerial understandability of functional interactions, a key requisite for enforcing JIT on a systemwide basis. Fifth, JIT did not predict layers, and the effect on the senior logistics executive span of control interacted with size. Thus the efficiency gains associated with JIT do not result in a significantly flatter organisational structure for the logistics function. Span of control does increase with JIT, but the relationship is dependent on the size of the firm: the effect of JIT on the span of control of the senior logistics executives increases as size increases.

Sixth, JIT is associated with improved perceptions of the firm's performance relative to the primary industry over the past three years. This applies to financial performance (such as average profit) and market performance (such as sales growth). Much has been written about JIT and performance, but the evidence has been mostly anecdotal. Empirical support is scarce. This research supports the frequently cited claim that JIT is associated with improved firm performance. Despite this support, our research is cross-sectional in nature, unable to detect causal relationships, and thus an initial, tentative step. Furthermore, we did not address the anecdotal evidence that the performance of some firms may decline as JIT increases. Further research should examine why some firms benefit while others do not when JIT is implemented. In summary, the organisation of the logistics function is dramatically associated with JIT implementation. Logistics managers have at their fingertips a greater volume of information on costs, productivity levels, service levels, and profitability levels. They have a better understanding of internal performance, performance relative to competitors, and supplier performance.

This provides logistics managers with a better ability to plan and to adjust plans based on actual performance. They manage a function that is more specialized concerning indirect logistics labour. Participation and involvement is increased by delegating responsibility for strategic logistics decision-making to lower organisational levels. Logistics strategy is better integrated with other functional strategies and with the overall strategy of the firm. Furthermore, more performance control, greater specialization, more formalized planning, and greater decentralization suggest that senior logistics managers in JIT firms possess a greater level of understandability of system components, system interactions, and the total system.

Such knowledge may be necessary to implement JIT on a total system basis. Finally, logistics managers should understand that these adjustments in the structure of the logistics function are not fruitless. Indeed, the performance of JIT firms is better than non-JIT ones, and part of that improvement may result from the greater understandability engendered by the changes in the organisation of the logistics function that accompany JIT.

5

Logistics Operation Management

Reverse logistics (RL) is a new logistics form which from the customers or distributors to the manufacturers is contrary with the traditional logistics. Concretely speaking, because some productions lost the obvious use value such as the packaging, or lost the function such as the spoiled products, or are difficult to sale in the general market such as the overstocks, or must be returned for some reasons, such as the cars with disfigurement, they have to flow reversely from the downstream to the upstream in supply chain. Reverse logistics management is the process of planning, implementing, and controlling RL activities. The rapid development of RL is along with the increased research both in practice and the theory. Some literatures have provided some feasible solving methods mainly reflected as follows: Operational management meaning. Literatures represented the impact factors such as determined automated pipeline, inventory and order-based production control system; cost or time; product life cycle etc.

Operational Model

The main works involved return models, network structures, inventory management, information technologies etc. In return aspect, such as compared with OEM takeback, Pooled takeback and third parry takeback; third-parry reverse logistics providers selection and evaluation; a contractor of fourth-parry logistics etc., As far as network structures, such as network design principles; the product return network structure; the strategic-tactic-operational decisions framework; the hierarchical model of RL network design; the mix integer linear program applied in reverse network; empirical study etc., To inventory management, the key work centralized in optimal methods, such as optimal control model based on double warehouses; newsboy problem; average cost approach; Lagrange function and so on.

For information technology, most of work reflected the definite role in RL, such as the superior performance through focused resource commitments to information technology; supply chain information system; material recovery and environmental impact through a Decision Support System. And, other works are represented in forecast; design of reverse distribution networks; disassembly and reassembly etc. In fact, RL has become one of important strategy for enterprises and even countries to seize the global plateau.

With the industrial ecology issues are extensive popularity among the fields of society, government and industry etc., such as 3R (reducing, reusing and recycling) strategies, cost-saving ecological ideas and plan, green production and so on. On the other hand, the leading actors in today's markets have transformed from sellers to buyers, whether or not meet customers' individuation demands become an important factor to show enterprises' talents in the competitive environment. The information asymmetry between enterprises and customers, the complexity in the business environment, the diversity of customers' demands and so on, all indicate that customer complaint is unavoidable.

Based on the modern organisational behaviour theory, the viewpoint of complaint reflects that an enterprise should admit customer complaint, even more advocates it. Customer complaint helps an enterprise win the customer again and provides with the change to improve product. Therefore, enterprises in supply chain must take active manners to treat customer complaint and manage it effectively. The complaint information such as the returned product from consumer is portion of RL activities; at the same time, complaint service management (CSM) in a supply chain needs to be analyzed.

From the strategic view, CSM is the crucial composing of RL strategy and an effective approach of reverse information, such as, CSM can help organisation build the customer loyalty and find the new value-added; an enterprise via successful managing complaint, it can improve its customer satisfaction degree, retain the old customers and allure the new customers; an enterprise via analyzing the customer complaint, it can find out its customer preference, so make for updating or developing product; the return product attached complaint information is just core activity in RL etc. Nowadays the computer technology, the communication technology and the information technology have been active and progressing aggressively. Those would give CSM important stimulus and prompting to perform more efficiently and effectively. Under the supply chain circumstance, based on online complaint management as well as auctions to sell refurbished or old parts are discussed by Rainer Alt (2000). If the partial order does not deliver on time, it is important to get the system to notify System Manager such that Kills can initiate the action instead of customer filing a complaint.

The service provider's reaction can either reinforce a strong customer relationship, or change a smilingly minor complaint into a major incident. The visibility concept into the domain of mobile information systems in a supply chain, it can offer when incorporated into business customer solutions and solves company related to certain complaint management problems.

Aspects of Social Dialogue, freedom of association and complaint management are clearly separated as distinct issues by another enterprise representative who fundamentally distances himself from the task of forcing union participation through the companies: As an enterprise representative, one did not want to assume a mediating role for unions at suppliers', representation being the task of the unions themselves. In fact, personal relationships play a fundamental role in business relations, in which technical aspects of communication prevail on emotional ones. From those literatures' results, we can see the main RL activities driven by the coercive conditions or enterprise' sustaining objectives. From the customer's behaviour, specially, CSM applied in RL rarely and combing the computer technology to managing complaint is unperceived.

RL operation management is restricted by the cost, the practice, the human resource and uncertainties in market etc. Considering the environmental consciousness and the policy impact, the outsourcing is the better selection for enterprises driven by economic profit. In order to make full use of the third provider services' advantage, a virtual enterprise (VE) fashion will be most appropriate.

The concept of VE was proposed by Kenneth Preiss et al. (1991). The way of only depending on a single enterprise to respond rapidly to changing market opportunities and intensely global competition have been inapplicable.

The key technique determined by utilising agile manufacturing practices is based on VE. With the urgent demand of implementing, it is significant to find an effective operation management mode for

RL. From presented works, we can see the main RL operation was presided over enterprise's oneself or cooperation fashion or third parry logistics supplier, CSM applied in RL rarely and combing the computer. How to consider the VE model in RL operation, it is significance. Therefore, we represent an operation management mode based on VEs.

CSM is an Important Reason of Engendered RL

As a whole, RL can be classified by return and reclaim in a supply chain. Return is "push" logistics produced by all distributors or end customers; and reclaim driven by manufacturers is called "pull" logistics. "Push" logistics mostly involves reverse flowed products and information; customer complaint is just aim at the product information feedback except the government policy.

One of causes for RL engendering is determined by fashion of an enterprise takes cognizance of complaint. If an enterprise is attention to the customer complaint information, throw into CSM, it will clean off obstacles of the return flow of product or information, whereas, if an enterprise disregards the customer complaint, RL service will be wave aside.

In fact, any complaint may trigger reverse activities in a supply chain. When analyzing the customer complaint information professionally, some bugs in product designing or production processes could be find out, enterprises must recall those products initiatively, i.e., results in the "pull" RL. It is obvious that CSM is an important reason for engendering RL.

CSM is the Crucial Portion of RL Management

Complaint information of customers is the feedback information, as well as products; those information and products flow conversely are just all RL activities. The drive force to implement CSM comes from customer, that because if considering the customers as the point of origin of RL, the enterprises act can be regarded as the "transfer" or terminal. Based on sufficient communication with customers, enterprises collect the external complaint information to track investigation and integrating analysis; different departments share information at the same time, such as client data, product status, processing flow etc.

From logistics management, RL activities are organised according to CSM, those activities include: Reuse-where packaging is reused or a product is returned to polish for resale to another customer; Repair/

repackage-where a moderate magnitude of repairs and/or repackaging will allow the product to be reused; Return to supplier-if the product was purchased from a supplier and is returnable, or materials from return disassembled product; Resell-where the product is resold in a secondary market "as is."

Some logistics companies have found a niche in matching sellers with buyers in secondary markets and say that there is a market for virtually anything; Recycle-where the product is broken down and "mined" for components that can be reused or resold; Renew-where a used product's utility is restored by replacing worn parts or remanufacturing in some manner, such that the product can reuse; Harmless disposal-where the unworthiness item is sent to a landfill, which can be fired with high temperature or buried.

There is a far more expensive choice than most organisations operation, e.g., transportation costs, disposal facilities and IT cost etc. When payment for goods or compensation has happened between enterprises and customers, the content of CSM involve financial management committed in RL. In fact, CSM will help enterprises to implement RL operation exactly.

CSM Objective is Based on Customer Satisfaction

CSM is aim to improve customer satisfactory degree, this is not contradiction to the objective of the enterprises' economic benefit in implementing RL. If enterprises want to win customers, customers enjoyable is necessary, there is need to provide the better service after purchased.

That is to say, RL strategy is of an important approach to meet customer demand involving repair, replacing etc. To develop CSM, enterprises can implement RL management to reclaim actively the spoiled products in customers or overstock in downstream distributors, these ways will be propitious to improve the relationships with downstream actors as distributors and customers, and then increase satisfaction degree availably. With satisfaction degree improving, a good brand will prevail widely, after then higher market share and production profit will be received. On the other hand, reproducing for spoiled, rebuilding for disused etc., form which enterprises can excavate more potential value.

Process Management of CSM

The different emergence patterns of RL in a supply chain affect the application of CSM in RL, which can be split into three aspects:

in manufacturing, in distribution, in use. We consider CSM of RL in manufacturing as an example.

CSM of RL in manufacturing activities refers to raw material surplus, quality- control returns and production leftovers etc. Considering a supplier as an "enterprise", a manufacturer then means the a "customer", there maybe some complaints form the manufacturer follows materials that supplier supplied, such as quality, fashion etc., so the supplier must respond to those matters quickly in order to meet customer demand. CSM of RL is one of the important items in RL strategy, via implementing process achieves three functions: collection, evaluation and disposal.

Collection

Complaint Collected: To capturing complaint information, enterprises need to lower "the threshold" to invite the voice of complaint.

Some inspirit methods can be used, such as the initiative consultation, using by gifts to encourage complaint etc; to customers, there are not airy proper routes to express complaint, so enterprises should open the relative channels, such as Internet, poster, phone or fax, E-mail etc. To unwillingness expression complaint customers, enterprises must launch some trigger strategies initiatively to search for the customer's dissatisfaction. The familiar forms are questionnaire, consultation, visit, promotion etc.

Product Return: based on the customer complaint information, enterprises can collect the returned product that dispersed in customers' hands. Those activities include collection, transport, and storage etc.

A convenient channel is very important to improve the response service to RL. Traditionally, the complaint channels that enterprises provide to customers are telephone, letter, fax, etc; nowadays, the web language, wireless information technology are new emerging field. These techniques all have their own advantages. To maximize the customer satisfaction, the integrated multi-channel service model should be a good choice. Before completely integration of the channels, let us consider a computer integration technique, the Computer Telephone Integration system called CTI for short. Generally speaking, the phonetic system is separate from a computer network system, but CTI technique can integrate the two functions together.

1. Customer-call-organisation switch equipment. The switch equipment receives the key request service number via Automatic Number Identification (ANI) and Dialed Number Identification Service (DNIS).

2. If Interactive Voice Response (IVR) equipment is available, the switch equipment will memorize the key-press information of customers automatically.
3. The switch equipment can transfer the numbers and key-press information from step (1) and step (2) to the CTI agency servers.
4. The information format is transformed in the agency servers, then the information is sent to the CTI application servers.
5. According to the input parameters, the CTI application servers will implement relevant logical operations, for example, search for the best responder in the database.
6. Return the search result (the best responder) to the CTI agent servers.
7. The CTI agent servers send the information of the best responder to the switch equipment.
8. The communication is turned into the best responder by the switch equipment.
9. After finished the communication, the switch equipment send the end-of-exchange signal to the CTI agent servers.
10. The success-of-exchange signal is transmitted from the CTI agent servers to the CTI application servers.
11. The CTI application servers transmit the data information to the terminal responder, such as pop-upping the calling prompt automatically, calling the videotext of customers, and so on.
12. The all related complaint information is recorded in the CSM database and repository.

We can design an integrated multi-channels collection routeway based on the CTI technique. The complaint information via the integrated mold-channels in CSM could achieve the CSM processing system which will be represented in detail in the next part.

Evaluation

Production Inspection/Sort In this phase, the returned products are being sorted based on their current quality, spoilage degree, etc., after that it is the enterprise's turns to determine the reuse manner of the products and then classify them. Those products can be divided into no spoilage, partial spoilage, or complete spoilage and so on.

(i) *No spoilage:* If returned products keep in the good state, then can often be reused directly by using cleaning or maintaining easily.

(ii) *Partial spoilage:* If returned products have been damaged partly, and need to be disassembled, inspected or tested, and repaired or replaced by parts, in this way their quality may be lowered. Usually, the products may be delivered to customers, or be sold at a discount in the secondary market.

(iii) *Complete spoilage:* If returned products are damaged or deteriorated badly, though they may include valuable components, but that can be reused restrictedly. So enterprises just implement the relative operation activities, such as recycle, remanufacture or harmless process etc.

Complaint Classification Customer complaints can reflect different information according to the diversities of customer preference, the types of products etc. Therefore, enterprises need to apply different processing techniques; it is necessary to classify the complaint information firstly. Based on the customer response, the complaint information is split up into three levels.

Level I: Customers feel the complaint is too inappreciable and do not want to unfold, such information is obtained often through questionnaires.

Level II: Customers have some tempered complaint or appeal, which they want to make enterprises known. The integrated mold-channels collection route in CSM could be their right choices.

Level III: The customers are with a strong fashion or conflict. When appeal to enterprises they may take violent attitudes and insist on own viewpoints all along.

The integration evaluation conclusions are determined by the comparison of customer complaint and product quality; it is the key gist for CSM of RL. The different customers have the different apperceptions of product and service utility. It is necessary for enterprises to discern the customer reaction based on the product spoilage degree, or the spoilage degrees based on the customer complaint levels in order to reply with the corresponding disposal countermeasure.

In modern times, the intelligent system is extensive applied to help decision-making increasingly. The intelligent "experts" based on the database and data-storage can respond customer complaint quickly. With the advance of complaint level, in order to respond customer complaint exactly, the database and data-storage should integrate more comprehensive information about customers and products. Intelligent decision support system (IDSS) is integration of artificial intelligence (AI) and decision support system (DSS).

By using expert system (ES) technique, we can make the traditional DSS more humanized and flexible. The framework of IDSS consists of three subsystems, inlaid languages system (LS), problems processing system (PPS) and knowledge management system (KMS), namely 3S system. In practice, enterprises may setup an expert team together with IDSS to evaluate the relative complaint. At the same time, utilising "the virtual expert team" based on Web (knowledge database) is good fashion.

There are some main advantages of IDSS: first, it is the synthesis of AI techniques, mathematics techniques and decision-making approaches, i.e., the integration of knowledge consequences and mathematics calculations to provide strong support to decision-making; second, it is based on the thoughts of ES or KMS (Knowledge Management System) to implement uniform preparation, uniform management, uniform control etc.; third, it makes full use of experts' knowledge, experience, judgement and decision-making cases. Consequently, the evaluation processing in CSM of RL will be supported by IDSS effectively.

Utility of CSM

Customers' responses to the spoiled product show the expectation of the purchased products, so the utility of CSM in RL reflecting the customer expectation can be measured by two factors, i.e., the product spoilage degree and the customer complaint level. The more serious complaint means the higher customer's expectation, here the utility of CSM in RL will be greater. The lower expectation of customer may be easy to satisfy, so the utility of CSM will not be great any more. It is obvious that the utility of CSM in enterprises have inverse ratio with the spoilage degree, and direct ratio with the complaint level. Here customers have high product expectation; CSM in RL is significant and implies a great utility. To improve the utility of CSM and increase the customer satisfaction, enterprises should take into more consideration the product design and marketing.

The CSM in RL Processing System

By receiving the complaint information and inspecting the products, the experts would give a reasonable disposal countermeasure. When the level of customer complaint is lower and the product spoilage is not bad, the feedback can be disposed in the place of distributors, such as wholesalers and retailers. Especially, the retailers must keep in touch with the customers directly, which are the chief and basic nodes for CSM in RL. For the complaint on Level I, the good customer service is necessary, such as the feasible propaganda in the right time. To reply the customer complaint on Level II and Level III, a lot of different means should be chosen based on the product status, for instance recycle the products at a discount, replaced by new products, and so on. Then the returned products can be resold in a secondary market after being repaired.

If the products are broken or even damaged badly, they should be transported to the manufacturers directly. The professional processing of manufacturers is significant for customer satisfaction. In a word, there is corresponding process for CSM processing system in RL. The CSM processing system in allusion to different disposal countermeasures is supported by the embedded information system; the real-time information exchange helps to provide the decision-making with support and improve the manufacture technique. Furthermore, the functions of the CSM processing system are controlled and supervised by related function modules, such as cost control, transport support, channel management, marketing, production operation etc., to help enterprises construct the resources economized and harmonious system.

Existing Barriers of RL Operation Management

RL operation management is a bran-new field for the modern enterprise, which their objectives of reducing risk and pursuing profit is conflicted by a great many of uncertainties and the large investment risks at the beginning. Comparing with the tradition logistics, RL is more complex and uncertain. The uncertainties of RL involve four characteristics mainly as follows:

The uncertain time: different people favouritism often result in products having different lifecycle, such that RL happening time is difficult to speculate. The uncertain place: The customers distribute all over the world, that means RL happening place is possible everywhere.

The uncertain reason: The reasons of RL is involved in multi-factors, such as changing market, product quality, usage method etc., which resulting in uncertainty. The uncertain disposal: The numerous reasons of RL done bring on different measures to dispose. The corresponding disposal can not be identified until inspecting.

Consequently, the flexibility and agility of RL operation management must be taken more attention, and we need analyze the characteristics of uncertainties in time, place, reason and disposal. For most enterprises, specially the RL operation based on themselves, so RL operation management needs to invest the large of money and resource, influence the enterprises in every ways, e.g. the planning is adjusted just for the potential reverse logistics; a new network need to design; the inventory management is impacted by the bidirectional flow; it must be supported by increasing the special equipment and training employee, etc.

Furthermore, the economic benefits from RL hiding in total profit cannot display obviously in account, which enlarges the investment risk for an enterprise. In addition, RL theory and application that is still in a developing process and few successful cases for references are also the barriers.

The Characteristics of a VE

To overcome the abovementioned barriers, we analyze some important characteristics in a VE as follows:

Virtual function: The theory of core competency figures that an enterprise is a set of resources and capabilities; the heterogeneous resources and the special capabilities are the key strengths, called the core competencies differentiating it from other enterprises. A VE is a function aggregation; the subdivided functions are assigned to several independent enterprises according to their particular competencies.

Virtual organisation: Nowadays, the rapid development of information technology and the computer technology bring an opportunity for the organising mode of modern enterprise. The VE is also a dynamic alliance, made up of independent enterprises, which can be self-organisation. They may locate in the world everywhere and communicate with each other via Internet and Internet, i.e. it is a virtual organisation without fixed place.

Virtual region: The advancement of science and technology also are impelling the development of transportation industries; the information systems applied in model logistics result in physical distribution among enterprises more effective and efficient, i.e., the distance is not the barrier any longer; the goods can flow among partner enterprises at arty moment.

The Advantages of RL Operation Management based on a VE

In today's competitive market, the enterprises should adjust their strategies, organisation structures, and operation management, i.e., change from the traditional competition strategy to the value-renovation strategy based on cooperation—from the pyramidal organisation structure to the flat organisation structure forming a dynamic network, from the close-operation management that considers competition in cost and quality, to the open-operation management that considers competition in time and speed.

VE, a dynamic alliance consisting of several quick (or agile) independent enterprises quickly, is triggered by sudden market opportunities in order to overcome the uncertainties of the RL, reducing cost and increasing profit by utilising the core resources of partner enterprises. The advantages of RL operation management based on a VE are focused on four aspects:

Rapid response: RL is often paroxysmal. When the affairs beyond the planning take place, RL management play the role of remedy (e.g. the cars recalled for disfigurement); sometimes the happening is foreseeable but it is hard to know the exact time and clear place (e.g. the electronic products of end-of-life). The outstanding advantage of VE is to respond the market changing rapidly, that will endow operation with agility. Based on VE obviating mass preparation, the operation management of RL can integrate the particular resources of partner enterprises together at once to cope with the changing environment, by improving the competition.

Flexibility: The flexibility motivation comes from two aspects: the uncertainties of RL require multiform disposal; for most enterprises, RL from begin to end is just a short-term process, so the flexibility and efficiency are regarded as the key factors. RL will benefit from the flexibility attribute of a VE.

The organisation structure formed by some independent enterprises provides more options of disposal. Besides we notice that a VE is from configuration to disbandment along with the appearance and disappearance of market opportunity. The driven-market feature will suit for the flexible operation of RL.

Reducing cost: Generally speaking, RL is often driven by legislation constraint and environmental responsibility. Nevertheless the enterprise with the aim at profit pays more attention to the direct or indirect economic benefits. The operation management mode based on a VE is an effective approach to reduce the RL cost, in respect that enterprises make use of the external strength to cut down cost by reason of homologous resource advantage.

Sharing risk: RL is also a large challenge for enterprises with respect to the long-term operation of traditional logistics. It induces several risks, e.g. the assets proprietary risk. In contrast with the high risk of single enterprise, the subdivided operation can share risk among partner enterprises. It has been noticed to elude the external manage risk resulting from many enterprises combination.

RL Operation Management Based on AVE

The difficulties of RL management are enlarged by lots of partners and their flexibility. Thus a "leader enterprise or organisation" is necessary to administer the VE, namely the leader enterprise. The sponsor manufacturer always plays the role of core enterprise, e.g., the large-scale enterprise or the fourth-party service provider is also an appropriate option.

Comparing with the traditional organisation structure, the VE organised by two layers (core enterprises and non-core enterprises) is flat, allowing interaction of partners. The flat structure is easy to respond the changing market, as well as to eliminate the information distortion effectively. There are three main reverse logistic functions: collection, inspection/sort, and reprocessing. Collection refers to bringing the products from the customer to a point of recovery, including return, transportation, and storage etc.

At this point the products are inspected, i.e. their quality is assessed and a decision is made on the options of disposal, then the products are sorted. The disposal of reprocessing includes the following options: direct reuse, repair, recycling, remanufacturing and harmless disposal. The type of recovery can be separated between product recovery, component recovery, material recovery and energy recovery etc. The abovementioned functions are necessary for RL. Based on the VE operation, subdividing the functions to several independent enterprises by integrating their core competencies is just the advantage we hope seek, e.g., lowering cost, evading risk, etc. Therefore, the organisation frame of RL operation management based on a VE can presented.

The Process of Operation Management

Identifying-Opportunity

In order to utilising the rapid response attribution of a VE with respect to the uncertainties of RL, enterprises have to track the trends of market development timely. A mass of collected data using for forecasting should be from enterprises, customers, industries, markets, legislation and so on. The useful information will be evaluated relative to reliability, worthiness, feasibility.

Organisation configuration: Based on abovementioned, a VE means the integration of the core competencies for participating in enterprises. Therefore identifying the core competency, evaluating the alternative enterprises and estimating the entire performance are crucial, that directly influence the operation efficiency of RL. The core competencies concerning RL reflect return channels, logistics capabilities, R & D technology, manufacture arts and crafts, assets proprietary etc., and are determined by the relevant decision support system (DSS). Information system and the logistics network are necessary absolutely to support the VE.

Organisation operation: The organisation form of a VE is at the expense of coordination among partners. It implies that the excellent organisation management is the precondition of the VE operation. The operation management is extended to the application of coordination mechanism, dynamic contract by stages, risk identification and control etc. As the dynamic developing, examine the running status continuously, and improve the process according to the feedback.

Organisation disbandment: The disbandment of a VE takes place after the disappearance of market opportunity. There is the assets liquidation among partner enterprises. The knowledge management runs through the whole operation management of the VE.

The Dynamic Durative of a VE

It is easy to see, depending on a VE, that there is every chance of RL in developing market. However, considering RL exist in enterprises at all times, the operation management based on the VE do not end after disbandment. Contrarily, it is the beginning of the new VE. Facing the uninter-rupted opportunities the independent enterprises broke from one VE, can then take part in another dynamic alliance immediately. In fact, the VE is that organisation of the older members left and the newer members' enter. So the VE for RL is the dynamic durative process organisation from the phase of opportunity identifying to the phase of organisation disbandment.

The Compare with the Traditional Mode

In contrast with the traditional logistics management, the operation management of RL based on a VE is improved in agility, flexibility, lowering cost and sharing risk as abovementioned.

Evaluation Method and Process

The evaluation of a VE for RL operation is based on the firms' multi-criteria which are qualitative or quantitative. AHP is often used in such problems. But, the unbalanced estimations, unconsidered the uncertainty and risk, the subjective judgement error etc., those show the technique exists some disadvantages.

Based on those reasons, we integrate the concept of fuzzy set theory with the AHP to overcome some above disadvantages in our proposed model. Fuzzy AHP approach is applied in some practical problems widely. In order to facilitate comparison, all elements of the judgement matrix and weight vectors are represented by the triangular fuzzy values. The VE for RL selection process are as follows:

(1) Determine alternative firms and construct the evaluating hierarchical structure. RL first choose the alternative VEs from those which can bear reverse activities, based on the basic requirements, such as Quality Certificated. Then, the hierarchical structure is constructed by the criteria of SCOR model and the chain which is linked by the product flow, the alternative VEs are considered as similar types on the similar phase. The SCOR (Supply-Chain Operations Reference-model) is a process reference model that has been developed and endorsed by the Supply-Chain Council as the cross-industry standard diagnostic tool for supply-chain management. SCOR enables users to address, improve, and communicate supply-chain management practices within and between all interested parties. SCOR is a management tool. It is a process reference model for supply-chain management, spanning from the supplier's supplier to the customer's customer. The SCOR-model has been developed to describe the business activities associated with all phases of satisfying a customer's demand. By describing supply chains using process building blocks, the Model can be used to describe supply chains that are very simple or very complex using a common set of definitions. As a result, disparate industries can be linked to describe the depth and breadth of virtually any supply chain. Considering that the full chain or part of supply chain can be selected by VEs, and many firms are involved in the scope and may operate different industries. So, there is more diversity among those, and SCOR model adapt to the cross-functional framework, the metrics of Level I of SCOR model as the criteria and sub-criteria of alternative will be referenced. These 13 sub-criteria can be categorized into the qualitative criteria and the quantitative criteria. Unmeasured indirectly through firms' historical data are called as the qualitative criteria. And measured directly are called as the quantitative criteria. The

quantitative criteria can be found from the historical data, and the qualitative criteria can be evaluated by experts and experiential managers, based the firm's correlative data and their experience, which can decrease the subjective errors.

(2) Evaluate the alternative VEs. Based on the defined scope, the experts begin to evaluate those alternative firms, based on the criteria of SCOR model. The quantitative criteria can be gained by the VEs historical data and the alternative degree measured by five scales from the worst to t he best, here we use 1-9 triangular fuzzy number (from (1, 1, 3) to (7, 9, 9)) that is similar to Wu Lei and Guojun Ji (2006). The qualitative criteria are obtained by the experts evaluating values. To reducing the experts' subjective effect, the following approach is adopted for the qualitative criteria.

(3) Evaluate the VEs relationship. The RL is constructed by selecting firms from VEs and the relationship among the firms is evaluated. The basic values in step (2) may be considered the average value of the VEs criteria, and that the effect of the upstream and downstream to the firms may be positive or negative. But the relationship among the firms is not determinant factor to some performance criteria. It happens that the double effect of performance. In addition, the negative effects produced by the relationship to the performance criteria cannot reach zero. Herein, these two situations need not discussed. The relationship Coefficients are from 0 to 2 ranked by 9, which are relevant to some sub-criteria from descending by 100% to ascending by 100%.

(4) Integrate the basic value of the criteria of the firms with relationship coefficients. Relationship coefficients just effect on the exterior correlated criteria and not on the interior correlated criteria. Let Z denotes that the subscript set of the exterior correlated criteria and let denotes that the subscript set of the interior correlated criteria. Relationship coefficients are measured the relationship between the firm and its nearness firms, thus the upstream firm and the downstream firm both effect on it.

Numerical Example

Considering a three-stage network of the electronic industry is incorporated by two VEs, two manufactories and one retailer. The VEs implement the reverse activities, and the manufactories perform assembly line work to achieve the finial products. The retailer sells these products.

It is easy to see the best VEs that formed chain are F11-F21-F31. At the same time, we can find that the chain relationship effect on the order of finial scores, i.e., VEs should pay attention to the chain relations in course of constructing the RL. In addition, VEs can comprehend the important degree of every criterion in the different industries by using the criteria weight evaluation, thus performance can be improved efficiently. In the same time, such technique can be used as a decision support system in VEs. VEs can provide more consulting service and realise the integrative optimization of RL.

In this chapter, CSM was considered in RL. Based on the computer telephone integration technology, an integration multi-channels collection has be designed; the evaluation of complaint and product is supported by intelligent decision support system; in accord with the different disposal countermeasures, the CSM processing system was established to implement corresponding disposal which reflects the utility of CSM. The operation management mode of RL based on a VE was analyzed. The organisation structure, RL functions and the framework were discussed too. The process of operation management based on a VE includes opportunity identifying, organisation configuration, organisation operation and organisation disbandment, in that the superiority of a VE in contrast with traditional management is unveiled. The evaluation of VEs for RL operation was based on the firms' multi-criteria which are qualitative or quantitative. By using Fuzzy AHP technique, the hierarchical and the multi-criteria decision making problems for VEs were considered and the optimized selection is presented. Our conclusions help to impel the development of RL in practice.

Transportation Management to Global Logistics

Global logistics in business operation is playing a critical role in responding to the changing market demand in a world of globalization and mass customization. The efficiency of global distribution holds the key to success in international trade.

Not only is collaborative transportation management (CTM) a new collaboration strategy between the shipper and carrier, it is also a new business model. This chapter presents a descriptive case study on the application of CTM to business global logistics. In-depth interviews were conducted with respondents from multinational electronic manufacturing service (EMS) corporations and transportation logistics service providers. Our analysis reveals that third-party logistics (3PL) service providers play an important role in global sourcing of multinational corporations. Integrating CTM with enterprise resource planning (ERP) via information technology (IT) can facilitate transportation capacity planning and achieve prompt delivery within the shortest time possible.

The positive impact of CTM on business logistics enables enterprises to gain competitive advantage in the global business arena. The rise of regional economies around the world as well as the development of globalization has caused the supply chain to face problems such as global sourcing, cross-country production, diverse needs of customers, short product life cycle, demand for rapid delivery, frequent order placement, reduced procurement quantity, high logistics cost and diminished revenues. Hence, efficiency in global distribution is the key to survival and success under the intensely competitive business environment, which demands adequate product supply, rapid delivery and low inventory.

Growing trend of mass customization and e-commerce are forcing manufacturers and retailers to shorten their planning cycles and delivery time. With smaller planning windows and the universal objective to minimize inventory in the value chain, transportation has become a critical opportunity in the process. Transportation consumes 5.5% of the U.S. gross domestic product (GDP), and approximately the same proportion of a company's sales revenue. Transportation service represents a major component of order lead time. Much of the variability in order lead time is attributed to variation in transit times.

Huge capital in terms of sunk cost is a unique feature of transportation industry, making it difficulty, if not impossible, to increase supply capacity or find substitutes within a short time. The success in supply chain management lies in whether the replenishment can be in the right place when it needs to be there. The supply chain is a complex system made up of many parties. Insufficient or unavailable carrier capacity provided in time for the shipper will cause disruption in the supply chain when the delivery will be in process but its status is unknown or delayed. Such uncertainty will cause both the buyers and sellers to maintain a larger inventory just in case. Hence, suppliers either have to face the pressure of excess inventory or run the risk of inadequate stock.

This jeopardizes the whole supply chain, posing problems of increased cost, time delay and negative impact on business. A single member of the supply chain alone cannot do much to resolve supply chain problems.

This is why collaboration among partners in a supply chain has become a topic of great interest for many and an essential element of company strategy for others. Previous studies on supply chain collaboration have focused mainly on the collaboration among supply chain parties including, the suppliers, manufacturers, wholesalers/ distributors and retailers. As a matter of fact, the supply chain consists of not only customers in downstream flows, but also third-party organisations, such as logistics and transportation providers.

Researchers including Sutherland (2003), Browning and White (2000), Esper and Williams (2003) and Bishop (2004) have all pointed out the need to incorporate Collaborative Transportation Management (CTM) with Collaborative Planning, Forecasting and Replenishment (CPFR) among trading partners in the supply chain. While CPFR is primarily buyer- and seller-based, CTM involves the transportation service providers including carriers and 3PLs to ensure efficient and effective shipment delivery.

Nevertheless, in order to reap the abovementioned benefits, CTM should be adopted and implemented to avoid logistics bottlenecks, to overcome inefficiencies due to the lack of interaction between the shipper and the transportation component, and to foster closer collaboration.

Collaborative commerce among enterprises is a relatively recent concept of business operation. Hence, enterprises that have developed CTM strategies are rare including only the few global 3PL service providers such as UPS, DHL and FedEx, large logistics and transportation management services provider such as Transplace, and well-know retailers such as Wal-Mart, Procter & Gamble. Although the relevant literature and case studies on CTM are scarce, the operation, applications and impacts of CTM are topics worthy of further investigation. The purpose of this study is to explore the application of CTM to business global logistics and discusses the roles played by third-party logistics providers (3PLs) and information technology (IT) in the CTM model. Finally, the value of CTM is assessed from the perspective of the shipper.

Collaboration has been defined as an attempt to fully satisfy the concerns of the parties involved in exchange, in order to achieve an integrative settlement. Collaboration is a process of decision making among interdependent parties. It involves joint ownership of decisions and collective responsibility for outcomes. As pointed out by Thomas and Griffin (19%), collaboration is creating significant value in the relationships along the value chain. Many studies have also discovered positive impact of strategic alliance between enterprises on their market performance.

Kordal (2002) indicated that collaborative commerce is a strategy for gaining competitive advantage. Not only is CTM a new partner strategy between the shipper and carrier, it is also a new business model. This model includes the carrier as a strategic partner for information sharing and collaboration in the supply chain. The application of CTM promises to reduce transit times and total costs for the retailer and its suppliers while increasing asset utilisation for the carriers. The programs benefits all three parties involved: the retailer, the supplier and the carrier.

CTM has been referred to as the 'missing link' in collaborative supply chain execution that adds value to the entire collaboration process in terms of reduced transportation costs, increased asset utilisation, improved service, enhanced customer satisfaction and greater revenues. Esper and Williams (2003) regarded CTM as a relatively new extension of CPFR; and just as in the early development stages, value measures for CTM have been difficult to find in the extant literature. Information technology (IT) has a significant impact on collaborative effort formation playing a dual role as 'supporter' and 'enabler'.

A descriptive case study of a third-party CTM systems provider is employed to investigate the processes and benefits of CTM. They found that CTM implemented through information systems could save transportation cost by 8.4%-20% through advance planning, optimization, and continual updates of shipment status, improve on-time performance ranging from 5% to 30%, increase regional fleet utilisation by 10%-42% because of complementary backhaul opportunities in an extended planning horizon to the carriers, lessen the chance of shipment damage, reduce administrative cost, and minimize financial risk.

Feng, Yuan and Lin (2005) developed a supply chain simulation model with CTM. Using the modified simulation model of "Beer Game", they applied CTM to the manufacturer, distributor and carrier and obtained a significant decrease in total supply chain costs, including inventory cost and backlog cost, an improvement in bullwhip effect, and enhanced utilisation of transportation capacity.

Tyan et al. (2003) analyzed the application of CTM by a 3PL provider in a notebook computer global supply chain in Taiwan using the case study approach. The implementation results show that the delivery cycle time and the total cost are simultaneously reduced. In sum, previous research has emphasized the value of CTM while little attention has been paid to exploring the impact of CTM integrated into business global logistics. As mentioned above, CTM is a relatively new concept and related studies are thus scarce. In this work, the application of CTM to business global logistics is examined using a descriptive case study.

In-depth interviews are conducted to obtain relevant data for analysis. The company selected as a case study was recommended by one worldwide computer corporation of Taiwan (FIC Global Inc) and one global integrated logistics service provider (UPS International Inc., Taiwan branch) as an outstanding example of global logistics and transportation collaborative management. The respondents are senior managers of the production, import/export and Customs operations departments. Questions asked during the interview covered the following issues. What is the purpose of implementing CTM? What kinds of problems are resolved by CTM? What does the CTM process involve? What are the roles of 3PL service provider and IT in CTM? What are the items contained in the CTM shipment agreements between the carrier (including 3PL service provider) and shipper? What kind of information is exchanged between the carrier and shipper? What are the exception events often seen during actual implementation and how are they handled? Which party undertakes the investment on establishing IT facilities for CTM? What benefits obtained.

Collaborative Transportation Management

This section provides an overview of CTM, lists the objectives of the study and illustrates the process of collaboration.

CTM Definition

According to the CTM Sub-Committee of the Voluntary Inter-Industry Commerce Standards (VICS) Logistics Committee, CTM is a holistic process that brings together supply chain trading partners and service providers to drive inefficiencies out of the transport planning and execution process.

CTM focuses on enhancing the interaction and collaboration between three principle parties (a seller, a carrier, and a buyer) in their logistics roles of shipper, carrier and receiver, as well as, secondary participants including 3PL service providers. Participants collaborate by sharing key information about demand and supply (e.g., forecasts, event plans, expected capacity), ideas and capabilities to improve the performance of the overall transport planning and execution proves, and assets, where feasible (i.e., trucks, warehouses). CTM essentially involves converting order forecasts development via CPFR into shipment forecasts, and insuring their accurate fulfillment.

The objective of CTM is to improve the operating performance of all parties involved in the relationship by eliminating inefficiencies in the transportation component of the supply chain through collaboration. Transportation service represents a major component of order leas time-the time that elapses from an order placement until the goods are ultimately delivered to a customer. Much of the variability in order lead time is attributed to variation in transit times. With more and more companies operating on a just-in-time basis, there is less room for error in the delivery process. It is important for companies to work together to eliminate inefficiencies, reduce cost, and ensure excellence in the movement of goods. In most instances, there is only so much that a single member of the supply chain can do to resolve the problems noted above. This is why collaboration among partners in supply chain has become a topic of great interest for many and an essential element of company strategy for others. In order to achieve the positive results of CTM, the processes between participating companies should be in real time, extendible, automated and cost-effective.

CTM Business Process

CTM involves the carrier at five key points comprising 14 steps, three of the key points are included in the CPFR, namely the creation of a joint business plan (Steps 1-2), order forecast (Steps 3-5) and order generation (Steps 6-8). CTM provides new additional steps after order generation; they are freight order confirmation including shipment creation (Steps 9-11) and carrier payment processes (Steps 12-14).

The process begins with an order/shipment forecast, and includes capacity planning and scheduling, order generation, load tender, delivery execution, and carrier payment. There are opportunities for collaboration between buyers, sellers and carriers in three major categories: strategic planning, forecasting and replenishments and physical execution. The CTM business process model is comprised of three distinct phases as follows:

- *Strategic phase (defining the relationship):* The strategic phase includes things like: specific process steps to be performed, what data will be shared and how, freight terms, geographic scope, distribution strategies, performance metrics, exceptional management protocols, and how benefits will be shared.

- *Tactical phase (planning for transportation equipment needs):* The tactical component focuses on all parties sharing a shipment forecast with the intention to help the carrier(s) anticipate future equipment demands by providing an advance look at expected shipping volumes.
- *Operational phase (managing actual shipment):* The operational component of CTM is a business process that focuses on planning, executing, and accounting for actual shipments.

Case Study of CTM

Electronic manufacturing services (EMS) are companies that design, assemble, produce, and test electronic components and assemblies for original equipment manufacturers (OEMs). Typically, OEMs retain ownership of product designs and brand names. Some electronic manufacturing services are contract electronic manufacturers (CEMs) that specialize in rapid prototyping or product testing. Others offer small, medium, or large production runs. Electronic manufacturing services vary in terms of production capabilities and comply with various quality standards and regulatory requirements.

Current development trend of the global IT industry are characterized by concentration of markets in Europe and USA with production highly localized in the Asia Pacific region.

Time Magazine has pointed out Taiwan own the main electronic manufactures of the world. Taiwan alone manufactures two-thirds of the world's LCD monitors, 75% of notebook (NB) computer and 80% of PDAs. These electronic devices are produced under the outsourcing contracts made with Global sourcing computer manufacturer such as HP, Apple and Dell.

In view of the cheap labour cost, most of the production lines of Taiwan electronic manufacturer have been moved to the Mainland, and some to Eastern Europe and South America. Production activities in the Mainland concern mainly Original Equipment Manufacturing (OEM)/Original Design Manufacturing (ODM) orders from multinational corporations, while the R&D, management and marketing activities are still conducted in Taiwan. Corporations involved in OEM adopt vertical division of work with Taiwan in the upper stream responsible for manufacturing of components and semi-finished products and the Mainland in the lower stream engaged mainly in assembly of the final products. This study conducted face-to-face interviews with the top executives of First International Computer Inc and UPS Taiwan branch. FIC is a leading company in manufacturing and sales of personal computer, notebook computer, pocket PC, motherboard, computer circuit, Bluetooth solutions and IA solutions.

The company has over 6,500 employees, with approximate US dollar 2 billion in annual revenue.

Its main manufacturing sites are located in Taiwan, China, Czech and Brazil and has set up branch offices all over the world, including America, China, Hong Kong, UK, Japan, Brazil, Middle East, Germany and Czech. The company is committed to delivering the latest products, solutions, service and support globally. UPS (United Parcel Service Inc) is a global company with one of the most recognised and admired brands in the world.

As the largest express carrier and package Delivery Company in the world, they are also a leading provider of specialized transportation, logistics, capital, and e-commerce services. Every day they manage the flow of goods, funds and information in more than 200 countries and territories worldwide.

The EMS Corporations Need CTM

Recent years has seen the life cycle of personal computing products becoming shorter and a sharp drop in product price. In view of such changes, the world's famous computer corporations like Dell, IBM and HP Compaq have begun to adopt new business types such as Build To Order (BTO), Configure To Order (CTO) and Taiwan Direct Ship (TDS) instead of Build To Forecast (BTF).

The shift in business types has greatly reduced the order lead time from 30-45 days for BTF to 5-7 days for BTO, 2 days for CTO and 2-4 days for TDS. Hence, over 98% of the products can be delivered into the hands of the end consumers 2-3 days after order placement.

The business trends of mass customization and e-commerce are forcing manufacturers and retailers to shorten planning cycles and expedite execution. The shortening of time taken for production and delivery has become more and more important for enterprises to remain competitive. CTM strengthens the strategic alliance between the shipper and carrier and fosters closer collaboration between them, thus improving the efficiency of physical flow and enhancing the operation performance.

The Role of 3PL Provider in Global Logistics

Global Logistics Management (GLM) integrates superior production conditions around the world using advanced information and communication technologies as well as efficient information flow. With GLM, industries engaged in global procurement, global manufacture, and global distribution can achieve competitive edge in the world market. The essence of GLM is to respond promptly to the changes in the market and the demands of customers, and to minimize operation cost, pressure of inventory and financial risk.

In the context of typical logistics relations, a third-party company is, beside the shipper or the receiver involved, a company that affects the relation between these two companies and takes over some part of the primary parties' role. Third-party logistics relationships are characterized by the following properties:

- Outsourcing of transportation and/or warehousing and some value-added services
- Long-term contract (normally-2-3 years)
- Solutions developed, based on mutual orientation
- Tailor-made solutions
- Win-win relationship.

Enterprises engaged in multinational operation face significant changes in transportation mode of products. The rapid development of the door-to-door mode of transportation is attributed to the consumers' pressing demand for the products. Many multinational trading companies want to establish links with global logistics service providers. Such partner relationships can enable the enterprises to face the constantly changing global environment with less uncertainty and complexity. Douglas and Mueller (1999) investigated several international 3PL service providers and concluded that partner relationship between multinational enterprises and 3PL service providers plays a crucial role in solving problems related to customer service and information flow. Hence, 3PL service providers, can help improve the relationship between supplier and customer.

Implementation Issues of CTM

CTM is a new business model for integrating transportation management with supply chain management. The primary implementation issues are benefits, technology and organisation infrastructure. The most obvious benefit to 3PL providers is the ability to develop business plans with their key customers to fulfill distribution requirements better. The manufacturers, in turn, benefit from better transportation transit times, visibility to shipment status, and the payment process. In order to foster collaboration, new information and technology (IT) is needed to link between the carrier and the manufacturer. Global supply chain is a highly dynamic system and any changes to it may impact the logistics activities. The core concept of CTM is to resolve these transportation exceptions collaboratively. In order to achieve the benefits, empowered designated personnel from each party are essential.

3PL Service Provider Implements CTM

In the planning phase of CTM, the shipping agreements were outlined to include the scope of shipment, freight rate, expected delivery cycle time, pickup cut-off time, maximum daily guaranteed volume, and tracking function.

In the forecasting phase, shippers provided monthly, weekly or daily shipment forecast updates to the 3PL provider for aircraft capacity planning. The 3PL provider gained sufficient time to acquire additional capacity for planned month-end or quarter-end peak shipment demands. In the execution phase of CTM, A new CTM integrator was developed by the 3PL provider to link with the manufacturer's Enterprise Resource Planning (ERP) system in order to retrieve shipping information during the shipment tender stage.

The information flow between the shipper and the 3PL provider involves the exchange of delivery-related information using EDI or XML via the Internet. The manufacturer received EDI order (Day 7:00) and release shipping order to 3PL provider (10:00). A shipping order acknowledgment was provided to manufacturer (11:00). The packing list and commercial invoice were tendered to the 3PL provider through the CTM integrator before the actual shipment pickup in order to prepare and submit customs clearance.

Upon picked up the shipments, a pickup confirmation notice will be sent back to manufacturer through the CTM integrator. The 3PL provider enabled the manufacturer to access the estimated and actual time of departure, and real-time tracking status via the Internet. At the same time, the consignee or end customer could then check the delivery status via the Internet of through customer service.

Resolution on Shipment Forecast Exceptions

Exceptional events that occur during the shipment tender and delivery can be resolved according to prior agreement between the shipper and carrier. A shipment forecast is developed from the initial product order forecast leveraging pre-determined load building strategies (e. g., aggregation or consolidation). Upon receipt, carriers review shipment forecast and plan equipment; if capacity is unavailable, exception management is used.

In actual practice, an exception shipment forecast often occurs when the actual shipment demand exceeds the planned transportation available capacity. In such case, the carrier adjusts equipment availability to eliminate or minimize the discrepancies in demand and supply of transportation capacity.

In case of insufficient capacity supply to meet the actual shipment demand, the carrier can try to resolve such problem in two ways. On the demand side, the carrier may change delivery requirements on some shipments or use pre-specified alternative carriers; while on the supply side, the carrier can release some capacity from the preceding or following stop or try to increase transportation supply capacity through co-loading. If these measures still fail to boost capacity supply, the excess shipment will have to be off-loaded and delayed.

The Benefits of CTM

As mentioned in the literature review, a strategic alliance between enterprises has a positive impact on their market performance. According to the respondents, CTM creates a 'win-win' relationship between the manufacturer and 3PL service provider through fostering rapid communication and efficient cooperation.

CTM offers FIC the benefits of transportation exception cost decreasing from US$140,000 to US$67,000 per month, shipment visibility improving from 35% to 91%, logistics service provider cost saving from US$8 to US$5 per shipment, on time delivery improving from 75% to 98% and providing real time cargo tracking cycle time.

Implementation Cost of CTM

The implementation of CTM lies mainly in establishing IT facilities for information exchange between various parties. Such expenditure is a kind of common cost that is not undertaken by a specific party but shared among the various CTM members on a long-term basis. Hence, the respondents find it difficult to estimate the actual investment in CTM and this constitutes a limitation of our study.

Large international logistics providers in Taiwan have been increasing their budget about 3%-5% per year for the development of value-added e-logistics services. Feng and Yuan (2006) conducted a questionnaire survey to examine the impact of information and communication technologies on logistics management and found that the majority of respondents (80%) considered that information and communication technologies do affect operation costs resulting in either an increase or decrease in costs within a 10% range.

Hence, regardless of the extent of investment of IT facilities, CTM would have an impact on the total operation cost.

In face of the growing trend of e-commerce, globalization and mass customization, global logistics management in business operation has become more important than ever. To survive and thrive in the highly competitive global business arena, enterprises have to maintain constant supply with low inventory and rapid delivery.

Failure of the carrier in providing sufficient transportation available capacity for the shipment plan of the shipper would cause delay in transit time in the supply chain, thus producing excess inventory in upstream and causing risk of out of stock in downstream.

As a result, delay in transit time and increase in supply chain cost will undermine the performance of the enterprise, thus affecting its competitiveness. Hence, problems of transportation cause bottlenecks in the entire supply chain. It is of urgent necessity to enhance the efficiency in transportation so as to achieve the goal of minimizing the supply chain cost.

In recent years, the change of EMS corporations from BTF to BTO, CTO and TDS has significantly reduced the order lead time from a month's time or longer to between 5 and 7 days, and even the shortest of just 2 days.

Hence, 98% of the order placement can be delivered to the end consumers within 2-3 days. Closer collaboration between different parties in the supply chain can ensure smooth transit of products, thus eliminating inefficiencies and decreasing cost.

This research is a descriptive case study on the application of CTM to business global logistics. In-depth interviews conducted with respondents from multinational electronic manufacturing service corporations and transportation logistics service providers reveal that 3PL service providers play an important role in global sourcing of multinational corporations.

Integration of CTM and ERP/CPFR using IT can facilitate intra- and inter-firm information exchange. Hence, more efficient transportation capacity planning can be achieved and prompt delivery can be made within the shortest time possible, thus enhancing the quality of service and gaining competitive advantage in the global market.

With the development of e-commerce and reengineering of the supply chain, CTM, with the benefits it can bring to different parties involved, will certainly become an important strategy in business global logistics.

To follow the inevitable trend and to reap the benefits CTM promises, small- and medium-sized transportation logistics service providers should enhance their application and capability of IT. Large international logistics providers in Taiwan have been increasing their budget for the development of value-added e-logistics services. Along with this, the government of Taiwan has also devoted great effort to promoting e-logistics in order to enhance the competitiveness of the enterprises in the international business arena.

6

Transport Infrastructure

The development of tourism requires a transport infrastructure to facilitate the free movement of tourist traffic, and much of the research in this context has focused on modal forms of travel (e.g., rail travel, air travel and car-based trips). One of the fundamental links that has been overlooked in the tourist transport system is the way in which demand and supply are brought together and managed, and the infrastructure used to ensure the system functions efficiently. In both the transport and tourism literature, terminal facilities, which provide the context in which the tourist embarks on the mode of transport, to ensure the interaction of supply and demand takes place smoothly, have been largely overlooked. Yet it is widely recognised that the 'holiday experience' begins when the tourist arrives at a terminal, ready to embark on a journey. In fact some commentators even suggest that the experience effectively begins when the traveller leaves their home environment.

This chapter examines the challenge of managing the interaction of supply and demand for tourist travel with reference to one type of terminal facility-the airport. Airports are probably the most complex environments and systems in which this interaction occurs and yet they often remain poorly understood in a tourism context. As Ashford et. al., (1991 : 1) argue, 'the airport forms an essential part of the air transport system, because it is the physical site at which a model transfer of transport is made from the air modes to land modes'. The chapter commences with a discussion of the management challenges posed by terminal facilities, emphasising the organisations involved in the management process. This is followed by a discussion of the locational and planning issues associated with airport development, particularly access to markets. Future development plans for world regions experiencing a rapid growth in tourist travel are then discussed, as arrivals are likely to outstrip existing airport capacity. But why focus on air travel rather than other types of terminal ? What literature does exist is airport-specific and ports, bus/coach terminals and railway terminals have not attracted much attention, with a notable exception being Bertolini and Spit. However, in Chapter the importance of the terminal environment for InterCity rail travel was discussed, albeit briefly, in relation to service quality and the travel experience.

In addition, ATAG (1993) provided a convincing argument for a focus on air travel: in 1993, the volume of air travel worldwide was equivalent to one-fifth of the world's population travelling once a year. The air transport industry also generated 24 million jobs and US$??? billion in gross output.

Therefore, while some of the principles and issues discussed in this chapter relate solely to air travel, some of the broader issues (i.e., developing a customer-focused approach) have a wide application to the management of the tourist-transport interface which occurs in transport terminal facilities.

The Management Challenge of Tourist Transport Terminals: Airports

To the uninitiated, occasional traveller, terminal facilities can be a bewildering, seemingly chaotic and unnerving experience. The semblance of chaos is conveyed by Barlay (1995):

> *The airport cavalcade can baffle or startle the inexperienced passenger...Laden with suitcases and packages, calm and rational people grow uptight, defensive with aggression, fail to allow themselves time to familiarise themselves with the layout or study the free guides to terminals.*

The entire psychology of travel and the change in the behaviour of the traveller in airports (e.g., tunnel vision or airport syndrome) embraces a whole series of emotions among the diversity of passengers: 'joy, grief, anxiety, expectations, aggravation, yearning and fulfilment'. From a tourists' perspective, numerous factors affect their experience, according to Barlay (1995 : 49):

- Speed of check-in.
- Efficiency of passport control and customs clearance (the UK government is now placing the onus on air-lines to check

outbound travellers' passports in order to devote more resources to inbound travellers).

- Luggage retrieval.
- Availability of shops, duty-free goods and associated services.
- A spacious and relaxed environment in which to wait prior to boarding the aircraft.

From the airport's perspective, operational issues have dominated its work. The management challenge is to recognise the tourists' needs and to minimise likely problems while ensuring the terminal operates as a smooth series of complex systems. Doganis (1992) defines airports as complex industrial organisations that

- ...act as a forum in which disparate elements and activities are brought together to facilitate, for both passengers and freight, the interchange between air and surface transport.

In some countries, for a range of historical, legal and other reasons, the scope of airport activities can vary from the highly complex and all-embracing to the very limited. In physical terms, Doganis defines an airport as :

- Essentially one or more runways for aircraft together with associated buildings or terminals where passengers... are processed...the majority of airport authorities own and operate their runways, terminals and associated facilities, such as taxiways or aprons.

Doganis distinguishes between the three principal activities of airports:

- Essential operational services and facilities.
- Traffic-handling services.
- Commercial activities.

Although 'at most, if not all, airports, the major consideration must be passenger flows' and this in itself requires management measures to ensure smooth operation (e.g., pricing and flow management. This comprises a broad range of activities within any airport environment, whether in an international gateway airport, a regional or local airport:

- Ground handling.
- Baggage handling.
- Passenger terminal operations.
- Airport security.

- Cargo operations.
- Airport technical services.
- air traffic control.
- Aircraft scheduling (takeoff/landing slot allocation)
- Airport and aircraft emergency services.
- Airport access.

Which are described in detail by Ashford et. al., (1991) in what remains the principal study on airport operations. Highlights some of the relationships which need to be managed in the airport system so that the airport-airline-traveller interactions occur in a professional and smooth manner. Indicating how the airport enables an aircraft to take off/land and to unload and load passengers. As part of these functions, it enables travellers to change their mode of transport and be processed efficiently (e.g., ticketing and documentation).

Each of these functions impinges upon the management of the tourists' experience, outlines the weekly pattern of scheduled departures from the world's top 30 airports, which are only a fraction of the ICAO list of 1,012 airports worldwide. Of the top 30 airports, 19 are located in the USA, confirming a pattern similar to that observed by Sealy (1992). This is followed by Europe and Asia-Pacific.

At a global scale, the management of airports is affected by government policy which, in part, determines the pattern of ownership. As Doganis (1992) observes, there are four main types of ownership. These are:

- *State ownership with direct government control,* characterised by a single government department (i.e., a Civil Aviation Department) which operates the country's airports. The alternative to a centralised government pattern of control and management is localised ownership such as municipal ownership.
- *Public ownership through an airport authority,* usually as a limited liability or private company. For example, the British Airports Authority (BAA) was one of the early examples of a national airport authority. Aer Rianta in the Republic of Ireland is another example of a national airport authority. There are also cases of regional airport authorities in the USA.
- *Mixed public and private ownership* is an organisational model adopted at larger Italian airports, where a company manages the airport, with public and private shareholders.

- *Private ownership* was a model of limited appeal prior to the wave of privatisation in the 1980s. One of the early examples in the UK was London City Airport in London Docklands, opened in 1987. However, Doganis (1992) points out that the major impetus to private ownership was the privatisation of BAA in 1987.

In generic terms, Doganis argues that a prime function of airport management is to determine the objective of any economic and management strategy for an airport by addressing four questions:

- Should airports be run as commercially oriented profitable concerns?
- How should one improve airport economic efficiency?
- Should profits from larger airports be used to cross-subsidise loss-making smaller airports?
- Should airports be privatised?

These four questions essentially raise the issue of what form of airport ownership a government deems important and the prime objectives which will affect the economic strategy each airport pursues. This in turn will require very different management strategies. For example, airlines and bodies such as IATA still argue that airports are public utilities when arguing against increased airport charges.

It is useful to examine a number of specific issues associated with airport management which will then be exemplified by a case study of BAA. As Doganis rightly argues, 'matching the provision of airport capacity with the demand while achieving and maintaining airport profitability and an adequate level of customer satisfaction is a difficult task'. One of the principal problems facing any airport manager is that of planning. The time lag between the decision to build and the opening of a new airport terminal is five to ten years, as the case of Heathrow Airport's planned Terminal 5 illustrates. In addition, planners also need to ensure forecasts of future growth are within realistic bounds so that terminal facilities can accommodate demand for at least another decade. However, for any airport development, probably the most fundamental issues to understand are :

- Costs.
- The economic features of airports.
- Sources of revenue.
- Methods of charging and pricing airport aeronautical services
- The type of commercial strategy to adopt

- Potential sources of commercial revenue
- The most appropriate management structure for an airport as a commercial/non-commercial organi-sation.
- Financial performance indicators

Costs and Economic Characteristics of Airports

Research undertaken in the 1980s and reported by Doganis (1992) identified the following costs of airports based on an analysis of European airports:

- *Staffing* accounts for 42 per cent of costs; it is normally the major operational cost for most airports.
- *Capital* charges comprise 22 per cent of costs; they include interest payments on commercial loans and the cost of depreciation of capital assets.
- *Other operational items* (e.g., electricity, water and supplies) comprise 11 per cent of costs.
- *Maintenance* accounted for 9 per cent of costs while *Administration* resulted in 4 per cent of costs.

Doganis (1992) also draws attention to the differences between US and European airports; airport costs are reduced by airline rental or lease agreements on terminal facilities in the USA. Likewise, many US airports are not directly involved in baggage handling, which is left to airlines. But financing costs for US airports tend to be a major element of expenditure, often 44 per cent of total costs if depreciation is included, although staff costs tend to remain at approximately 22 per cent.

Which indicates the significance of the direct employment-generating potential of such infrastructure. Three airports (London Heathrow, London Gatwick and Manchester) employed over half of the airport workers in 1994/95. In addition, Langley (1997) provides detailed data on UK airports from an operational and financial perspective.

Two of the principal economic characteristics of airports are that:

- Economies of scale exist as the volume of traffic increases, though congestion can lead to increases in unit costs.
- Development programmes for airports increase unit costs, particularly when new terminals are opened and are operating below their design capacity.

Prospects and Challenges for Tourist Transport

The relationship between tourism and transport by developing the concept of a tourist transport system as a means of analysing the processes shaping the provision and consumption of transport services by tourists. Throughout the book, transport is emphasised as a dynamic and active element in the tourist's experience of travelling because it is a vital part of the process of tourism. Some of the first-generation tourism textbooks (e.g., Mathieson and Wall 1982) regarded tourist transport an essential part of tourism but not worthy of study in its own right. In fact, a number of subsequent texts (e.g., Cooper et al. 1993, 1998) continue to view transport as a passive element in the tourist experience (Ryan 1996) and it remains a descriptive feature of most texts.

In the scope of multidisciplinary research on tourism and transport is reviewed in terms of the concepts and methods of each discipline (economics, geography, marketing and management) use to analyse tourist transport. However, the different philosophical backgrounds of researchers from these disciplines mean that their approach to tourist transport is not easy to synthesise into a holistic framework. Moreover, the tendency for researchers to retain their disciplinary training–whether in economics, geography, marketing or management–has simple contributed to the growing body of knowledge on transport and tourism.

For our understanding of tourist transport systems and the tourist's experience of travel to grow, a greater degree of coherence and a theoretical basis needs to be developed. This means that research will need to be interdisciplinary in nature. Interdisciplinary research requires people from different disciplines to collaborate and focus on a specific research problem, where different questions are asked about the topic without each researcher losing sight of the problem under consideration. This may help to integrate the contributions which different disciplines can make to the analysis of tourist transport systems in order to achieve a more holistic understanding of the operation, management and use of transport services by tourists.

Although there is not space within this introductory book to undertake a comprehensive review of transport and tourism, it has sought to focus on how the consumer, provider and other agencies (e.g., national governments) interact in different transport systems. The concept of a tourist transport system was developed as a framework in which to understand the interrelationships between different elements in such systems. Using a system approach to the analysis of tourist transport also highlighted the importance of *inputs* to the system (e.g., the demand and supply) as well as *controlling influences* (e.g., government policy) and *outputs* (the tourist travel experience) and the effect on the environ-ment. The book has also sought to identify a number of process which characterise the tourist transport system.

For example, deregulation and privatisation is a process now affecting tourist transport systems in North America, Western Europe and Australasia (Button and Gillingwater 1991) as well as communist states such as China (Tapling 1993). Within the existing literature, the discussion of tourist transport systems has remained fragmented and dependent upon generalised and empirical studies or extremely specialised studies of both tourism and transport. The interface between tourism and transport has not been integrated into a holistic framework. Wilst tourism is now regarded as a complex phenomenon by educators and researchers, its frequent association with transport has meant that social science researchers have failed to integrate these issues in a framework where the complementarity between tourism and transport could be explored further.

The tendency within tourism research to focus on typologies of tourism and tourists has led to a critical separation of the tourist from the mode of transport they use. This has the effect of contributing to the separation of tourism and transport research, with tourist motivation to travel viewed in isolation from the process of travelling. The result is that tourist travel is divided into two discrete elements (transport and the tourist) rather than being conceptualised as a conti-nuous process using a systems approach. But what are the process shaping tourist transport in the new millennium?

One of the overriding themes affecting the tourist transport system is globalisation especially in those sectors which deal with the management and logistics of international travel (Lovelock and Yip 1996). Globalisation inevitably produces 'winners and losers's in the pursuit of business and four distinct processes are associated with it. There are :

- *Deregulation,* where the entry barriers to many sectors of the tourist transport business have been removed and large oligophilies are challenged the new entrants (Pearce 1995b). As the example of the US domestic airline industry illustrates, in newly deregulated indicters, competition increased at a rapid pace. However, there is debate within the American dome-stic airline industry as to whether consumers have been the main beneficiaries, with lower prices. Goetz and Sutton (1997) explain that the benefits of deregulation have accrued to those passengers travelling on trunk routes, while business travellers and passengers travelling to/from more peripheral locations have experienced higher fares.

- *Technological change,* which has revolutionised the organisation, management and day-to-day running of tourist transport businesses with the introduction of information technology (IT). IT has also helped reduce some of the costs of business operations. The introduction of CRSs and GDSs have certainly assisted with the globalisation of the supply of tourist transport services. The introduction of the Internet has also had a major impact on the supply of transport services (Macdonald) Wallace 1997). In fact many of the world's airlines now have Internet sites and as Whitaker and Levere (1997) show, some are being used for bookings, but 'the scope and standard of airline-related material on the Internet varies drama-tically'. In fact the evolution of Internet sites and their use in marketing has now moved beyond a tool simply to advertise and sell tourist transport services.

  This traditional use, based on sales and marketing, is reflected in the UK express coach network site—http://www.national-express.co.uk. However, there is evidence that some companies (e.g., Red Funnel Ferries is Southampton) are developing a more holistic approach to transport and tourism and using the Internet to address the impact of competitive force such as rival carriers.

  The company's Internet site –http://www.redfunnel.co.uk contains the traditional sales and marketing function. But it also moves into a tactical marketing role where bookings can be auctioned and place-marketing is undertaken in relation to the main destination they serve–the Isle of White. The website provides ideas for theme itineraries and the main attractions to visit which complement the tourism marketing activities of the public sector (e.g., the Southern England Tourist Board). This is certainly leading the way in providing a seamless tourism experience facilitated by technology and the activities of the transport operator. Some airlines also often sophisticated system allowing passengers to plan book and pay for their flights other can master little more than sketchy corporate information (Whitaker and Levere 1997 : 27).

- *Regional change :* The highest costs for air travel remain in Europe and North America whereas in other trading blocs such as ASEAN, lower costs exist. For tourist transport providers in the global economy, it can mean airliners are competing on a different cost basis as Halon (1996) observes in terms of regional wage rates and remuneration of airline employees.
- *Hypercompetition:* Within the global marketplace, tourist transport provider are facing pressures conti-nually to improve products and to remain competitive. In some case, organisation and constantly struggling to remain in business as experience in the international airline industry suggests. As the privatisation charac-teristic of the 1990s and deregulation seem set to continue, established industry leaders and find their position challenged or destroyed by fierce completions. According to D'Aveni (1998), this hypercompetition is typified by:
- Rapid product innovation.
- Aggressive competition.
- Shorter product life cycles.
- Businesses experimenting with meeting customers' needs.
- The rising importance of alliance.
- The destruction of norms and rules of national oligopolies.

D'Aveni (1998) identifies four processes which are fuelling hypercompetition :

- Customers requiring better quality at lower prices One of the innovations airlines have pursued to develop improved quality at lower prices is in-flight catering (Jones 1995)
- Rapid technological change, especially the use of IT.
- the rise of aggressive large companies willing to enter markets for a number of years with a loss-leader product in the hope of destroying the competition and capturing the market in the long term.
- Government policies towards barriers to competition are being progressively removed. This is evident in the tourist transport sector throughout the world, albeit to differing degrees

depending on the political persuasion and commitment to deregulation.

At first sight, D'Aveni's (1998) processes are not particularly different from those listed under globalisation (e.g., deregulation, technological change, consumer preferences and regional change). But the fundamental different lies in the business strategy of hypercompetitors.

As D'Aveni (1998) argues, hypercompetitors tend to destroy the existing competencies of businesses. Those affected by such change are often trapped by an inability to think laterally and to adopt new competencies. Even when new competencies are introduced, businesses often have difficulty in diffusing them throughout their organisation. Some belatedly look towards the concept of 'change management' but this can sometimes be too little action too late. Often firms are so severely affected by hypercompetions and their action, that their reponses are bound by age-old relations based on previous rules of completion, However, the hypercompetitor can only remain in a competitive position while it retains the advantage.

According to D'Aveni (1998), hypercompetitors enter the market by disrupting the competition in some of the following ways :

- By redefining the product market, thereby redefining the meaning of the quality while offering it at a lower price. This is the strategy adopted by EasyJet in the UK which entered the market with low-cost air travel from Luton Airport to challenge the market leaders (e.g., BA, British Midland and KLM UK).
- By modifying the industry's purpose and focus by bundling and splitting industries. BA's response to EarJet was to reduce fares in the short term, but then it provided a splitting action by establishing a similar low-cost operation based at London Stansted, with lower landing fees. This avoid eroding profit margins and using high-cost airline capacity from Heathrow and Gatwick. In other words, BA can operate a loss-leader small business to compete head on which FasyJet on equal terms. A similar response occurred in New Zealand in the mid-1990s when Air New Zealand established a low-cost airline (Freedom Air) to compete with the Hamilton-based airline Kiwi Air.
- By disrupting the supply chain by redefining the knowledge and know-how needed to deliver the product to the customer.

- By harnessing the global resources from alliances to compete with the non-aligned businesses. This in particularly acute in the airline industry although to data the term 'hypercompetitor' has not been used to describe the business strategy of key players.

The process of globalisation and hypercompetition are powerful forces affecting the tourist transport sector and a number of themes emergy which are worthy of further discussion :

- The role of the consumer.
- The growing significance of service quality.
- The introduction of Total Quality Management Systems.

Much of the rhetoric and hype associated with the rapid expansion of popular business books and the elevation of individuals to 'guru' status in the 1980s and 1990s is characterised by one consistent theme : that businesses need to understand the customer and to get near to them as 'end-users'. Swarbrooke (1997) reiterates the importance of consumer behaviour research in tourism, since from a tourist transport perspective it allows businesses to plan infrastructure developments, identify product opportunities, set price levels for products and identify market segments and the best marketing medium to promote the product. Consumer behaviour research also allows businesses to modify their product and its delivery to align it more closely with consumer expectations.

For the tourist transport business, understanding how tourists make their purchasing decisions and the factors affecting their choice of product is critical. In particular, the travellers' predisposition towards certain forms of transport will obviously affect their overall satisfaction with the product. For the tourism sector in general, Swarbrooke (1997) identifies a number of weakness in consumer behaviour research in the UK which are particularly relevant to the transport sector (although the exception may be the major airlines who commission in-house research that emains confidential and commercially sensitive). The main weaknesses are :

- An absence of reliable and up-to-data a feature emphasisted.
- A lack of longitudinal studies to trace the evolution of consumer behaviour in tourism through time.
- The methodologies and techniques used to collect data on consumer behaviour in tourism remain relatively crude and unsophisticated.

- The most robust data collated by private sector companies remains inaccessible to researchers.
- Methods of segmenting the market remain outdated due to a reliance on the lifecycle concepts and age, despite major societal and value changes which have questioned their validity in the late 1990s.
- Cross cultural differences in tourism markets and a predisposition towards using specific tourist transport mode remain poorly understood. The research identified by Lumsdon (1997), in prt, addresses some of these issues in relation to cycling.
- There are few media available to disseminate results to the practitioner audience.

As a result, consumer behaviour is one area which tourist transport operators will need to focus on if they seek to understand what motivates tourists to travel and to select specific modes of transport. Tourist transport systems are likely to be affected by various opportunities and constraints on tourist travel in the late 1990s and beyond. For example, congestion of airspace in developed countries such as North America and Western Europe (French 1994, 1997b) will remain a persistent problem for policy makers and transport planners in late 1990s and new millennium.

At the same time the demand for long-haul travel is developed for transports provides and tours operators if cohstraints cannot be covercome, Environmental issues will also feature more prominently in tourist transport systems as a new generation of travellers, having become familiar with green issues in the 1980s, emerge as consumers of tourist transports services. Understanding the relative importance of these factors in shaping the tourist's desire to travel on different modes of transport will be a major challenge for service providers, as the sustainability debate (Weiler 1993) focuses on more environmentally sensitive and novel modes of transport. Increasingly, the patronage of tourist transport service is going to depend upon the ability of providers to differentiate their services on the basis of image market positioning and reputation for service quality. The 1990s are emerging as the decade of the consumer in relation to tourist travel, the providers responding to legitimate requests for higher standards of comfort, reliability and courtesy as part of the travel experience. The new millenium is also set to see a continuity and intensity of these processes of change, while the discussion of globalisation and hypercompetion indicates the pressure on transport provides will intensify, Passengers are now recognised as customers and their rights and needs are beginning to gain a higher profile in the provision, quality and management of tourist transport services.

Service Quality Issues in Tourist Transport

The concept of service was introduced in the context of marketing. While that discussion provided a broad overview of the importance of service issues in tourist, transport, it is evident from the processes affecting the tourist as a consumer, that service quality is assuming a greater role in their purchasing decisions any travel behaviour. Irons (1994) argues that services are relationships and that whether that relationship is a transient one or a longerterm proposition, it needs to be conducted in a professional and consistent manner. As Irons (1994 : 13) shows,

- Such a relationship will be based on a series of contacts or interactions. It is from these interactions with the organisation that consumers form their perceptions... to assess value, decide to buy, repeat purchase or recommend to others.

Such interactions are also repeated within the organisation and Irons (1994) expresses this process as a triangle Irons explain the triangle in the following way:

- An organisation need to associate its internal culture with the one it portrays externally and this underpins the relationships evident.
- Within the organisation, power needs to be devolved so that the relationships can be developed and the appropriate skill and know-how is provided at the point where customer satisfaction is met.
- The organisational values and culture need to be clearly understood by all employees so that they affect their actions and activities in relation to customers.
- Managers need to lead the process, empowering people at the various levels in the organisation to achieve customer-related targets. In other words, managers need not only to exercise a degree of control in the management function, but also to lead the organisation in this era of the consumer.
- A customer focus is critical rather than a focus first on the product and then its purchasers. To create a service culture in an organisation, Irons (1997) identified the following key points :

- Service businesses need to identify what the priorities are for the customer. Irons (1997) cites the example of Southwest Airlines in the USA which saw a set or priorities–reliability, low fates, personal treatment–and set about 'rigorously building the airline around meeting these needs and cutting out those things the customer did not want's.
- Organisations need to develop a clear vision of 'what they stand for and where they aspire to go...This vision should be for the customer, for the staff and for the owners'.
- Organisations and employees need to communicate so that they understand what is to be achieved, why, how and the role of employees in the corporate vision.
- The organisation needs to learn from its experience through problem-solving and how this can benefit its vision.
- The service culture needs to be led from the top in the organisation rather than through passive forms of managerialism.
- It is at the point of interaction between the market and the consumer that value can be created.
- Service delivery is an integral part of the process for service organisations and it should drive the business.

While the principle outlined by Irons (1994, 1997) may be useful in outlining how businesses may create a service culture, at a practical level the service requirements of the tourist transport sector need to be examined in more derail. This is because in certain sectors of the tourist transport business, service qualities offer particular challenges to operators because of the nature of the service interaction. It should also be emphasised that in some case, tourists' expectations are rising beyond the reach of mass transport providers and their ability to meet these needs. Within the literature on tourism and transport there are comparatively few systematic reviews of service quality. While studies reviewed on rail travel highlighted the experience of InterCity prior to privatisation, few other reviews exist.

Those studies which have been undertaken have largely focused on the airline sector. Probably the most influential publication to date is that by Witt and Muhle-mann (1995) which not only reviews the previous research in the area, but also identifies the idiosyncrasies and conditions which influence service quality in airlines.

7

Strategy in Transportation

Nature based tourism is one of Australia and the world's fastest growing tourism markets, as residents and visitors go to natural and cultural areas and sites to experience beautiful landscapes, flora and fauna and our European and Indigenous culture. In the ACT, even without significant promotion, visitation to natural areas and cultural sites is steadily growing.

Nature based tourism is tourism focusing on visitation to natural or near natural area, including recreation, visits to European and Indigenous cultural sites and simple sightseeing. As a nature based tourism destination the ACT is unique within Australia and possibly the world. Compared to a national average of 8% for land designated as parks and reserves, 53% of the ACT is made up of either national park or nature reserves with a further 10% of the Territory composed of plantation forests.

Given this wealth, the ACT's natural areas represent significant recreation and tourism resources. Indeed, experiences of unspoiled natural environments, unique landscapes and wildlife, as well as significant Indigenous and European heritage and cultural resources, offer considerable potential to contribute to the Territory's tourism promotion and positioning.

Canberra's high quality urban environment also provides an opportunity for the ACT to develop an image as a diverse and healthy leisure destination. The Bush Capital's open spaces, parks, walking and cycling trails as well as close proximity to substantial and significant nature parks and reserves provide a wide range of opportunities for Canberrans and visitors to relax, recuperate and revitalise. This Strategy sets out the ACT Government's directions and priorities for the further development of nature based tourism in the territory. The Strategy has been developed as one component of the ACT Tourism Master Plan. Ongoing community involvement in both experiencing our wonderful assets and in working with the Government in refining and developing the Strategy is actively sought.

Why an ACT Nature Based Tourism Strategy?

Nature based tourism can deliver a range of environmental, social and economic benefits to the ACT community, including:

- Increased community and visitor environmental awareness and understanding;
- Promotion of environmental and cultural values;
- Generation revenue for the conservation and management of natural and cultural heritage;
- Greater community and visitor enjoyment of natural and cultural sites and facilities; and
- Employment opportunities, utilising local knowledge and facilities.

In addition, nature based tourists tend to be high yield tourists, spending more, and staying longer in a destination than general tourists. Importantly, as tourism, and in particular nature based tourism, is essentially about the environment in which we live, work and play the ACT's natural assets also represent significant community resources and recreational opportunities. Many of those visiting the Territory's natural and cultural sites and attractions are and will continue to be Canberra residents and their visiting friends and relatives.

What is Nature Based Tourism?

Nature based tourism can be defined as visitation to natural or near natural areas. This includes ecotourism, adventure tourism, rural tourism, visits to European or Indigenous cultural and heritage sites, and simple sightseeing and recreation. Ecotourism is a niche component of nature based tourism, with a focus on education and interpretation of the natural and cultural environment. The ACT has a wide range of significant nature based tourism assets and resources, including Namadgi National Park, Tidbinbilla Nature Reserve, Canberra Nature Park, Murrumbidgee River Corridor and Googong Foreshores. Other assets include:

- The Australian National Botanic Gardens;
- The National Aquariums and Australian Wildlife Sanctuary;
- Canberra's city parks and lakes, managed by the ACT Government and the National Capital Authority;
- European and Indigenous cultural heritage sites and objects; and
- Plantation pine and native forests managed by ACT Forests.

Who are the Nature Based Tourists?

We are all nature based tourists. Most of us enjoy getting out into the natural environment, and most of us seek a range of experiences, from wilderness trekking and bush walking through to less demanding activities such as scenic driving and casual visits to nature reserves and parks. Bureau of Tourism Research (BTR) data notes that:

- The appeal of nature based tourism experiences are similar across most age and life cycle groups;
- Educative and interpretive experiences are of similar appeal amongst both sexes and across age and life cycle groups (although people with children are more likely to see learning about nature as important than those without children);
- Nature based and ecotourists tend to be more educated than non-ecotourists and often have higher incomes; and
- As experiences become more physically demanding, more expensive or specialised the nature based tourism market quickly narrows.

Thus there is no single nature based tourism market, rather a range of markets and market segments that flow into one another as the tourists seek a range of experiences. These experiences range from what can be described as 'hard' nature based such as wilderness trekking and bush walking through to less demanding or 'soft' nature based activities such as scenic driving, and casual visits to nature reserves and parks. Many visitors to natural and cultural heritage sites are Canberra residents-families and friends wishing to simply experience nature and culture.

Plantation Forests

Approximately 10% of the Territory is plantation pine and other forests managed by ACT Forests. About 1.1 m residents and visitors come to the forests each year. These areas are managed as multiple purpose forests, being both commercial forest and available for a wide range of recreational activities. Of the 26,900 hectares managed by ACT Forests, about 16,000 hectares is pine plantation. The remainder comprises nature reserves, native vegetation corridors, water bodies and streams and over 1200km of forest roadway.

The range of activities available in these areas is much wider than in the national parks and nature reserve areas, and includes car rallies, paint ball, sled dog trials, horse riding, cycling, orienteering and off-lead areas for dogs. ACT Forests offer a range of activities including bush walks, fishing and camping. The forests also contain a diversity of European and Aboriginal heritage sites, as well as several arboreta and the largest cork oak plantation in the southern hemisphere. The less restricted use of the forests also reduces any pressure to use the more sensitive natural areas for more intensive activity, for example the FAI Rally of Canberra, a major car rally, is also held in ACT Forests areas.

In contrast to the other states and territories, the ACT's bush parks and forests are relatively close to our urban areas, enabling easy access for both residents and visitors to experience the ACT's natural and cultural heritage.

The Environment Green Evaluation Programme

Balatonfüred managed environment protection as an important mission even before the political –economical changes of '89. But the real progress started only in the nineties. The Self-government created its own Local Order of Environment amongst the first towns in the country, introduced selective waste collection subsided financially by EU after a successful PHARE submission, joined local forces of NGOs interested in environmental issues. As a continuation of this progress the Self-government participated in a large international environmental project led by the Union of Baltic Cities along with Siófok and Lake Balaton Development Coordination Agency.

The goal of the project is to create and introduce an up to date, environment conscious managing system in the participating cities for a sustainable urban environment. Dr. Bóka István, the mayor of Balatonfüred signed the co-financing statement on 26th March 2004. The Kickoff meeting was held in Riga on 13th-14th June, 2005, where the most important steps and the frameworks of cooperation of the three years long project were discussed. Only after this meeting, on 21st July, 2005. The Partnership and Grant Agreement was signed by UBC and Balatonfüred. Yet in Riga on the starting plenary conference the frameworks and the forms of cooperation and the schedule of work were determined. First of all the preparation of a Baseline Review and then a Strategic Program were decided. After having collected the available necessary local documents and refreshing data Balatonfüred has compiled its Baseline Review.

As a part of this work, the SWOT analysis gives a proper starting point for the Strategic Program of the town, as it formulates step by step the strengths to be exploited consciously better in the future, weaknesses we have to eliminate as far as possible, or to reduce their negative effects and the possibilities we are to make the best and the threats which are to avoid. This Strategic Program was compiled following the structure of the BR. In the process of creation of SP the still existing documents (City Developing Concept, Urban Organization Plan, for Public Health, etc.) and the newest developing ideas were highly taken into consideration Evaluation of the present situation (SWOT analysis) Environmental elements

The natural environment of town Balatonfüred belongs to the most beautiful and most precious sites in the country. This beauty has not only aesthetic but a high economic value, as it considerably contributes to the tourist attractiveness of the town itself. Thus protecting and improving the natural environment is a basic interest of the community.

The Koloska valley, the Tamás hill and the Malom valley are the most precious outskirt areas of Balatonfüred. These sites along with the other outings are threatened mostly by two main dangers. The first is building up and fencing (illegally or evading the law) and the illegal waste deposits. Building up and fencing endangers mostly Tamás hill and the other higher areas where the beautiful panorama induces such needs and intentions. Illegal waste deposits have been occurring in decades long on certain places well accessible by cars and lorries, mainly by the roadsides leading out of town.

The Strategic Program is to preserve the natural environment by the following measures: On the non built green areas of Tamás hill total ban of construction is to introduce except those improvement involved in the Strategic Program. It is to acquire the ownership the areas around Jókai lookout tower and the paths leading to the summit. More frequently emptied and more numerous waste containers are to be placed on the most often visited illegal deposits by the roads leading out of the town-The control of these area must be realized by joining forces of official and voluntary environmentalists. Besides preservation of the natural environment it is to make efforts to a careful and cautious exploitation of these values, as the improving ecotourism, and with raising incomes increase the city welfare. The Strategic Program supports the following improvements: Ecological recreation of the streambed of Malom valley brook and establishment a fee fishing pond above the Dobogóhid section of the brook. Previously or simultaneously The recultivation of the neighbouring dumpsite is to be completed.

A cable lift is to establish on the slopes of Tamás hill. Its incomes are to ensure the costs of a permanent warding of the natural environment. It is a further benefit, that heart patients and disabled people can enjoy the beauty of the panorama. On the still existing forest paths of the northern slopes a system of jogging tracks is to establish. This can also be used as cross country sky courses in winter. Summer bobsleigh course is also supported by the Strategic Program. The excursion centre in the Koloska valley needs a better and easier access and a higher level of services and more comfort. The Strategic Program supports such improvements. Besides this a cautious riverbed recreation on the lower sections of the brook is allowed. On the upper sections it is only the installation of small wooden barrages to retain water what is supported by the SP. The middle section of the brook is to remain in its natural condition. The renovation of the Füredi Kiserd (Small Forest Park) is supported but the old and precious wood stock must be preserved. The Balaton shoreline is to be protected.

Further concrete walls and stoning is allowed only sections where the Shoreline Rehabilitation Plan indicates boat jetties or yacht harbours. Reeds and natural shoreline are to be protected even at that sites. A mobile, floating aquarium and ecological showplace is to be built and placed between Tagore Promenade and the Annabella beach Efforts are to be made for the most detailed mapping of underground mineral carbonic water bases. Further research drillings must be carried out in order to substantiate an improving medicinal spa culture. Constructed environment The three historical centre of the town, Fured Old Village, the Resort Quarter and Aracs historical village core is to preserved and developed according to the traditions.

At a different extent these three areas became city centres by the commerce, catering and services focused here. Further improvement is possible and desirable mostly by the private investments attracted here, but for the preserving renovation of public places financed by municipal and granted funds is also necessary. The "Mainstreet program" aims at the development of the main street of the Old Village besides preserving the picturesque values, strengthen the functions of town centre. The improvement of the historical village centre of Aracs has already commenced. It must be completed by reconstructing the municipality owned buildings into a centre of education, culture and services.

The partly finished renovation of the Resort Quarter is to be extended with the reconstruction of Gyogyter (Medicinal square), and east and westward continuation of the Tagore Promenade. In the eastern section of the littoral zone between the two main beaches on the plot of the Anglers' Association a municipal water sport centre is to be established. This places will afford possibilities for fishing rowing and sailing first of all for the local people. The former Huray –market (once the village football ground in the old times) building up is allowed only with establishments for only cultural and/or entertaining activities.

On the public plots behind it recreational or educational establishments are to be built. Building areas for economical activities which are not desirable in residential districts will be provided primarily by the northern side of Aszof road, towards the dumpsite and on itself the dumpsite after its restoration.

The building of the west bypass road is the most important traffic task. Renovation of pavements and urban streets must be continued. The number and the length of bike roads are to be increased. This improvement is desirable primarily in the case of bike roads joining to the Balaton Bike road and leading north out town, thus the background settlements, the stations of wine routes, and the values of nature can get an easy access. The total renovation of the rainfall system is vitally necessary. Humane factor First rank task is to increase the number of birth.

It can be realized by increasing the certainty of existence (creating new places of employment, flat building programs) education and by the financial support for young mothers and newborns We have to protect our fundamentally good education system of the unfavourable effects, spreading from outside. Further cooperation of our primary schools is desirable. In health aspect the conditions of the environmental elements are generally suitable. Occasional air pollution from traffic will be reduced by building bypass roads, and the sporadic water and soil pollution will also diminished by perfecting the sewage system.

The main mortal risk factors are to be reduced by proper and effective health education and by the extension of screening tests. At present only the State and the local Self-government play essential role in social care. It is desirable to establish and support civil organizations with a vocation to such aims and goals. The crime status is rather suitable in the city.

The main figures in crime reports are ceasing year by year. The Self Government, NGOs and enterprises support effectively the work of the Police and other crime pursuing organizations through the Foundation for Property Defence. To counter against drugs and other addictions prevention is the number one tool, and secondly a more effective crime pursual work and a rising social support is to be achieved. The seasonal (autumn, winter) unemployment is a very characteristic and impending factor on city development.

Thus the main goal is to increase the numbers of permanent work places. City function and management The Mayor's Office, which is responsible for city function and management carries out its task profoundly suitable. Its cooperation with the elected city management, the Self-government is also proper. Within the Office the cooperation between the departments must be strengthen.

Regular heads of departments meetings-are to be held, where they report on the achievements and where the tasks for the next period will be shared out. Reinforcement of environmental affairs with minimum one new staff member is absolutely necessary. In the case of public space wards the situation is similar. Employment of an additional staff member is justified as well as the widening of their authority and competence. The clarks' ability of communication in a foreign language are to be improved. Employment of a new civil servant ought to be conditioned by a communicative skill in a foreign language. It is the PROBIO zRT which performs definitely the communal duties of the town in a suitable and a improving way. This company is responsible for collecting, transport and deposit of communal waste on a dumpsite operated by itself. The dumpsite is to be operated until the start up of the regional waste management system including the new dumpsite. Then the old dumpsite must be recultivated and environment friendly activities are to be settled here.

We have to stimulate and increase the selective waste collecting and the in situ composting on the detached estates with a garden. The self-government has to review the whole city function especially the energy supply of the town. It is vitally important to compile an energy concept and an energy action plan. The Self-government and the Mayor's Office are to be committed to be the vanguard promoting the utilization of alternative energy resources. Therefore an action plan must be worked out for the installation of public buildings with solar collectors. The Self-government is to encourage the establishment of small local di-and trigeneration power stations for new public establishments and bigger private buildings.

For the realization of this program a conscious and well prepared project strategy is to be compiled. This is the way to acquire the majority of the necessary financial funds. A local program is to be worked out for the renovation of public and private buildings introducing more efficient heat isolation technologies. Economy The economy of the city is mostly based on summer tourism. This must be changed in two ways. First the tourist period must be widened, and secondly other economical activities must be settled in the town. The extension of tourist season has already begun. The Balaton Congress and Leisure time Centre has built and organises diverse programs, the year round functioning Aqua park opened for the public.

Three four star hotels affording high level services all the year are going to be finished and opened at the end of this year. The still existing older hotels are to be renovated thus joining to the season elongating program.

The sport tourism is also improving thanks to the new possibilities by the opening of BCLC and by building new yacht harbours. Former institute offers place for sport events all the year, sailing life is restricted to the period from the late spring until early autumn. Establishment of an ice stadium would give an additional push to the development of sport tourism.

As this establishment needs much energy it is to be built and operate by the most modern and effective energy utilization. The cultural tourism also has got a huge possibility by the opening of BCLC. A new theatre performing all the year around would significantly animate the cultural life in the town. The traditional wine tourism is the only economical activity what is based on agriculture and has significant role in the town. Its quantitative improvement is hardly possible. Further development seems to be possible in the still existing estates, achievements of a better access to the wine route stations and improving better services. Fishing tourism is to be also improved. The Balatonfüredi Horgasz Egyesulet has to get a possibility to build a new jetty and fishing clubhouse, which can afford a proper level of services for guest anglers. The careful improvement of natural environment mentioned under will also contribute to the prolongation of the tourist season.

For the sake of creating new jobs, it is also vital to attract other economical activities in the city. First of all economical, logistic and financial centres are to be settled as they won't spoil the tourist appeal of the town. Different kinds of environment friendly artisan manufactures are also welcome Certain faculties of high school education according to character of the region (environmental, nature protection, hydrobiology or tourism and economy, possibly faculty of law) would animate the local economy and the whole spirit of the town. The growth in alternative forms of tourism has occurred simultaneously with an increased recognition of the need to implement the concept of sustainable development. Ecotourism has been widely assumed to be inherently sustainable, although few attempts have been made to verify this assumption. Ecotourism incorporates environmental and cultural conservation objectives, and emphasizes economic benefits to local communities. Hence, eco-tourism would appear to be, and is increasingly presented as, a tool for sustainable development.

However, it also has the potential to be more environmentally damaging than mass tourism since it typically occurs in fragile environments and opens up previously undiscovered destinations to the mass market. By the late 1980s, a shift in the tourism industry's marketing strategy occurred alongside the emergence of the global environmental movement. In the decade of "green consumerism", critical consumers were soon leading the demand for "environmentally sound" holidays. Tour operators and travel companies began to promote themselves and their products as "environmentally friendly", and a number of companies published ethical and environmental codes of conduct and guidelines for travellers as well as guidelines for self-regulation. Tour companies also started to promote eco-tourism holidays to all corners of the world, to coincide with the inclusion of the environment on the mainstream political agenda. At the same time the tourist hunting industry has expanded dramatically.

Literature Survey

Sustainable Development

In the 1987 Brundtland Report of the World Commission on Environment and Development, sustainable development is defined as the "development that meets the needs of the present without compromising the ability of future generations to meet their own needs" (World Commission on Environment and Development, 1987:43). To meet the needs of the present, the new development has to provide ground on which the basic necessities of all humans and the opportunities for a better life can be satisfied.

Sustainable development is being discussed for the last two decades, mostly among academicians. The core elements of these discussions are:

- The idea that the needs of present and future generations must be considered;
- The need to ensure that renewable and non-renewable resources are conserved, not exhausted;
- The requirement that access to and use of natural resources must take fair account of the needs of all people;
- A recognition that issue of environment and sustainable development must be treated in an integrated manner.

Sustainable Tourism Development

The tourism and recreation industry is at a crossroads in its development. Now as one of the world's largest industries, it is increasingly confronted with arguments about its sustainability and compatibility with environmental protection and community development. Consideration of tourism, the environment, and concepts of sustainability should consider four key challenges:

(1) a better understanding of how tourists value and use natural environments;

(2) enhancement of the communities dependent on tourism as an industry;

(3) identification of the social and environmental impact of tourism; and

(4) implementation of systems to manage these impacts.

The tourism and recreation industry is confronted with serious and difficult choices about its future. The decisions made now will for decades affect the lifestyles and economic opportunity of residents in tourism destination areas. Many of these decisions are irreversible because once communities lose the character that makes them distinctive and attractive to nonresidents, they have lost their ability to vie for tourist-based income in an increasingly global and competitive market place.

Owen (1993) characterizes sustainable tourism development as:

- Tourism should be one part of a balanced economy.
- The use of tourism environments must allow for long-term preservation and for use of those environments.
- Tourism should respect the character of an area.
- Tourism must provide long-term economic benefits.
- Tourism should be sensitive to the needs of the host population.

Butler suggests the following working definition of sustainable development in the context of tourism: "tourism which is developed and maintained in an area (community, environment) in such a manner and at such a scale that it remains viable over an indefinite period and does not degrade or alter the environment (human and physical) in which it exists to such a degree that it prohibits the successful development and well being of other activities and processes".

The growth in alternative forms of tourism has occurred simultaneously with increased recognition of the need to implement the concept of sustainable development. As with "eco-tourism", "sustainable development" is another environmental catch phrase with no single definition.

On the face of it, no other economic activity would appear to lend itself to sustainable development better than tourism. Alternative forms of tourism that incorporate environmental and cultural conservation objectives with an emphasis on economic benefits to local communities would appear to be a panacea for sustainable development. Because damage to the environment threatens the resource base on which alternative forms of tourism depend, it would be logical to expect all involved in tourism to ensure the protection of these resources. All forms of tourism consume resources such as land and energy. However, when practiced against the standards of its definition, the small scale and dispersed nature of eco-tourism, combined with connotations of sound environmental management, means that it has the potential to consume far less basic resources than other forms of tourism or other developments.

A recent article in the UK Youth Hostel Association's magazine, Triangle, takes up this theme: "Spending your holiday in one of the latest artificial all-weather tropical pleasure domes or in intensely developed but properly managed holiday resorts like Benidorm and Torremolinos can be more environmentally friendly than indulging in trips to remote or fragile areas where tourism is more likely to be environmentally and culturally damaging and puts little or nothing back into managing and protecting the environment" (YHA, 1996).

Quoted in the same article, the popular conservationist David Bellamy comments "Ecotourism is already a dirty word. Hill walking, jungle trekking and all the rest are just as potentially harmful as conventional resort holidays, if not more so. Most of the tourism industry is simply sponging off clean water, fresh air, the natural and cultural environment and is putting nothing back in. But there are praiseworthy exceptions, which not only do not damage the environment, but also actually help to restore it. This is real eco-tourism." (YHA, 1996).

In addition to the potential damage caused locally to tourist destinations, the air transport of tourists to remote areas of the globe seriously undermines the concept of sustainability of the industry as a whole. For example, air travel contributes 2-3 percent of global emissions of fossil fuel derived carbon dioxide, the principal greenhouse gas, as well as nitrogen oxides, which contribute to low-level ozone formation. Paradoxically, nitrogen oxides released at high altitudes also contribute to the thinning of the protective ozone layer over the earth.

Not all of the impacts of tourism are necessarily negative. If development and change are bound to occur in a particular site from some activity or other, tourism may be a far less damaging alternative than many other more polluting industries. The Overseas Development Association (ODA) Manual of Environment Appraisal (1996) provides a checklist to help develop management strategies to minimize negative impacts and maximize positive benefits. Therefore, alternative or other forms of tourism are not necessarily a panacea for sustainable development, unless well planned and well regulated.

In most countries, there usually is no coordination between programs that promote and market tourism and those that manage environment and culture. On the other hand, agencies dealing with the promotion of tourism are not involved with the evaluation of its effects or with advance planning and management of the adverse impacts of tourism through avoidance, mitigation, and compensation strategies.

Ecotourism

The term "eco-tourism" is often assumed largely to alternative tourism that involves international travel by people from rich developed countries to developing countries, as a means of providing much needed foreign exchange for hard-pressed national economies, and earnings for poor rural people. The notion of these interrelated conservation and economic benefits has led to much confusion surrounding tho variety of terms currently in use that appear to have similar meanings and aims. These include "alternative tourism", "sustainable tourism", "soft tourism", "special interest tourism", "green tourism", and "eco-tourism". Some of these terms frequently appear to be used interchangeably, while others may be defined in a variety of ways.

In reality, eco-tourism has become widely adopted as a generic term to describe tourism that has, as its primary purpose, an interaction with nature, and that incorporates a desire to minimize negative impacts. Implicit in the term is the assumption that local communities should benefit from tourism and will help to conserve nature in the process. In this study, the term "Ecotourism" will be used to generalize all the other terms, and if a specific section of eco-tourism like wildlife tourism or alternative tourism is explained, then those terms will be used specifically. The terms "eco-tourists" and "ecotours" will be used in this study to summarize the group of tourists and the tours created for them in the name of eco-tourism.

As with the term "eco-tourism", there is similar confusion regarding the term "alternative tourism" that is often used as a generic term encompassing a range of variations such as eco-tourism and green tourism, all of which purport to offer a more benign alternative to conventional mass tourism. Indeed, eco-tourism has been described as "one of the most widely used and abused phrases of the last decade", which it is argued can mean anything to anyone.

A few definitions of "Ecotourism":

> *"An enlightening nature travel experience that contributes to the conservation of the ecosystem while respecting the integrity of host communities".*
>
> *"Responsible travel to natural areas, which conserves the environment and improves the welfare of local people".*
>
> *"Purposeful travel that creates an understanding of cultural and natural history, while safeguarding the integrity of the ecosystem and producing economic benefits that encourage conservation".*

Ecotourism can contribute enormously to the management of protected areas. Benefits include foreign exchange revenues, employment opportunities, improving awareness of conservation objectives and stimulation of economic activity. While protected areas are major destinations for eco-tourists, private enterprise is playing an increasing role in the eco-tourism sector. In addition, eco-tourism is a major vehicle for realizing tangible benefits of conservation for local communities with wildlife populations occurring on their land. However, the benefits accruing to local communities from tourism have so far been overstated. The type and magnitude of the environmental impacts associated with eco-tourism vary with the type of tourist activity pursued. Some impacts are obvious and easily identifiable, while others are indirect and difficult to quantify. Strategies to manage the impacts arising from eco-tourism may also be direct or indirect. Direct strategies include limiting the total numbers of visitors to an area; dispersing visitors; zoning; using fixed viewing points; and setting guidelines for minimum viewing distances. Indirect strategies are those that aim to modify the behaviour of tourists. One of the most important ways of achieving this is to educate visitors about the potential disturbance they can cause and to provide advice on how to reduce it.

Ecotourism has the potential to be more damaging than mass tourism since they often occur in fragile or unique environments. Small-scale operations in environmentally sensitive locations may eventually turn into much larger and more destructive operations. Ecotourism may simply represent the early stages of the conventional tourist destination life cycle. The life cycle concept essentially revolves around the premise that, unless intervention occurs, tourist destination areas and resources inevitably will become overused and, consequently, will decline. The six stages of the cycle are as follows:

- Exploration (few tourists, poor access and facilities, environment unchanged);
- Involvement (local initiatives, some promotion, increasing numbers);
- Development (many tourists, locals lose control, deterioration of environment);
- Consolidation (tourist numbers exceed local residents, all major chains represented);
- Stagnation (numbers peak, destination falls out of fashion, environmental and social problems);
- Decline or Rejuvenation (or intermediaries).

This cycle has a number of obvious implications for sustainability, based on the consideration of factors such as carrying capacity, local participation, ownership, social and environmental impacts.

Mass tourists may have less impact than eco-tourists, because they tend to limit themselves to well known, easily accessible areas and insulate themselves from the local people. In some instances, the zoning of mass tourism (or enclave tourism) is adopted as a deliberate policy by a host country. For example, tourists in the Maldives are confined to self-contained, purpose built resorts on isolated, often formerly uninhabited islands, in order to avoid a culture clash between bikini-clad tourists and the conservative, Islamic islanders. Bhutan limits the annual foreign tourist entrance to their country to 3,000 pax only.

Ecotourism proved to be a very lucrative sector of the industry, and commercial considerations of marketing the latest "undiscovered" paradise quickly overshadowed any concerns for environmental or cultural degradation. Indeed, the marketing of eco-tourism may well have accelerated social degradation, because more and more previously unknown destinations were discovered and subsequently opened up to mass tourism.

Turkey and Sustainable Tourism Development

Without giving due regard to the underlying principles of eco-tourism, tour operators and even governmental agencies seem to be securing the short-term economic benefits to sell regions or products.

As a developing country, Turkey's choice of pursuing a tourism development strategy is to create opportunities for economic improvement, since it suffers from deficit in the balance of payments. Tourism is also a tool for decreasing unemployment, because it is a labour-intensive industry. Turkey is trying to secure the short-term inflow of the foreign currency by increasing its bed capacity and trying to attract more tourists. Although the industry is centralized as being governed by the ministry, there are not any records available of any act for sustainable tourism development. Some accommodation units and travel agencies to a certain extent, as a tool for revenue generation, only use sustainable tourism.

Accommodation units try to decrease the operational costs like usage of sun energy. Some demand less usage of towels. Clearly, the aim of these acts is not to maintain sustainable tourism, but to minimize their costs. Indeed, the travel agencies' main concern is to maximize the total number of tourists to increase their profit. Therefore, the carrying capacity is totally ignored.

Like many other developing country governments, Turkish governments have helped the fast development of tourism without taking into account the factors of local culture and environment. All governmental acts have been related to monetary gains, since Turkey have been used to economic crises during the last decade. Even IMF has expected certain tourism income figures in order to give credits.

Research Methodology

The purpose of the research was to explore the perceptions of and the possible commitments of Turkish travel agencies engaged in eco-tourism to sustainable tourism development. An exploratory study were undertaken since not much was known about the situation at hand, and there were not any information available on how similar problems or research issues have been solved in the past. In other terms, there were not any previously defined theoretical framework and any hypothesis to test, so this research was to develop related subjects and their groupings by content analysis.

In order to address the quality of information obtained about nature tour operators, substantial attention will be given to survey design and administration. The aim of the research was to examine how travel agencies perceive the impacts of their development and to evaluate their level of response to environmental concerns.

In order to satisfy these aims, the objective was to obtain rich data. This pointed towards using a qualitative method involving relatively few people. According to Oppenheim (1992) 'the longer, the more difficult and the more open-ended the questions schedule is, the more we should prefer to use interviews.' In the light of this, a decision was made to undertake face-to-face, in-depth interviews.

In order to reach desired information, directors or senior personnel of ten TURSAB member agencies who are engaged in eco-tourism as the unit of analysis were interviewed. Having obtained the booklet of TURSAB listing the agencies as the population frame, the initial intention was to undertake systematic random sampling; however, this method of sampling proved unsatisfactory due to the high number of companies unwilling to participate and the fact that only around one-third of the population were in Istanbul, making the rest impossible to reach regarding the time limits. The choice of researcher was, therefore, very much decided on by the respondents' willingness to participate, i.e. the first ten agencies in Istanbul to agree. Given the seniority of all the interviewees, this was effectively 'elite interviewing': the individuals are influential and in a position to report on their organizations policies and future plan. Furthermore, 'elites respond well to intelligent, provocative, open-ended questions'.

Among the total population of 362, 135 were located in Istanbul and the rest 227 were located especially where eco-tourism activities took place. A limitation should be noted that the number of agencies rapidly change and figures of 2000 may not be the exact values of today, yet helped us for a fair idea of the population, since links on TURSAB website of the updated lists of agencies did not work during research process.

The research was a cross-sectional study with respect to time horizon, because data were gathered by the interview once, for a period of days. In-depth, face-to-face interviews with managers of travel agencies engaged in eco-tourism have been used as the data collection method. Other data sources were used during the literature survey such as publications, manuals, archives, journals and related books.

For qualitative data analysis, systematic coding by content analysis was used to analyse the transcripts of the interviews. In this method, the researcher analysed interview answers and prepared a list of subjects. The researcher and one independent sorter categorized these subjects independently. After a discussion between the researcher and the independent sorter, who was a manager of one of the visited travel agencies, a common categorization was agreed upon. For reliability testing, two independent graduate students who have studied research methodology also categorized the subjects.

According to the reliability test, the results of the content analysis came out to be significant.

Findings and Discussions

Types of Tours

According to the segmentation like mass tourism and eco-tourism, travel agencies engaged in eco-tourism also sell tours for the mass market. When the respondents were asked to compare the two types of tours with respect to sustainability, there was a clear dichotomy between the two segments.

At the first glance, special tours and ecotours might be considered more sustainable; their volumes are lower, they are more likely to use local accommodation, local guides and services, and attract more environmentally aware clients. However, a differentiated tour for the mass market may attract eco-tourists as well. On the other hand, some specialist markets are evolving into mass markets, because of the increase in volume and the rapidly changing markets. This shows the danger of using broad statements, as ecotours are more sustainable.

Types of Activities

According to the frequency order derived from the answers of the respondents, the following activities are marketed by the travel agencies: Walking/rambling, alternative water sports, trekking, golf, adventure, cycling, hunting, safari, photographing, mountaineering, rafting, horseback riding, fishing, alternative winter sports, bird watching. Many of the agencies sell more than one type of tours.

Why to Sell Alternative Forms of Tourism?

Travel agencies sell alternative forms of tourism in order to earn more money. Other reasons are to reach the young generation, to increase the variety of products and to enter a new market. Travel agency executives feel that their companies should be considered like markets or small shops in evaluation of any effects of operations, but they forget the fact that they do not sell products of another company like a market, but they produce the ecotours themselves and sell them. Since those tours selling the nature are their products, they are responsible for the positive or negative effects of their products.

These effects may be to the environment, to the local culture or to other aspects related to sustainable tourism. Travel agencies do not seem to accept the fact that some of the activities they make are acting against sustainable tourism by opening new areas to tourism without considering carrying capacity, using the nature as a marketing concept and allowing uncontrolled contact with local culture and tourists.

Sustainable Tourism

Sustainable development is a new subject of concern that many of us are not familiar with. Sustainable tourism development is also new, but it is being discussed in meetings of many international organizations. The first and obviously the main finding was that most of the interviewed senior personnel or managers of travel agencies in Turkey that are engaged in eco-tourism do not even know what sustainability is all about. Interesting answers on the definition of sustainability, which were totally unrelated to it, reminded the researcher the fact that many of the employees and managers in the tourism industry are uneducated or did not have their education on tourism. This was proved by the respondents' education levels, which were mostly high-school graduates.

The most interesting answer for the researcher was: 'Sustainable tourism, should be related to renovations of the hotels, planes it should not be related with travel agencies, we sustain tourism'. No matter the answer is funny or dramatic, but it seemed to be the reality for general knowledge of travel agency executives in Turkey related to sustainability.

So, the respondents did not take into consideration the important aspects of sustainability like local culture or environment, since they did not know the term.

Who is More Responsible for Realization of Sustainable Tourism?

Economically, travel agencies feel that any attempt to take steps on sustainable tourism will put them at a commercial disadvantage because of increasing costs. They agree on helping the realization of sustainable tourism only if the tourists accept to pay more.

Therefore, they feel that governments are more responsible for imposing restrictions, limiting growth and controlling volumes and so helping sustainable tourism.

The result of this study showed that, travel agencies are willing to comply with regulations if governments impose them to the whole sector. Another point that Turkish travel agencies engaged in eco-tourism mentioned is their operations are too small with respect to the whole market to make any influence.

Conclusion and Implications

This study has examined the social, environmental and cultural impacts of alternative tourism activities with regard to the travel agencies in Turkey engaged in eco-tourism. First conclusion is that it has become harder to segment the market into mass tourism and eco-tourism, since the two segments are becoming more integrated into each other and there are products, which cannot be put under a certain category.

Second conclusion is that, although these travel agencies sell ecotours and earn money, they believe that government has the major responsibility to ensure sustainable development. The third general conclusion is the fact that most of the travel agency executives has learned the definition of sustainability after the general explanation of the researcher.

It is easy to make an assumption like because travel agencies are small enterprises; their responsible behaviour may have a very small effect on sustainable tourism. Yet, specialist tours take tourists deeper into nature and sensitive local culture, and import the necessary skills instead using local work force.

Environmental policies and sustainable acts have become nothing more than a marketing ploy and a vehicle or eluding regulation. Environmental departments and affiliations with glossy campaigns have arguably become a PR exercise designed to meet the growing awareness in some markets to appear environmentally sound and to attract higher spending tourists. For sustainable tourism to be a marketable concept, tourists themselves have got to really buy on it.

To conclude, the researcher wants to point out that sustainability is mostly considered as an utopia and will probably never be achieved.

8

The Importance of Transport

Virtually all tourism is based on experiencing different locations, for which transport facilities are essential. Not so widely recognised, however, is the scale and extent of the transport businesses that underpin that travel. For international tourism, airlines are the principle mode of travel (although globally, ground travel—by car or train—remain the most commonly used forms of transport) and, for example, British Airways—the largest airline in the UK— in 2000 had a turnover of £8,940m, employing 65,640 people. Even so, BA is small by comparison with the giants of the US industry.

At the same time, transport investment and infrastructure are vital to the commercial development of tourism in an area. Indeed, the historical role of the railways in the development of the British seaside resorts in the 19th Century was mirrored by the contribution of air travel to the emergence of many international tourist destinations, such as The Gambia, the Maldives and the Caribbean islands, during the 20th Centuary. For example, traditionally the few visitors to the smaller Greek islands arrived by ferry from Athens (Piraeus) and the more adventurous still do, but the time taken (and inherent complexity) would be unacceptable to the mass market. It was only when an enterprising tour operator persuaded the authorities to allow military airfields to be used for charter flights that large-scale commercial development could begin.

This illustrates the important concept that, after cost, the main constraint on people's ability to travel is not distance but time; certainly, the growth of long-haul holidays shows that distance is not necessarily a deterrent as long as the journey can be made easily and rapidly. Conversely, some destinations, such as the St. Moriz area of Switzerland

and Positano/Amalfi on the Neapoliltan Riviera, have remained exclusive partly because they are difficult to reach quickly and are, thus, only available to those with time to spare or fast personal means of transport.

Transport is a Product of the Travel Industry

Despite the growing importance of Internet sales, travel agents generate a large proportion of their income from selling transport services, as distinct from holiday packages —in particular tickets for air and rail travel, together with car hire, coach and ferry services. World-wide, typically 75 percent of all air tickets are sold by travel agents. Commission is paid on these sales, and it is necessary for the travel agent to have knowledge of services and facilities available.

There is Overlap between Components of the Travel Industry

Some travel agents and tour operators are offshoots of transport companies, and vice-versa; the same organisation which puts the package together or sells it may be involved in providing the transport. Ferry companies, airlines, railways and coach operators offer extensive tour programmes of various kinds, while most charter airlines are connected financially with tour operators (the outstanding UK example being Britannia Airways, a subsidiary of Thomson Travel Group). The Virgin Group controls hotels, long-and short-haul aviation and two UK rail franchises, in addition to other activities outside transport.

The Quality of Transport is Important in the Travel Business

A tour operator contracting hotel accommodation seeks assurances about the standard of rooms, meals and other facilities. Less attention tends to be given to the choice of transport, but poor transport arrangements can spoil a holiday just as easily. However, people are increasingly conscious of quality and expect service of a high standard. Where that quality is lacking and an operator refuses compensation, successful legal action is possible—as occurred after a coach driver smoked throughout a holiday.

Elements of Transport Systems

Although various modes of transport perform different functions and have individual strengths and weaknesses, they all feature five essential elements in common:

- a *Way* or route on which travel occurs;
- *Vehicles* that perform that movement;
- *Terminals* between which they travel;

- *Control and communication systems* through which safety is ensured and those involved are kept informed; and
- *Skilled management and staff* who bring the element together.

All these make up a transport system, and it is important to recognise the contribution of each.

The Way

In the case of sea and air travel, the way is natural and 'free'. In principle, therefore, it can be used without restriction or cost, although safety demands that most air movements are subject to an air traffic control system, while ports and inland waterways usually involve artificial works which are charged for. Roads require construction and maintenance to reach a standard suitable for modern traffic; this is normally done by a public authority and the cost recovered by taxation on fuel and the use of vehicles. Occassionally, as with French autoroutes, a private company builds and maintains the route and then charges users a direct toll to use it. Rail systems similarly require construction and, by their nature, can only be used by very specialised vehicles. Historically, most railways were built by the companies which owned and operated vehicles on them, but nowadays it is increasingly common for the track to be in different hands from the operator. Since the way is exclusive, the congestion found on roads can be avoided but the specialised nature of rail construction incurs high costs which can only be justified by high levels of traffic.

The Vehicle

This is the carrying unit on which people travel—the train, ship, coach or aircraft. Sometimes separate 'motive power' is used to haul carrying units, the obvious example being railway engines, but usually the power to achieve movement is produced within the carrying unit itself. Over the years, the trend has been for the average size of vehicle to increase in order to accommodate increased demand and obtain economies (for example, the introduction of the 'jumbo' jet in the 1970s). However, this can result in the inability to service some destinations (as with cruise ships) or demand heavy investment to accommodate them, such as in longer airport runways.

The Terminal

The terminal could be defined as the place where people begin and end their journeys but, in practice, this is rarely true; few people live next to transport terminals and even fewer would like their holiday hotel to be next to the airport (although airport hotels do of course exist for other purposes). In fact, the terminal performs two functions. Firstly, it facilitates transfer or interchange between modes. For example, passengers boarding an international flight at a major airport might arrive by one of a variety of means, including:

- railway,
- their own or a friend's car,
- taxi,
- another aircraft (interlining),
- hire car,
- scheduled bus or coach,
- touring or transfer coach.

Thus, a major function of an airport is to allow the smooth interchange from and to these other modes of transport. The second function of a terminal is to consolidate traffic. Passengers normally 'interline' or change aircraft, because no convenient direct service exists. Therefore, the airport acts as a hub, a process which exists in most forms of transport and is becoming increasingly common. In this case, aircraft from regional centres feed into a major interchange, maximising the range of through-journey opportunities for passengers and creating higher passenger numbers for carriers.

Control and Communication Systems

For safety reasons, aircraft are subject to air traffic control systems which monitor not only take-off and landing but their movement while airborne. Similarly, railways are subject to control systems, traditionally referred to as 'signal-ling' but usually far more technically advanced than this suggests. It is these systems which make air and rail relatively safe in terms of accidents per passenger-kilometre.

In contrast, we enjoy a right to take a car or other vehicle onto the road system, however busy and congested it is. The purpose of control here is to improve safety and restrict movements once we are there, through traffic lights, roundabouts, speed limits, and so on. Similarly, once out of port ships can generally sail where their owners wish, although rules of navigation dictate how they should move when close to each other, and masters use navigational aids to avoid shallows and other dangers.

At airport or rail terminals, there are usually information screens which not only list arrivals and departures, but also give "real time" information stating when the next or delayed services are expected to arrive. This is possible because those operating the control systems are permanently in contract—through radio and electronically—with the aircraft or trains they monitor and thus know exactly where they are. This is not usually the case with road vehicles, unless they are linked to a tracking system which reports their movements back to a control centre and so on to waiting passengers.

Management and Staff

It is easy to underestimate not just the numbers of personnel involved in a major transport business but also the complexity of management. For example, a company such as GNER, the franchise which operates trains between London, North-East England and Scotland, employs 3,000 to operate its 112 departures per day and carries 14m passengers each year, requires all the usual management functions, such as HR, finance, IT and marketing, in addition to those carrying out specialist operating duties. The following sections now consider different modes or forms of transport.

Road Transport

The Private Car

In most developed countries, the private car is the most popular form of transport for leisure travel. Not only can it reach most destinations easily and luggage can be easily handled, but also car owners can make extra 'marginal' journeys at a low cost which becomes lower still as more people are carried. This popularity and convenience of the car is demonstrated by a survey of visitors to Stratford-on-Avon which found that 66 percent arrived by private car; 17 percent by touring coach; 6 percent by hire car; 5 percent by train, and 6 percent by other means. More generally, over 80 percent of visitors to the English countryside travel by car, a proportion which rises to ninety percent in some national parks.

The car's widespread availability has brought about two major developments within tourism:

The Use of a Family car for Holidays Abroad

There has been a rapid growth in independent overseas travel by private car, although crossing water adds disproportionately to total holiday costs, thus discouraging both island residents from holidaying abroad and those on 'the other side' from coming in. For this reason, together with the attraction of warmer weather, residents of France, Germany and Holland are much more likely to use their car for a holiday on the European mainland than to travel to the United Kingdom.

Car Rental

Because people value the use of a car for mobility at home, but a destination is beyond the possible range for taking one's own, the car hire business has developed rapidly in resort areas. Hire cars are also available at airports and rail terminals for business or leisure use. Some holidays include 'fly-drive' as an integral part of the package, while others offer optional car hire at discounted rates within the resort. Given the rapid growth in car ownership and usage, attention is inevitably focused on the environmental impacts of the car, particularly in more fragile areas.

Many national parks, for example, are developing policies to encourage the use of alternative forms of transport. At the same time, one approach to 'managing' independent car-borne leisure travel by tourism bodies is to designate recommended routes. These can be lengthy stretches of major roads passing through scenically attractive areas, such as the Romantischestrasse and Weinstrasse in Germany, where the object is to persuade travellers to stop and spend in historic towns along the route.

On a more local basis, 'scenic drives' may be promoted along a common theme such as fruit trees in blossom. These are geared more to the 'Sunday afternoon' motorist looking for somewhere to go, and may have the ulterior motive of attracting drivers away from popular destinations and roads which become congested.

Taxis and Private Hire Cars

The role of taxis is, in effect, halfway between private and public transport. Visitors may well use taxis on a casual basis to reach locations where they lack the confidence to use public tansport, whilst they may also find it the easiest way of reaching a city centre from an airport. Equally, a taxi may be an alternative to a hired car to reach an attraction which is not accessible by public transport. Sometimes it is accepted practice, for example when cruise ships call into a port, for visitors to hire a taxi with a driver for the time available; the driver knows the main attractions and takes his passengers for a personalised tour. Taxis are also used by tour operators and their resort representatives for transferring small numbers of visitors between airports and hotels.

Cycling

For the first half of the twentieth century, cycling was one of the commonest forms of transport, used for travel to work, school and leisure alike. While that has continued in some places (notably in some University cities and in Holland), the growth in car ownership has both led to cars replacing cycles for these journeys and made conditions more dangerous and unpleasant for the cyclists remaining.

Nevertheless, cycling has more recently re-emerged as a leisure activity, particularly in the form of 'mountain' bikes. Families often travel by car on holiday or for a day out with cycles fixed to the back or roof of their car to an area where quiet roads or tracks are available, whilst some bus and rail operators adapt vehicles to carry cycles and so offer a public transport alternative. Opportunities for leisure cycling have also increased.

In the UK, for example, the charity Sustrans (Sustainable Transport) is using funds raised from local authorities and others to develop a national network of cycle routes.

The National Cycle Network is a visionary project to provide a 10,000-mile network of cycle routes. Originally launched with a £43.5 million grant from the Millennium Commission, the Network involves the active participation of more than 400 local authorities, the Department of the Environment, Transport and the Regions, and other public and private bodies.

The Network is a linked series of traffic-free paths and traffic-calmed and minor roads connecting urban centres and the countryside, and reaching all parts of the UK. These will provide a safe, attractive, and high quality network for cyclists and a major new amenity for walkers and wheelchair users.

More than 5,000 miles of signed and mapped routes opened in June 2000. Ten thousand miles will be completed by 2005. The Network will connect with hundreds of further extensions. Among the 10,000 km already open, a 'Sea to Sea' route from the Irish to the North Sea has been created and the target is to achieve 17,000 km of track.

The routes are not all in open countryside; it is estimated that over 20 million people will live within 3 km of a point on the network, so it will be possible to use it for local leisure and travel to work or education. Inevitably, some of the network will be in the form of cycle lanes along roads carrying other traffic, but the maximum use is being made of disused routes, such as old rail tracks and canal towpaths.

Scheduled Bus and Coach

Scheduled services are those that run to a fixed timetable and are not subject to cancellation if demand is insufficient. These are the forms of transport normally used least by tourists, but are important for particular locations and purposes:

Long-Distance Leisure Journeys

In the UK, this market is dominated by two organisations, National Express and Scottish Citylink. Both run networks of inter-urban coach services and are, primarily, planning and marketing bodies which charter in coaches to meet their needs from large and small operators across the country.

However, the image of one large organisation is created by a requirement that coaches on long-term contract are of a specified design and painted in a standard colour scheme. Virtually all demand is leisure-oriented in some form and its scale is such that National Express schedules around 700 coaches on an average day, with more on a short-term basis to meet peak demands. Most European countries do not have long-distance coach networks of the same kind because their Governments have preferred to encourage use of their railways, but they are expanding slowly.

Local Services

These are used by tourists principally for short-distance travel within towns and cities; London Transport Marketing (1996) found that about 45 percent of overseas visitors used its buses during their say, while just under 40 percent used taxis. Buses are also used to an extent to reach rural attractions from the bigger accommodation centres. For example, in North Wales a 'Snowdon Sherpa' system of connecting minibuses was originally intended to help solve parking problems at the foot of Snowdon, but has been developed to provide longer distance access from towns such as Liandudno and Portmadoc. In some countries, particularly Switzerland, extensive and high quality rural services are promoted strongly to tourists and are used as an environmentally-friendly alternative to local car hire.

The bus has a fairly captive market among visitors to some islands, the systems in Tenerife, Malta and Majorca all being well used. That in Tenerife (TITSA) is modern and professional, while the Maltese system traditionally uses ancient buses which are almost a working museum and tourist attraction in themselves; however, modernisation is now taking place.

Also included in this category are local sightseeing tours, which are common in larger cities but have also been expanding in smaller historic centres. The London survey mentioned above found these to be used by over 20 percent of overseas visitors. In the UK they commonly use old double deck buses with the roof removed, which have a low purchase price and are a novelty for most visitors.

'Touring' Coaches

These refer to non-scheduled services offered for leisure purposes. At one extreme is the day trip, designed either for the resident population or to take visitors to attractions in the wider area; the latter, of course, are often organised in conjunction with tour operators and sold by resort representatives. Within the resident market, demand has moved away from the traditional seaside resort towards theme parks and locations associated with television series. Major shopping centres and developments can attract large numbers. The Metro Centre near Newcastle can accommodate 370 coaches and receives close to this number in the weeks before Christmas, while the hypermarkets of Calais are popular further south. Other growth sectors have been open-air museums such as Beamish and Ironbridge, where the school trip market is important.

The total value of the market for UK residents taking coach tours (i.e. at least one night away) is estimated at £643m per annum, with a further £396, coming into the UK from overseas groups. Beyond the day trip come weekend and mid-week breaks and extended tours of between seven and fourteen days. These include both more traditional tours and also 'shuttle' operations, where parties are ferried to their accommodation with a minimum of stops, and then return home one or two weeks later.

Structure of the Industry

The road transport industry includes all sizes of operator, with fleets varying from one coach to a thousand or more. However, the bigger fleets, which outside the UK are still often publicily owned, tend to concentrate on local bus work, and in the coach sector small firms predominate, many of whom sell direct by word of mouth, newspapers or through a small number of local agents. The elderly form a large part of the coach tour market, but growth can be achieved provided new customers are attracted; it is an expanding and increasingly prosperous sector of the population.

As coach operators do not normally have the bargaining strength to negotiate attractive rates with hotels and ferry companies, specialist tour wholesalers offer to coach firms a package of accommodation, if necessary with overnight stops, and ferry bookings at reasonable prices expressed as a figure per head (subject to a minimum break-even number). Operators have then only to add coach operating costs and a profit margin to arrive at a selling price for the tour.

Rail Transport

The railways no longer hold the dominant position in leisure passenger transport they enjoyed in the nineteenth and early twentieth centuries. Although demand still exists for rail transport to traditional coastal resorts for day trips and holidays, commuters and business travellers are now more numerous on these routes than holidaymarkers.

However, rail is important in certain niche markets and, where investment in new vehicles and infrastructure takes place, it can increase ridership and market share. Most European systems have developed more commercial approaches which identify distinct styles of operation, and set appropriate targets for them. We shall consider each of these principal sectors in turn and then look at the involvement of the private sector in preserved and narrow-gauge railways.

Inter-City Services

The main characteristic of Inter-City services is that they provide fast, high-quality regular services—often running every hour—between principal centres. Business travellers are an important market and for them first-class coaches are provided with restaurant cars and possibly other services such as computer plug-in points. Fares are relatively high, through a higher charge for First Class, discriminatory pricing on the busiest trains and possibly a premium for travel on Inter-City trains as opposed to others. Not surprisingly, perhaps, Inter-City services are normally the most profitable in a rail system.

Most West European countries have invested heavily in new high-speed rail systems, some running internationally. (e.g. the Thalys service from Paris to Brussels, Cologne and Amsterdam). Maximum speeds of up to 300 kph enable these trains to compete effectively not just with the car but with airlines, and they have taken much of the airlines' previous market share for centre-to-centre traffic. On Inter-City routes as a whole, however, few trains can be filled with business customers alone and other types of customer are encouraged through pricing mechanisms such as Senior and Young Person's Railcards and APEX tickets. Sales to visitors from overseas can also be important, for which most European railways maintain international offices. Unlimited travel tickets (in Britain the Britrail Pass) are also available, but are normally sold only through these offices to avoid their use by domestic customers. For example, many young Americans use the British system to attend the Edinburgh Festival each summer.

Regional Services

These are passenger routes outside the main conurbations that are slower, make more stops and sometimes offer lower standards of comfort. Although it is hard to distinguish precisely, there are two broad categories, which we might call 'Express' and 'the rest'. Express routes are those which come closest to Inter-City in terms of fast services between regional centres, using trains of a high standard with limited catering services; examples are Newcastle-Leeds-Liverpool in the UK and Dusseldorf-Kassel in Germany. These Express routes also come closest to Inter-City in their financial performance, being expected to cover at least their direct operating costs.

The rest are a financial liability to any rail organisation and exist mainly for political and social reasons. They may fit the description 'branch lines' although, in the UK, most such lines were closed in the 1960s; an exception is in Cornwall, where a number of branch lines remain open because of a continuing role in bringing visitors to the area. More commonly, these routes are 50 km or more in length, connecting outlying towns and remote areas to the core system. It is accepted that these lines cannot be profitable and are therefore, subsidised by central or regional Governments.

However, opportunities exist to improve their financial performance because, as rural tourism and interest in outdoor activities has grown, so too has the potential for their use by visitors. Many such lines pass through National Parks and other scenically attractive areas where environmental pressures make it sensible to encourage access by rail rather than by road. The cost structure of railways means that it costs little or nothing to carry additional leisure traffic, and the income can be used almost entirely to reduce losses. Well-planned marketing programmes to increase such patronage are therefore likely to be highly cost-effective.

Urban Services

Urban railways are often operated by local as opposed to nationally-controlled organisations. In much of Europe, new systems are being built and existing ones adapted. For example, in Stuigart and other

German cities the traditional street trams run by city authorities have been modernised and diverted underground in city centres, while the suburban trains of the state railway (DB) also run in tunnels under the centre. Visitors to cities, who often do not have private transport with them, will use local rail services if they are made attractive enough and promoted as an integrated system. In London, 9 percent of all journeys on the Underground system are made by tourists and a survey found that 76 percent of visitors had used the Underground system the previous day. Additionally, nearly 30 percent of all overseas visitors to London used the national rail system at some time during their stay.

Ownership and Control of Railways

Historically, most large railways, like major airlines, have been owned by the state, not only because they are seen as having political or strategic importance, but also because they tend not to be commercially viable. Most railways are still Government-owned, although they may be set more specific commercial targets and be run in a more businesslike way than hitherto.

The international trend to privatisation has not yet affected most rail systems. However, the EU has encouraged member states to separate the provision of *infrastructure* (track, control and stations) from the *operation* of the trains themselves. Some countries are, therefore, setting up track-owning companies or authorities from which train operators 'rent' paths or slots.

The UK Government's decision was firstly to separate the various elements of service provision and then privatise them in turn. An infrastructure company (Railtrack)—recently nationalised by the Government— own all public track (other than that locally run in the major cities), the control systems and some stations. 25 Train Operating Companies (TOCs) pay access charges for use of the system, own the remaining stations, and lease the trains they run from leasing companies. Their income is obtained from fares and Government subsidy. However, the ownership of trains is of little interest to passengers, who seek reliability, reasonable fares and comprehensive and unbiased information. These factors are particularly important to tourists who are unfamiliar with a system, and integrated charging can be important in marketing rail-based travel.

For example, tour operators sell packages based on accommodation together with rail travel, which is periced on a zonal system according to distance from the destination. It would seriously undermine the marketing of these packages if some TOCs excluded their services or charged on a different basis.

Tourist and Private Railways

Although the large, public rail organisations make an important contribution to the movement of tourists, there are also railways which exist purely as tourist attractions or holidays in their own right.

Firstly, it is possible to run privately-owned locomotives (usually steam) over parts of the public rail system; the number of preserved locomotives makes this commonest in the UK. Secondly, the national rail systems can be used for luxurious trains, of which the Venice-Simpton Orient Express (VSOE) is the best known example. Here, privately-owned coaches are hauled by electric locomotives provided by the various national railways.

Alternatively, a private organisation may run a self-contained railway. These normally involve steam locomo-tives and, usually, these are lines which have been closed to conventional traffic, although some were never intended for passenger travel at all. For example, most of the narrow-guage railways in North Wales, collectively promoted as the Great Little Trains of Wales, were built to carry slate from quarries to the sea. The popularity of such lines can be increased by attractive scenery and nearby major tourist attractions. The Keighley and Worth Valley Railway in West Yorkshire, for instance, has its headquarters at Haworth where visitors to the Bronte literary associations are numbered in hundreds of thousands.

The appeal of these preserved railways which are open throughout a season must be to a mass market where they compete with totally different attractions. However, although they must meet the same safety standards as a 'public' line, which involves considerable expense, they are helped by only having to run when they judge the market demands it and by the use of volunteers to carry out driving, manual and clerical work.

The Channel Tunnel and Eurostar

The Channel Tunnel between Folkestone in Kent (UK) and Coquelles near Calais (France) opened in May, 1994. It is a rail tunnel through which two distinct types of passenger service operate – the Shuttle and Eurostar. The Shuttle service is designed to carry cars, coaches and goods vehicles with their drivers and passengers, and operates only between terminals at either end of the tunnel. It competes directly with cross-Channel ferries, particularly those between Dover and Calais, but its effect has also been felt on the longer crossings north and west of the Straits of Dover. In 2000, the Shuttle carried 2.8m cars and 79,000 coaches.

Conversely, Eurostar is a high-speed Inter-City service which operates principally from London to Brussels and Paris. Jointly owned by the National Express Group and British Airways in the UK, and by the Belgian and French state railways, its scheduled time of 3 hours from London to Paris and 2 hours 40 minutes to Brussels makes it particularly attractive to business travellers between city centres.

By 2000, Air France had lost 60 percent of its Paris-London market to Eurostar, which carried a total of 7.1m passengers in that year. However, competition between Eurostar and the airlines has succeeded in expanding the total market.

Between Folkestone and London, Eurostar trains currently run over the slow and congested tracks also used by local commuter trains. A fast Rail Link to continental standards is under construction, the first section of which should be completed in 2003, with the more difficult London section to follow in 2007. This will further improve journey time and reliability, so increasing the threat to the airlines.

Shipping

Much of Britain's growth as an industrial nation and as the centre of an empire was connected with its shipping industry. In the Victoria era, large companies such as Cunard and P&O emerged, involved in the transport of goods to and from overseas centres and the movement of emigrants and business people. However, while cargo shipping still exists in a modern, mainly containerised, form, the greater speed of aircraft made it impossible from the 1950s onwards for ships to compete for passengers, and this business has largely disappeared. Shipping is now important to tourism in three forms:

Local Ferries

These operate principally inland on lakes but also over short distances along coastlines and in long inlets, such as the Norwegian fjords. These features often occur in mountainous areas which are attractive for tourism, and the lakes are part of the scenery that is marketed. Such terrain often makes overland travel difficult and it can be much quicker to travel from one side of a lake to the other by water than round the edge (for example from the French southern side of Lake Geneva to Lausanne in Switzerland on the northern bank). Similarly, it is an easier journey by water from one resort to another along the Italian Riviera than on land by road. Thus, ferries may form part of a local transport network for residents, but use by tourists is likely to predominate.

Such ferries have been a feature of the English Lake District since late Victorian times. The Furness Railway, wishing to reach the heart of the Lakes at Bowness and Ambleside, built a branch from its main line to the southern tip of Windermere at Lakeside, where a terminal and an imposing hotel were built, and its passengers could then travel by steamer along the lake. Today, the Lakeside and Haverthwaite Railway runs steam trains along the northern part of the line, connecting with the ships of Windermere Lake Cruises. The fact that original craft are still in use is one of the attractions, and in this way visitors are offered a package of travel by vintage train and ship.

Sea-going Ferries

These are distinguished by typically longer crossing times and, particularly with islands, their history is much more of necessity as opposed to leisure.

Traditionally, people wishing to travel from Britain to Europe or from Ireland to the UK mainland reached the port by train. Crossed by ferry and continued by rail on the other side. Nowadays, however, the majority of passengers travel with vehicles which are also carried on the ferry these being known as 'Roll-on/Roll-off or 'RoRo' ferries. Domestic routes, such as those to Ireland and the Scottish islands, continue to be important. Just under a million cars and many foot passengers travel by sea to or from Ireland every year, while the Scottish services, operated by Caledonian Macbrayne (West Coast) and P&O (Orkney and Shetland), in addition to being 'lifelines', have also become involved in tourism travel. Between them they carry about 250,000 cars annually.

Holidays involving taking the family car, and some-times a caravan, to or from the European mainland enjoyed steady growth for many years and packages were developed, including ferry crossings and either fixed bookings or a series of "go-as-you-please" hotel vouchers. In recent years, however, the ferry companies have experienced increasing difficulties. Over a ten year period, traffic on the Straits of Dover and English Channel routes began to fall in 1995, while on the North Sea the decline began earlier in 1993 (although a recovery can be seen from 1998 onwards). The Principal cause of this was the opening of the Channel Tunnel, where the shuttle service between Folke-stone and Calais takes 35 minutes compares with at least 75 minutes by ferry. By mid-1996, the Shuttle was estimated to have around 45 percent of traffic across the Straits of Dover, equivalent to the combined business of the two largest ferry companies, and the over-capacity led to fierce price competition, particularly at off-peak times. Thus, although the total market continued to increase, ferry turnover fell, a problem aggravated in 1999 by the ending of duty-free sales within the EU.

Cruises

Like ferries, cruising has a long history. Developed from the luxurious liners that sailed across the Atlantic and so far-flung colonies, cruise ships traditionally had an image of being expensive and oriented towards rich, elderly passengers.

The strength of cruising is that it combines the opportunity to 'sample' a variety of destinations with an elegant lifestyle, with the added benefit that the accommodation travels to the destination. The main disadvantage is that, due to the labour costs of providing high standards of service, cruising is expensive. For example, the average price of cruise holidays bought in the UK in 1995 was an estimated £1,049.

Sometimes, cruises may depart from and return to tourists' home country but, since most cruise destinations are a substantial distance from customers' homes, it is often impractical to sail from the country of origin. As a result, the 'fly-cruise' has become increasingly popular accounting for around 70 percent of the UK cruise market. Not only to customers can fly to join the ship at a suitable point, but also the cruise is able to consolidate passengers of different nationalities and so maximise carryings. For example, the world's largest cruise market is the USA and its principal cruising area the Caribbean; most cruises start at or near Miami, which both American and European customers can reach quickly by air.

In recent years, the traditional image of cruising as an expensive form of travel for more elderly customers has been addressed by cruise operators. The Caribbean, for example, has become an attractive destination for the young, partly due to the water-sports opportunities offered and partly by changing the style of shipboard activity towards the gym and swimming pool, and by moving towards healthier food. At the same time, the problem of high costs have also tackled by introducing short 'mini-cruises' at a low cost and hoping customers will then trade up and by reducing levels of service, including food (although in surveys, high standards of food and drink are highly rated). Moreover, tour operators have increasingly featured cruises in their brochure range, normally by selling the products of an existing operator. Airtours took this a stage further in 1995 by introducing cruises under their own name, targeted at the market in which the company already traded. As a result of these changes, UK sales of cruises increased from 30 1,900 in 1994 to 740,000 in 2000; as new destinations were brought on stream, the Caribbean lost some of its dominant position but still accounted for 41 percent of UK sales in 1999 (Coulson 2001).

For destinations, cruise ships do not always represent a suitable form of tourism. Cruise passengers tend to buy relatively little on shore, whilst the arrival of a cruise ship with 1,500 passengers can put enormous strains on local facilities. Thus, some Caribbean islands having developed an exclusive image for a small but wealthy market, fear that cruise business may lead to environmental damage and loss of this clientele. At least one island has withdrawn facilities for berthing cruise ships and, as shipping companies introduce new ships able to carry up to 6,000 passengers in their pursuit of economies of scale, this is likely to increase if indeed ports are able to accommodate vessels of this size.

Air Transport

Air travel is the means of transport most associated with the tourism industry, since it is a fundamental element of the mass package tour. This perception is confirmed by figures showing the number of UK residents leaving the UK by the three alternatives of air, sea and the Channel Tunnel. The figures also demonstrate that, while business travel and visiting friends and relatives (VFR) are important, holidays are the predominant reason for travel by all the modes. However, the UK aviation market is small by comparison with that of the USA, as can be seen by comparing passenger numbers passing through major airports and carried by the largest airlines.

Only a small proportion of its passengers fly internationally. British Airways, though eleventh in terms of total passengers carried, has the highest figures for *international* passengers and passenger kilometers. Similarly Heathrow, with 54.8 million international and 7.1 million domestic passengers in 1999, has the world's highest number of international users.

The USA's dominance can be explained by its advanced economy and its large geographical area, which not only contains a large population but creates a greater market for domestic travel within the country. The relatively high cost of air travel and the need to site airports at some distance from city centres mean that the greater speed of aircraft only becomes an asset above a certain distance, usually about 500km. Below this rail, and sometimes car, can achieve comparable centre-to-centre time, the exception being where water forms a barrier. This is why, until the Channel Tunnel was opened, air had a near-monopoly of business travel over the fairly short distances between London and Brussels or Paris.

Of the 151 million passengers who passed through British airports in 1999, 133.5 million were making international journeys and only 17.5 million domestic. The latter market comprises principally:

- Journeys linking cities over the magic distance where air becomes advantageous (e.g., London-Giasgow).
- Services to offshore islands as in Scotland, Northern Ireland and the Channel Islands.
- Interlining, where passengers transfer to or from an international flight.

Scheduled and Charter Aviation

The air passenger market can be divided in principle between scheduled traffic, where seats are purchased individually, and charter, where blocks of seats or the entire capacity of an aircraft, perhaps for a season, is sold to an intermediary. Most charter operations are in the form of Inclusive Tour Charters (ITCs), and it is the growth of these which made the European package holiday available to a mass market. More recently, long-haul destinations have been included in charter operations.

Charter operators achieve a much lower seat cost than the conventional scheduled flight, for a number of reasons:

- They usually fit more seats into a given type of aircraft than would a scheduled airline; a Boeing 757 would typically seat 180 for British Airways but 228 in charter use. The extra space is an important selling point to scheduled passengers, so it is difficult for the same aircraft to be used for a mix of scheduled and charter flights.
- The charter operator achieves a greater number of flying hours per day from its aeroplanes. The Managing Director of Monarch Airlines, claiming 11.7 flying hours per day compared with 6.8 hours at British Airways, commented:

By a combination of differential pricing and clever marketing by the tour operators, charter airlines are able to sell capacity at times of day that are unthinkable for scheduled carriers and thus achieve very high levels of utilisation.

For example flight plan for a Boeing 757 of Britannia Airways as it was scheduled to operate on Fridays during summer 1997:

- Whereas the scheduled airline may assume a relatively low load factor (i.e., percentage of seats filled), the charter operator assumes that 95 percent or more of seats will be filled. Furthermore, if this seems unlikely to be achieved, the operator will 'consolidate' groups of customers from different flights in a single departure. This results in the last-minute changes to flight arrangements that are unpopular with customers but keep costs down to the price they are willing to pay. The scheduled airline's lower load results from the fact that it must fly at scheduled times, irrespective of demand. Conversely, the charter operator flies only when the break-even load factor (typically 95 percent) has been achieved.
- Charter airlines are usually much smaller then scheduled airlines, which are often national 'flag-carriers' and in many cases state-owned, and therefore have relatively lower administrative costs. In particular, because the charter airline sells its seats in blocks to a few customers, its marketing costs are much lower. For example, Monarch Airlines claimed an advertising budget of £10,000 in relation to a turnover of £111 million, and that its only other marketing costs were the salaries of a sales director, three salesmen and a typist-altogether no more than 0.2 percent of turnover. Conversely, British Airways' 2000 turnover of £8,940m was much greater, but its 'selling costs' were 13 percent of this figure, mainly as a result of agent commissions and its reservation system.
- They normally offer a lower standard of in-flight catering and, unlike many scheduled operators, charge for all drinks and other services, such as the use of headphones.
- They generally use smaller and regional airports, where handling and landing charges are lower than at the major international airports.

Despite the low prices achieved by charter operators, under certain circumstances scheduled operators also serve the ITC market. For example, blocks of seats on scheduled flights are commonly sold at discounted prices to tour operators willing to pay above the charter rate (for example, fly-cruise customers), whilst some tour operators offer destinations where demand cannot justify charter flights and, therefore, there is no option but to buy scheduled capacity. Some scheduled airlines also mount their own holiday programmes using existing flights, and switch aircraft which fly business routes during the week to serve holiday destinations at weekends.

Conversely, some charter airlines, knowing they will have spare capacity on particular flights, now sell 'seat-only' tickets, but their development has been limited. Despite the demand for cheap individual bookings to holiday destinations, charter operators sometimes feel it is not worth the cost of setting up the necessary distribution system, whilst countries wishing to protect their scheduled airlines discourage 'seat-only' sales through their regulatory system.

'No-frills' Airlines

Perhaps the most significant recent development within Europe has been the growth of 'no-frills', or low-cost scheduled airlines such as Buzz, EasyJet, Go and Ryanair. This has been made possible by the relaxation of regulatory controls within the EU, but what distinguishes these airlines is the adoption of the same cost-cutting practices as charter airlines. There are variations in their systems, but generally:

- They use Internet or telesales bookings, thereby avoiding commissions to agents.
- They aim for high utilisation of aircraft through a long operational day and short turnrounds (20 minutes in the case of Ryanair). This is facilitated by carrying no cargo and limited catering.
- If catering is provided at all, it is basic and charged for, leading to a smaller cabin crew requirement.
- Regional airports are used, where low handling charges are negotiated.
- Aircraft have a high seating density similar to charter airlines.
- Tickets are only sold for single sectors, eliminating complex financial reconciliation, handling of baggage and transfers at connecting airports.

Although the 'no-frills' airlines carry out extensive promotion of very low lead-in fares, they also charge at levels closer to their established rivals—but still good value—at peak times and when demand enables them to. Thus, while in April, 2001 it was possible to fly with Ryanair from Stansted to Frankfurt/Hahn for £7 each way (plus airport departure tax), a flight to Ancona on a summer weekend in July, 2001 was priced at £77 each way.

Currently, these airlines hold no more than a 6 percent share of the total scheduled market within Europe, and not all are trading profitably. However, the leading operators are introducing new routes and expanding capacity at rates exceeding 20 percent per annum and it is clear that a large market is awaiting the opportunity of low-cost European travel.

Regulation in Transport

Regulations is important because it has a major effect on the price, availability and quality of transport services for tourism.

Forms of Regulation

Traditionally two types have been recognised:

Safety or Quality Controls

External safety control, such as the high standards of maintenance and operating procedures required with aircraft, is generally accepted as socially beneficial and, therefore, this form of regulation generally attracts controversy only when it is shown to be absent. For example, the sinking of SS Titanic in 1912 led to regulation ensuring that every ship carries sufficient lifeboats for all its passengers. Quality controls include the professional qualifications of ships' masters, airline pilots and coach drivers, their working hours and the mechanical condition of the equipment they use.

Quantity Controls

These may restrict entry to a route, the timetable offered or fares charged and are, therefore, far more controversial. Where deregulation has occurred in recent years, as in the US domestic air market and the British bus and coach industries, it is primarily the removal of quantity controls that has taken place. In recent years, regulation has been imposed for further reasons—consumer protection and environmental reasons. Operators of air-based holidays are required to hold an Air Travel Organiser's Licence (ATOL), which is issued by the Civil Aviation Authority (CAA) in return for a financial bond. The purpose is to protect customers against the risk of either losing holidays they have paid for or of being stranded at the destination.

All such organisers must display an ATOL number and logo in their publicity. Scheduled airlines carrying inclusive tour passengers and coach tour operators are now also subject to bonding.

The prime example of environmental controls is where limits are placed on night movements of aircraft at airports in the interest of local residents. Coach operators can also experience restrictions on the routes they use in areas congested by high levels of tourist traffic.

Who are the Regulators?

The task of regulation is carried out partly by public bodies and partly by private or industry-based organisations, although often to meet a Government's wishes.

In the UK, Government bodies include the CAA, which exercises both 'quantity' and 'quality' control over British air carriers, is responsible for the Air Traffic Control system and operates a number of airports. Traffic Commissioners issue Operators' Licences (now issued according to safety criteria only) to bus and coach operators, and monitor their behaviour.

Local councils control the issue of licences to taxi operators and, through powers to subsidise, can secure the availability of tourist-oriented bus and rail services.

Governments also support international bodies, among which is the International Civil Aviation Organisation (ICAO), a United Nations body which is mainly concerned with the technical side of air operations. In particular, it is concerned with the improvement of technical standards and with helping developing countries to bring their facilities to international standards.

Similarly, following marine disasters such as the loss of the 'Herald of Free Enterprise' at Zeebrugge in 1987, the International Marine Organisation (IMO) has been studying the design of RoRo ferries, and new requirements of bulkheads to divide up vehicle decks are being brought into effect.

ICAO works closely with the International Air Transport Association (IATA), a trade organisation representing most international airlines. IATA is concerned with technical matters (hence its liasion with ICAO), and also provides financial and legal services for its members.

However, it is best known as the body which still decides many of the fares charged by international airlines, a task which is delegated to it by individual Governments.

Regulation in International Air Transport

While control of domestic air routes is determined by the individual state, the international industry requires regulation at various levels. Indeed, whether a route between two states should exist at all is, firstly, a political decision made by the Governments concerned rather than the airlines. This is known as a *bilateral agreement* and specifies the number of airlines that are to operate the service. It is normally either 'dual designation', in which case only two airlines may operate (usually one from each country), or 'multiple designation', which allows a number of airlines to fly the route. The agreement sometimes specifies that the fixing of detailed times and fares should be delegated to IATA, subject to Government confirmation. It also specifies which of a number of possible 'freedoms' apply. These 'freedoms' grant the airlines of one country the following rights:

- 1st the freedom to fly over another country's territory without landing.
- 2nd the freedom to land for technical, non-traffic reasons, such as refuelling.
- 3rd the freedom to set down passengers, mail and freight taken on in the airline's the home country.
- 4th the freedom to pick up passengers, mail and freight destined for the home country of the airline.
- 5th the freedom to start flights in the home country (A), pick up passengers, mail and freight in country (B) and convey to country (C). An example of this 5th Freedom would be an American airline operating New York-London-Frankfurt which was permitted to carry London-Frankfurt traffic.
- 6th the freedom to start in country (A), and operate via the home country (B) to country (C). Here an example would be a route operated by the Chinese airline Cathay Pacific from Bangkok through its base at Hong Kong and on to Tokyo in Japan.

The granting of the first and second freedoms is nor-mally automatic. The third and fourth are negotiable, although possession of these freedoms forms the basis of most international services. The 5th and 6th freedoms are less commonly agreed although the deregulation of air services within Europe should in principle mean that all European airlines now enjoy all of these freedoms. An airline wishing to take advantage of a bilateral agreement must next satisfy the licensing requirements of each state involved. This is normally a formally but gives the 'host' country an opportunity to ensure that visiting airlines meet its own quality standards. Similarly, the aspiring airline must meet its own state's requirements, partly on a quality basis but also to be recognised as a party to the bilateral agreement relevant to its intended destination.

The above applies to scheduled routes, but it cannot be assumed that a free market exists in the charter business, about which each state makes its own policy decision.

Quality controls still exist to the same standards and in the USA, for example, where quantity controls are absent following deregulation of the domestic industry in the 1970s, there appears little need for a charter industry. On the other hand, most European countries favour charter flights as encouraging the growth of tourism whilst, until recently, Australia discouraged them, thereby delaying the growth of long-haul holidays.

Regulation within Europe

Despite the existence since 1993 of a Single European Market within the EU, the aviation industry is still strongly oriented to individual states. In 1992 the EU agreed its 'Third Aviation Package', which was a complex series of liberalisation measures. However, the most important points may be summarised as follows:

- In general, Governments can no longer control the fares charged by airlines.
- The bilateral agreements between EU member states are replaced by the freedom for airlines based in one state to fly between any of them. Not only can an airline fly any route from its home state to another EU state, but it can fly between two others; for example, the Irish-registered Ryanair flies between the UK and Germany. This is sometimes referred to as the 7th freedom.
- An EU-based airline can now also fly internally within another member state. For example, Lufthansa could operate on the Paris-Nice route. This is known as 'cabotage' or the 8th Freedom.

However, it must be remembered that at least one of most city-pairs served by airline routes lies outside both the USA and the EU, where most deregulation/liberalisation has occurred. In these cases, bilateral agreements normally still have dual designation and the route can be served only by the two partners' national airlines.

Strategic Alliances

The nationally or place of ownership of an airline is important in determining where it is permitted to fly. In the past this was not a problem, because most international routes were 'dual designation' with access limited to the national (and usually state-owned) airlines of the destination countries. Now that other airlines are permitted to compete on these routes, and that they are increasingly owned by the private sector, the issue of nationality becomes, important. That is, if an airline, through changes in shareholdings, loses its national status it also loses the right to operate on routes based in its 'home' country. Aviation, like most industries, is becoming global and economies of scale are identified from having worldwide coverage. However, the obvious approach of mergers between airlines may be closed to them because of their effect on national status. Airlines have, therefore, taken the alternative approach of forming strategic or marketing alliances designed to achieve the benefits of scale without losing national identity. There is no rigid formula but the following are common features:

- Cross-shareholdings at a level below 50 percent.
- Collaboration in maintenance of aircraft and stocking of spare parts.
- Mutual provision of handling services at "home" airports.
- Code-sharing, that is, the attachment of the flight code of one partner to the operation of another. For example, a KLM flight from Amsterdam to Berlin may also be listed with a flight number of its American partner North West Airlines. This is to encourage a concept of through or connecting flights and to give a stronger presence on computer reservation screens.
- Jointly-planned scheduling to optimise connections at hub airports and maximise utilisation of aircraft.
- Inter-availability of tickets, standardised pricing and common reservation systems.
- Shared Frequent Flyer programmes, encouraging brand loyalty among customers.

Cost Structures, Capacity and Utilisation

Fixed and Variable Costs

Like any business, transport experiences a mixture of fixed, variable and semi-variable costs. Similarly, what the economist calls 'joint costs' are experienced, the most important of which is that at some time a vehicle will probably have to return to the place where it began its journey. Therefore, the cost to a carrier of operating a journey must include coming back, and purely one-way traffic must pay exceptionally well if it is to be. This does not necessarily mean returning directly; airlines, for example, often perfect are known as 'W formations' where routes are linked together, either to give good or to serve destinations where the airline lacks back-up resources.

The incidence of fixed and variable costs determines what marginal costs will be, that is, the cost of providing an additional unit of capacity or the saving from removing a unit. Transport's units of production come in 'lumps' of fixed sizes; if a coach tour operator runs only 50-seat coaches, the minimum that can be added to or removed from an operation is this number. Marginal costs can be very low or very high.

The cost to the operator of an additional passenger on a train or plane which has empty seats is minimal; in the case of the train it is literally the carboard in the ticket, while an airline must pay airport handling charges for each passenger and provide meals, but other cost changes are negligible. However, the point is eventually reached where no capacity remains and the marginal cost of the next passenger is then extremely high.

The significance of marginal costs varies between the modes of transport. Variable costs have traditionally formed a much greater proportion of total costs in road transport than rail, because rail provides its own track which must be paid for regardless of the level of use. Road users, on the other hand, pay for their track through taxation, which (especially fuel tax) varies directly with use. Variable costs are also high for airlines because of the high fuel consumption of aircraft. These differences are important because they affect the benefit to the operator from increasing or reducing the level of service.

Utilisation and Load Factors

We have already noted that one of the ways in which charter and 'no-frills' airlines are able to keep costs down is by maximising utilisation of their aircraft. This is because the high fixed costs remain the same regardless of distance or sectors covered; the fixed cost per flight or per passenger falls as it is spread over a greater number. Similarly, we have seen that total cost varies little with the number of passengers being carried and that costs are at their lowest per head when the load factor is maximised. It is therefore in operators' interest:

- To maximise the distance operated in service.
- Given fixed vehicle capacities, to maximise *use* of that capacity profitably in terms of the number of passengers being carried. Thus, it is usually not in operators' interest to create more capacity if it will remain partly unused.

Contributory Revenue

When assessing the financial performance of a route, it should not necessarily be considered in isolation. Frequently, one part of a transport system feeds another, passengers transferring from a local to a long-distance service at an interchange point. If the local service, such as a rail branch line, is deemed to be uneconomic and closed, passengers using it for access to Inter-City routes will not necessarily make their own way to the railhead and many are likely to use cars for the whole journey. Thus, if the capacity of the Inter-City service remains the same, the seat stays empty and the fare income (much more than that for the local service) is lost. For this reason, it is worth looking at the contributory element in a loss-making service, since it could well be worth retaining as a 'loss leader' for the commercial route. Many airlines' domestic routes are loss-making in themselves but are retained because they feed traffic, which might otherwise be lost to a competitor, to profitable international routes.

Industry Performance and Marketing

The glamour associated with air travel and the enormous investment in aircraft and airports may suggest that aviation is highly profitable but, in general, this is not so. Scheduled airlines rarely achieve significant profits, and no large rail system is commercially viable. The challenge for these businesses, therefore, is to improve their load factors to nearer the levels of charter airlines. However, whilst this could easily be done by filling seats at low fares, it does not necessarily maximise revenues; for example, business travellers on airlines making last-minute journeys and willing to pay & hire fare may find their chosen flight is full. The answer lies in yield management.

Reference has already been made to transport capacity being in 'lumps' of fixed sizes. The problem for operators in filling that capacity is that, with a few exceptions, demand for their product is 'derived'—it is not wanted as an end in itself but as a means to something else. People fly to Spain to acquire a suntan and, therefore, want a flight in August and not February. The carrier thus experiences peaks in demand which hinder attempts to secure full utilisation of capacity and which may mean that some equipment is not in use for part of the day or year.

Operators must first ensure that the costs of any under-used equipment are correctly allocated and fully recovered, probably in the form of peak premium charges. However, action can also be taken to minimise the effect of the peak. Some of this action may be operational, for example, by leasing extra vehicles for peak requirements, but the price mechanism can help towards this objective too, both by persuading some peak customers to switch and by generating new business outside the peak.

Provided again that costing is accurate and fixed costs are allocated to the peak operations, lower but still profitable prices can be offered for this new business because only the marginal variable and semi-variable costs, plus ideally some contribution to fixed costs, need be recovered.

Elasticity of Demand

Use of the price mechanism to influence patronage levels presumes that the public will in fact respond—what economists call 'price-elastic' demand. However, a number of hurdles must be overcome by the transport operator. Firstly, elasticity of demand can relate to factors other than price, in particular quality of service issues. Therefore there are limits to the extent to which price alone will affect patronage.

Secondly, it is important not to be too successful. Low prices which result in demand exceeding supply will bring a call for extra resources with a high marginal cost that would not be recovered. Finally, every operator has its existing customers who are paying the full price. It is vital not to allow these to 'trade down' to lower prices, a process known as revenue dillution, and so some kind of barrier or distinction must be created between the high-and low-price products in order to retain high-price traffic. This is the explanation of many of the restrictive conditions attached to reduced fares, which will now be examined.

Product Differentiation and Price Discrimination

Transport operators have long practiced branding in the form of separate First and Second Class or Economy provision, Pullman cars and so on. These maximised revenue by ensuring that customers willing to pay a higher price did so, and the revenue is secured by a providing higher quality in some way—more comfortable and guaranteed seats, availability of meals, a quiet atmosphere for working, and so on. Much more widespread than in the past, however, is the carriage of passengers in the same facilities at widely diffe-ring prices, where barriers of an invisible kind are erected.

The best illustration of this are the rules conventionally attached to airlines' APEX fares, which are sometimes as low as 30 percent of Economy. These are subject to a limited number of seats on particular flights, often around midday when demand is low, a minimum advance booking period of 14 days, which is unsuitable for urgent business trips; a 'no refund or cancellation' condition; and, a rule that a Saturday night must fall between the outward and return journeys, which conflicts with the business traveller's normal desire to be home for the weekend but is acceptable to leisure travellers.

These all minimise the 'dilution' of revenue from the valued business market but, as the number of reduced price offers has increased, can lead to a situation where passengers seated alongside pay fares varying by up to 300 percent. Airlines have therefore developed a 'business' or 'Club' class for those paying the full Economy fare, creating a separate cabin with better meals and other privileges. In turn, this has undermined the need for First Class and most airlines have now abolished it within Europe.

However, the operator's objective is to maximise not just seats filled but revenue, and both can be achieved by skillful use of market intelligence and sales data. Just as a tour operator observes sales carefully before deciding when and how far to discount, an airline can decide when, where and how many APEX seats to release. Thus, the ratio can vary not just between flights but day by day, the process aided by equipping aircraft with moveable screens and curtains to adjust the balance between Business and discounted passengers. Information from Computer Reservation Systems assists airlines in making these decisions, and load factors can be further improved by the use of Standby tickets, which are only validated close to the time of departure and when seats have not been filled by other means.

Seat Reservations and Overbooking

Air passengers assume that when a booking is confirmed a seat is assured, but this is not necessarily the case. Full-price scheduled tickets have a refund facility which airlines are anxious to retain for fear of upsetting high-fare regular business travellers. These, uncertain when they will be able to travel, sometimes buy several tickets in the knowledge that they can obtain a refund on those not used. The loss resulting from 'no-shows' can be considerable, so a practice has developed of systematic overbooking, whereby levels of 'no-shows' are established from records and a flight for which 5 percent of passengers typically fail to report might be overbooked by 3 percent. Sometimes the gamble fails and passengers with valid tickets find there is no room. On long-haul flights, it may be possible to upgrade some to First, while others are encouraged or obliged, with a variety of inducements, to transfer to other flights. The European Union has introduced a Regulation fixing levels of compensation for overbooked passengers and setting priorities in selection.

Environmental Impacts of Transport

All tourism activities have their damaging effects on the local and wider community, but transport has some of the most visible and severe of these. Few would consider airports and their surroundings physically attractive, air pollution levels are normally high, and the route to resorts is often littered with the ugly but necessary support business on which mass tourism depends. Even in the resort itself, we may notice large areas taken up by car parking both on and off the street, the smell of vehicle exhausts and nose-to-tail traffic at busy times. There are also the less obvious consequences, such as climate change.

Ample evidence exists of people's concern at these problems. For example, a survey of residents' attitudes to tourism in Stratford-on-Avon confirmed that traffic congestion, parking problems and general environmental damage were seen as disadvantages of the town's tourism business. 88 percent of residents believed that traffic congestion needed to be relieved, but there was not the same consensus on how to achieve it! As car ownership grows, both visitors and residents find it more difficult to imagine a lifestyle without it, while business in host areas consider car-borne trade vital to their prosperity. As a result, people's desire for action in general is contradicted by a wish that it should not affect them personally.

Nevertheless, attitudes may be changing slowly. A view has emerged in Europe that, rather than restrictions on car use deterring visitors, *too much* traffic can be a deterrent. Switzerland has a group of car-free villages which promote themselves jointly on that strength, and they have experienced growth in their share of the tourism market. An economic as well as an environmental case therefore exists for promoting sustainable forms of transport. Also, it is easy to forget that not everybody owns a car. Ownership rates vary widely between countries and regions but, even in prosperous areas, 10-15 percent of households may have no car, a figure which rises to over 50 percent in cities. Therefore, a resort or business which limits itself to car access ignores a substantial part of the market whilst, at some attractions, scarce land has to be devoted to car parking which, if visitors arrived by other means, could be put to more productive use.

A number of approaches to environmentally-friendlier transport are possible. Greater use of walking, horse-riding and cycling can be encouraged by the development of specialised routes. Local traffic management and restriction schemes can be implemented, but these tend to have no effect on the total number of cars coming into an area. The signing necessary to advise motorists of a restriction can itself be visually intrusive, but perhaps the biggest problem is the likely objections from businesses and residents.

An alternative approach is to encourage use of public transport, either for the 'trunk' journey to the holiday area or for local journeys within it. However, car-owners take their motorised lifestyle for granted and find the alternative inconvenient, probably expensive and unsuited to their image, and many projects have failed to achieve their objectives. As a minimum, in order to attract car users public transport must offer high quality in its operation and promotion, have reasonable and simple integrated pricing, appear 'seamless' and create an impression of user-friendliness. It helps if it can be sold as an attraction in itself, for example through the use of vintage equipment. Even this may not be enough and, therefore, to achieve any significant transfer from cars, it may be necessary to introduce traffic restrictions alongside. Here, here the pill can be sweetened with assurances that funding is committed to a high-quality alternative.

Two kinds of location lend themselves particularly to intervention of the kind described, namely, historic towns and protected rural areas, such as National Parks. In both cases, visitors are attracted by the traditional and 'heritage' aspects. Thus, conventional approaches to traffic planning, involving the widening of roads, demolition of buildings and construction of car parks, would remove the essential attraction of the visit and so threaten visitor numbers. As a result, many historic town centres are now pedestrianised, and the removal of traffic to achieve this is often by a Park and Ride scheme which allows car users to park on the outskirts and use a dedicated bus (occasionally a train) to the centre.

National Park areas have found it more difficult to achieve progress, but the Lake District, for example, is currently developing a 'Strategic Gateway' west of Kendal. This will seek to intercept car traffic approaching the congested centre of the National Park by providing a Park and Ride facility on its outskirts.

Marketing for Tourism

The complexity of the many different organisations and industries which provide services and products for visitors or travellers of all types. This mixed bag of service providers is often termed 'the travel and tourism industry' or 'the tourism industry', despite the fact that it encompasses many different classifications of industry and organisation, and serves many different consumer groups. This chapter will, therefore, refer to other industries, such as accommodation and tour operations, as 'sectors' within the more global definition 'tourism industry'. Hotels, restaurants, tour guides, tour operators, tourist boards and other businesses or organisations involved in tourism often act cohesively in order to market their products and services more effectively. Indeed, many of the major tourism marketing events, as well as more general promotional activity, are undertaken jointly by tourism organisations, such events or activities including tourist board promotions; overseas trade missions (for example, those undertaken by the British Tourist Authority); trade shows, such as the The World Travel Market, and joint advertising.

As Seaton (1996) observes, those business defined under the 'tourism industry' banner are able to achieve greater visibility by acting cohesively together, although in subsuming them under one label, we ignore the fact that there are few common denominators aside from their provision of services for tourists or local visitors.

From the outset, therefore, it should be recognised that each industry involved in the activity of promoting tourism has slightly differing characteristics and approaches to marketing. Assistance in understanding these differences can be found in texts which examine the subject of marketing in more detail. However, it is beyond the scope of this chapter to examine these differences in depth and, therefore, further reading on distinct areas are suggested at the end of this chapter.

Definitions of Marketing

Firstly, it is important to define what is meant by the term marketing, for to do so helps to clarify its overal purpose as well as presenting a more holistic picture of the marketing process. The Chartered Institute of Marketing, a professional and awarding body for practioners in marketing, defines it as follows:

- *Marketing is the management process responsible for identifying, anticipating and satisfying customer requirements profitably.*

This statement has a number of important indicators as to the scope, purpose and process of marketing. Firstly, a business must identify for whom it is designing products and services, and it must anticipate the needs and wants of both existing and potential and consumers. Assuming that these needs and wants of consumers have been forecast correctly and that a product has been designed to suit them, the business should then focus on satisfying their needs successfully satisfy so that they will want to return and give the company more business. More simplistically, therefore, marketing can also be described as providing the right product, at the right place and the right time.

The central focus of marketing, then, is the consumer. In other words, the popular notion that marketing is to do with advertising and promotion, or that it is really selling in disguise, oversimplifies the total process. In reality, marketing is a broader, logical process consisting of many activities which are central to satisfying the consumer and ensuring the future prosperity of the organisation.

Marketing Activities

Marketing involves not just the department or function responsible for marketing activity but whole organisation, and marketing planning takes the form of both strategic and operational (or tactical) planning. Whilst the operational plan for any business or organisation usually covers a period of approximately one year, the strategic plan covers a longer time scale, generally three to five years. However, a particular feature of some sectors of the tourism industry where competition is most intense, for instance tour operating, is the emphasis on tactical planning-it could be argued that the dynamic nature of the business renders longer-term strategic planning an almost impossible task.

Therefore, this chapter will concentrate on the marketing activities which are considered to be primarily operational or tactical. Nevertheless, this specific focus helps to highlight and explain the preliminary and formalised planning processes that most market oriented companies undertake. McDonald explains the relationship between the two planning (operational and strategic) stages as follows:

- *A written strategic marketing plan is the backcloth against which operational decisions are taken on an ongoing basis (McDonald 1995).*

The former part of the planning process, therefore, involves preparing for strategic planning-a simple explanation of this process is that it explains 'where we are now' as an organisation and 'where we want to be' at a point in the future. This chapter is more concerned with the processes which follow strategic planning and the techniques which marketing can employ to determine 'how' the organisation's objectives can be achieved, or how it can get to where it wants to be.

The activities associated with longer-term strategic planning and operational planning are fully outlined in McDonald (1995). However, the key activities in marketing are summarised in the following sections.

Situation Analysis—External and Internal Audit

Situation analysis involves research into both the company's external operating environment and its own structures, processes, aims and objectives. The results of this research may affect what the company decides its course of action should be in the long-term, or what its strategic plans should incorporate. A situation analysis will cover, amongst other things:

- The organisation's position in the market.
- Market forces which will affect the organisation's position and abilities.
- Competitive activity and analysis.
- Internal analysis or audit of the organisation and its functional abilities and resources.

There can be a number of variables over which the organisation has little or no control, and the results of the audit tend to dictate the parameters within which an organisation can operate. It also gives an outline structure for future short-term plans and objectives.

Market Research

Before any marketing activity can be planned, an organisation needs basic information on which to base its future plans. Therefore, one of the primary roles of marketing is to conduct research. All of the primary activities involve research and there is a constant loop or feedback which enables organisations to make both strategic and tactical decisions.

Analysis and Activity—Market and Consumer Research

Before detailing its marketing plans, an organisation requires some of the following fundamental information.

Market Research

- The size and nature of the market.
- The nature of products and services on offer.
- The nature of competing products and services.

Consumer Research

- Identifying consumer groups to whom the product will appeal.
- Identifying the validity (size, reachability, etc.) of target consumer groups.
- Identifying consumer tastes and preferences.
- Identifying consumer behaviour and changes—i.e. forecasting.

The results of this research will largely determine what the organisation produces, for whom, when and in what quantities. In other words, it principally determines how and on what the activities of the organisation will be focused.

Characteristics of the Tourism Industry and Positioning Strategies

The tourism industry, like many others, reacts to the particular nature of the environment and the structure of the market in which it operates. This brings about differing approaches to segmenting the market, and differing strategies for segments and product groups. Companies sometimes work on determining 'competitive market structures'—that is, grouping products or brands on the basis of competition boundaries. It can be recognised that, in the tourism market, there are specific areas where brands compete more strongly with one another than with other similar products.

For example, stronger brands and vertically integrated organisations, such as JMC or First Choice, may concentrate their marketing effort on dealing with the competition offered by others operating on a multi-market, multi-product basis (such as Thomsons or Airtours), rather than on smaller operators using the same destinations and offering similar packages. Similarly, major tourist destinations in the world, such as Greece and Spain, may compete more directly with one another for various tourist segments from the UK than do France and Spain as two of the largest destinations for UK tourists.

Differing Market Strategies and Mixes in a Fragmented Market

A recent feature of the market for tourism is that many tour operators and destinations which catered for what was termed the 'mass market' are now attempted to respond to the growing trend towards a more fragmented market and tourists who require more individually tailored holidays (niche markets). This they have done by bringing out a wider variety of products to suit individual market segments and, as a result, in some product areas the larger operators might see their more direct competition to be a specialist or smaller operator.

This highlights the need for distinctly different marketing strategies for particular market segments and products, with a different marketing mix. As an example, the competition between JMC and Thomsons for their main multi-product summar programme might be such that they are forced to manipulate price rather more than other elements of the marketing mix. They might also have to concentrate a higher degree of their marketing budget on advertising and promotion. On the other hand, a smaller specialist operator, such as Abercrombie and Kent, competing with Thomsons in a tourist location may offer added value and expertise and a greater personal service element to the product.

Thomsons may, in turn, may have to manipulate its product mix or perceived value in order to compete with the smaller operator. In this case, either operator may invoke the extended marketing mix and the emphasis may be on elements other than price, such as people and the service they give. Similarly, destinations such as Spain have the challenge of remaining appealing to the established market segments of the 'Costas' whilst promoting to smaller, and potentially more lucrative, segments who require differing product benefits. The marketing mix they invoke for these segments may therefore have to be very different.

The Control of Variables—The Nature and Characteristics of Services and Tourism Marketing

In the marketing of tourism products, it is acknowledged that there are a number of variables over which the industry has little control and which characterise the tourism product. These variables tend to focus on economic and political influences over which organisations in the tourism field have either little or no control. These variables, such as PDI (personal disposable income), are used by market intelligence agencies, such as Mintel, to forecast the nature of the market. Mintel maintain, for instance, that pdi has a direct correlational effect on the number of holidays the consumer is able to take in the year, and anticipated growth or decline in PDI will, therefore, have a direct influence on trends in holiday taking (Mintel 2001).

The level of activity and spend in the tourism market are also affected by potential changes in the economic and political environment, including inflation, levels, mortgage rates, interest rates and exchange rates, all of which may have a greater or lesser effect on consumer confidence and spending. Other variables of particular concern to those involved in tourism are wars and political instability.

All organisations, therefore, seek to reduce risk by research; that is, they undertake economic forecasting and acquire other market intelligence which enables them to make realistic strategic and tactical plans. Once organisations have defined those variables which will have most influence over the ability of the consumer to purchase, they must decide upon ways of overcoming some of the difficulties and then decide upon more direct activities.

These direct activities focus on those variables which marketers are more able to control and are more widely known as the marketing mix, the extended marketing mix or services marketing mix. Marketers must seek to find the correct 'mix' which will achieve success for the organisation and satisfy consumers.

The Marketing Mix and Extended Marketing Mix

As discussed above, the most widely accepted and used definition of the marketing mix is the four 'Ps', which incorporates product, price, place (distribution) and promotion. In service industries and in tourism in particular, it is considered that this mix can be extended to include other activities and that these can assume just as much importance. Indeed, the four 'Ps' approach has been widely criticised for its limitations and many commentators have offered advice on the application of an extended mix and the nature of services.

Cowell emphasises that the marketing mix is a guide and a framework for action, not simply a theoretical idea. Marketers should, therefore, be prepared to adapt and adopt the correct mix according to their particular industry and organisational conditions and, most particularly, according to the needs of the target market segments they have decided to cater for. One of the principal reasons for adopting an extended mix is the nature of the delivery of services, such as tourism, where in order to differentiate one product from another, factors such as the management of service quality through *people, processes and physical evidence* are important. These additional variables in the production process can affect the response of the consumer more readily. As far as possible, marketing must influence performance and delivery of the product.

The role of customer service and the control of quality are, therefore, heavily emphasised in tourism organisations. Companies such as British Airways spend sizeable portions of their marketing budget ensuring that the product is made more tangible and that customer experiences and percep-tions are more consistent. The extended marketing mix of people, processes and physical evidence provide more ways in which marketers can control the delivery.

Product

The Nature and Characteristics of the Tourism Product

Inseparability and heterogeneity : As has already been observed in the discussion of marketing mix, one of the features of tourism products is that production and consumption are not entirely exclusive. This inseparability is created because services which are part of the production process are only 'produced' at the time of consumption. For example, a night in an hotel or a flight on an aeroplane only occurs the service is 'consumed'.

Because people are so much a part of this production process, another feature of tourism products is their lack of standardisation or 'heterogeneity'. As previously stated, marketers must try to make the product conform to the same standard so that it perceived the same by all users.

Intangibility : Tourism products incorporate many elements, but a particular feature of tourism is that many of these elements are intangible-they are not physical goods, but experiences and feelings. In short, the nature of many holiday products is such that consumers could be said to buy on trust. As demonstrated in the above section, the producer seeks to control as many of these intangible variables as possible in order to make the product more tangible for the consumer.

Perishability and seasonality : Tourism products are highly perishable; unlike manufactured goods, they cannot be stored and sold at a later date. Therefore, the costs involved in their production can increase if, for example, tours are not filled to capacity, some departure dates remain unsold, or aircraft seats remain unsold. These are some of the factors which affect the pricing of tourism products, since producers must sometimes allow for a level of unsold capacity which can increase the individual costs of a holiday.

It is sometimes the seasonal nature of the tourism product which increases the risk and, therefore, tourist attractions and tour operators must ensure that they are able to make the most of peak seasons. Cash flow tends to be poor and sometimes non-existent in shoulder and off-peak seasons, whilst for those with high fixed costs or assets which remain dormant (aircraft, ships, coaches, hotels), the problem of seasonality is greater.

Marketing efforts must, therefore, be focused on achieving prices which achieve the highest rate of return in peak season, and prices which stimulate demand in low seasons, thus increasing the likelihood of full use of assets.

Product Analysis

Product analysis is an element of the marketing process that helps an organisation to identify the ways in which it can adpt and improve products in relation to customer needs and competitor products. It also assists the organisation in identifying features and benefits which can be highlighted in promotional campaigns.

Shoashtack (1977) has attempted to analyse products by identifying their relative importance to the core service, demonstrating how important some of the more peripheral services are in making the product more tangible for some consumers. The importance of components within the structure may change for different consumers—with airlines, for example, business class travellers may value reclining seats and more leg room, whilst a leisure passenger may value speed of service and ancillary services, such as duty free shopping. Both, however, experience the same core service—the flight.

The concept of a core which satisfies the most fundamental or basic needs arises from Kotler's (1994) Five Product Levels model, in which he suggests that marketers should attempt to enhance the set of attributes and conditions that customers normally expect with and augmented level, one which distinguishes their product from others. By augmenting the product, marketers will be satisfying more than the basic needs of customers and be supplying additional benefits which also differentiate the product from its competitors.

There are many other useful models which assist organisations in comparing and improving upon products. A SWOT analysis (strengths, weaknesses, opportunities and threats), for instance, may prove useful in comparing competing products. Alternatively, an analysis of the benefits which consumers derive from products helps the organisations to distinguish them from the integral features, thus providing marketers with material for promotional campaigns.

It is harder is to develop new products for the tourism market, as opposed to other markets, since it is generally much more difficult to pretest service related products. Some tour operators will pretest new products by pilot launches to specific geographical regions or release programmes with limited departure dates. Hotels and purpose built attractions may test concepts and reactions to interior decor. The retail trade and tourist boards can attempt to simulate the holiday experience through videos and computer generated graphics. In general, however, much of the industry relies on experience and the post-purchase evaluations of consumer satisfaction. When compared to some industries in manufacturing, the costs of the research, introduction and testing of new products for tourism are relatively low.

Product Life-cycle

Since manipulating the features and design of the product is one of the primary ways in which marketers can ensure success, it is inevitable that they will also be interested in how much adaptation of the product can take place before consumers tire of the product and it becomes obsolete. The product life-cycle concept proposes that every product has four basic stages, namely, *introduction, growth, maturity and decline.* It is the job of marketing to assess the life of individual products in order to:

- Assess and predict the length of the adoption stage of a new product.
- Determine at what stage in the process each product in the organisation's portfolio is.
- Adapt products to stem the decline or renew interest (extending the lifecycle).
- Assess when products need to be deleted.
- Assess when new products need to be introduced.

There are a number of pitfalls in predicting the life-stages of products, and the intense competition in the tourism industry with its characteristic price wars could lead to a misinterpretation of the pattern of growth and decline. The popularity of products is clearly not just influenced by their path to obsolescence and caution is needed in interpreting the pattern of sales. At the introduction stage, cost is the primary factor and it is not until the growth stage, when sales begin to rise, that marketing can be sure of some return on their investment. A mistake that some companies make is to underestimate the length of the adoption process and pull to the plug on new products too early. Equally, overestimation will increase costs with no return. Growth may also be affected by a number of other factors, such as the introduction of competitive products. At the maturity stage, it may be that a smaller number of producers battle it out for market share, during this stage it may be difficult to tell whether sales have reached saturation and a decline is likely.

Price

Influences on Pricing

There are many influences on pricing, including:

- demand;
- supply (availability);
- costs;
- competition;
- government policies on pricing;
- consumer legislation; and
- competition.

In addition, there are many other constraints which influence the way in which organisations price their products. These include the health of the economy, personal disposable income level, exchange rates, interest rates, mortgage rates, and so on. Corporate objectives and the margins required by shareholders and other investors will also be influential on pricing policy. Whilst it is important that marketers decide upon the correct price for the product which suits the market segment at which it is aimed, it must be remembered that many constraints influence their ability to use price as a tool to manipulate consumer response.

Supply and Demand Pricing Policy

Some sectors of the tourism industry are said to be characterised by price was. These are, sometimes, the inevitable result of overcapacity in airlines, shipping, and to a lesser extent, hotels, and reflect the extent to which supply or demand influences pricing. Principles or producers with spare capacity resulting from lower demand or increased supply will sell at cheaper rates in order to cover existing or high fixed costs, or cut prices in the belief that a reduction in price will lead to a subsequent increase in sales.

Market Share and Pricing Policy

In recent years, price wars and discounting have been the major characteristic of the larger, vertically integrated companies who combine the functions of tour operator, travel agent and charter airline.

These reflect the extent to which both perishability and the fight for market share influences pricing. These larger companies have produced larger tour operating programmes, sometimes flooding the market with products, in order to preserve or win market share. When these efforts fail, products often have to be put back on the market in different forms or through different distribution channels and, generally, at lower or discounted rates.

Those companies without adequate resources cannot generally price products for market share. Nor should companies with either substantial borrowings and poor performance pursue pricing for market share, as banks may 'pull the plug' at the wrong time whilst shareholders may object to policies which reduce margins. Thus, market share is not a realistic option for many companies; indeed, some markets may remain stagnant with little growth in volume. Nevertheless, growth can be achieved not only by selling more of product but also by selling the same volume, but at higher prices. For some, but relatively few, organisations in the tourism industry, this is the only option.

Pricing Methods

Target rate of return : Prices are decided on the basis of achieving a particular return on the assets employed in an organisation. Investors in a business may simply set a target with which they will be happy.

Cost based methods : Based on accounting disciplines of costing, this method is easy for many organisations to understand and use. Costs can be split into two types, fixed and variable. Fixed costs are those which do not vary with 'output', or the amount of the service provided. Variable costs, conversely, are those which do increase as more of a service is provided.

These two cost elements can be combined with revenue-which should increase as the service is sold-to give a picture of when an operation becomes profitable. Known as Break Even Analysis or Cost/

Profit/Volume (CPV) Analysis, the interaction of these elements can be shown graphically.

In reality, in some businesses it may be difficult to allocate overheads or fixed costs to some products. Some businesses may want to be flexible and operate differing prices and pricing methods to achieve different objectives which stimulate demand.

Therefore, contirbutions to cost (marginal cost pricing) is a more realistic proposition for some companies, as the range offered may support the sale of other products, or utilise spare capacity (e.g., transportation).

Promotional and psychological pricing : Promotional pricing may be employed to destroy rival products or pricing policies. It may also be used as the lead-in price for a brochure where, for example, £399 is perceived as removing a barrier price of £400 or over. However, it would normally be viewed as a short term strategy as its objectives are achieved at the cost of profit.

Competitive based pricing : Some industries are constrained in the way they price products and can only sell at what is termed the going rate, that is, the rate which the competition is charging. However, this method should be used with caution as it also means that costs should be relatively the same for both parties. Many organisations are forced into this situation when competition is intense and the public have got used to what they consider to be the 'going rate' for a product—as is very much the case with the mass, package holiday market.

Premium and destroyer pricing : These methods represent the opposite ends of a scale. More successful companies with well-known brands and highly regarded products are in a position to be price leaders in a market and achieve a premium price over others. Generally, there are good reasons for being able to achieve this, such as providing a higher quality service or providing a specialist or unique service.

At the opposite end of the scale, destroyer aims to undercut competitors in order to remove them from the market. This type of pricing can result in negative implications for the consumer as, once competition is removed, so too are the barriers for increasing prices and, therefore, such actions may be swiftly followed by price rises.

Place

Distribution and promotion often play interrelated roles in the marketing of travel and tourism products. The decisions facing most organisations are either to market direct to the consumer or to market their products via an intermediary, such as a travel agent. This still leaves the problem of how to distribute information and inventory (available capacity) to the travel agent.

The nature of distribution services has changed considerably in the past twenty years as more and more ways of delivering the product direct to the consumer or more speedily business to business have been developed. For example, on a business to business basis CRS's—global reservations networks—allowed travel agents and producers to access interrelated products, such as airlines, hotels and other services and for organisations to communicate. These systems are now becoming redundant as agents are able to access inventory and information on the Internet via separately controlled networks (which the public are not allowed access to).

Importantly, time is often saved and fewer brochures are needed if the public is able to access information direct from producers' web-sites and make some decisions before contacting travel agents. In these instances, the consumer is going direct to the producer for information but is still using the agent for booking purposes. Many organisations have developed call centres for the same purpose.

There has been much discussion on the value of the Internet tool. Before making any decisions on more direct methods of distribution and promotion, it is necessary for marketers to decide what use the majority of people will make of the these services. For example, it must be ascertained whether consumers will use services, such as the Internet, as a tool for collating information (accepting promotional material) or whether they would with to undertaken transactions using the Internet (a distribution tool). Air travel is one product which has been successfully distributed on the Internet. Ryanair, for example, have achieved 70 percent of their bookings through their web site another 23 percent are made by phone and only 7 per cent through agents.

One of the major advantages of the Internet is that it may lower the cost of distribution for many organisations. For products such as ferry crossings, it offers another method of distributing information on fares and sailing times which are quicker than brochure distribution and more flexible. The Internet has also provided an opportunity for new types of distribution service which differ from retail agents. These distribution services may concentrate on one type of service or one consumer segment. They aggregate services to capture whole product or consumer markets, whilst providing an opportunity for a more efficient service for consumers wanting to compare services, prices and times (Barrass 1998). Thus, sites such as Ferrybooker.com are able to offer information on all ferry services on one site (Mintel 2001: 23).

Keynote maintain that four times as many tourists considered the Internet and travel books a better source of information than travel agents and tour operators (Keynote 2001: 51). Nevertheless, many organisations still believe that there are limitations to distributing products through the Internet. These limitations are: a reluctance to use technology; security concerns (with credit card transactions, bank details); ease of access to inventory; ease of access to correct information; and the lack security associated with dealing face-to-face or verbal communication.

Travel agents are still the primary method by which people in the UK access information on holiday products and make reservations. Agents can provide a professional service with additional information and advice, which should be impartial. There has been much discussion as to how impartial this advice can be when many agents are part of vertically integrated companies who have an interest in promoting their own products.

Therefore, the European Competition, Commission have taken an active interest in the growing integration of the European travel industry and have issued guidelines for agents which enable the public to identify where an agents is offering products which are owned by the group. The nature of travel agents is changing and many companies are developing new types of agency which no longer perform traditional roles but, which offer the benefits of new technology, such as the Internet alongside personal contact.

Whilst it is the marketer of tourism products who must decide on the best method of distribution for their product, it is still the consumer who makes the decision which method they prefer to use. Most organisations now seek to determine how particular market segments will react to and use different distribution systems and the preferences of important target market segments are taken into account. The type of holiday product and the typical consumer give some indication—for example, the Internet is apparently the ideal method for adventure travel operators as the profile of their consumers closely matches that of consumers likely to participate in adventure travel. It also suits the many small companies involved in this area, as distribution through agents would be difficult if not impossible. Indeed, approximately 85 per cent of sales for adventure travel companies is by direct booking (Millington 2001).

Specialist tour operators in general are hoping to develop their brands via the Internet, whilst the Association of Independent Tour Operators (AITO) has used it to raise the profile of its members and their products and as a communications tool (Mintel 2001).

In addition to consumer preference, tour operators and others must consider the cost of distributing products. If distributing through travel agents, they must decide whether they will distribute on a blanket approach to each agent or whether they will selectively distribute to a small number of agents or selected chains. Many organisations do not have the choice as, with such a wide variety of products on offer, travel agents must be selective about how many they stock and some producers may have no option but to sell direct.

Promotion

It is the responsibility of marketing to communicate factors about an organisation and its products. The purpose of communications can vary; for instance, it may be used for establishing an identify for a product, creating a corporate image for an organisation or creating awareness of a destination. The promotional efforts of organisations should generally be focused on their selected target market segments. It is one of the responsibilites of marketing not only to identify the various audiences but their characteristics. They also need to analyse the characteristics of their products and the appeal they have for their audience.

This knowledge will enable clear directions to be given to those preparing the promotional plan as to the purpose of the campaign. The purposes of campaigns are very varied. Tour operators or destinations, for example, may find it necessary to place advertising which raises awareness of a destination whereas established consumer segments, who are already knowledgeable on products and destinations, may need more persuasion to choose the product in preference to others. The purpose of the campaign, therefore, may be to create more favourable attitudes or to stimulate consumers to purchase. As discussed shortly, there are a number of ways in which we can communicate with chosen audiences. However, the choice of the promotional effort or mix of the communications package will depend upon many factors, including:

- the size of budge;
- the objectives of the promotional campaign;
- the size and nature of the target audience; and
- the geographical spread of the target audience.

The primary concern is to establish clear objectives or goals for the campaign and then to monitor and measure the responses to it. Without monitoring and measurement, no organisation can clearly determine whether its success is due to marketing effort and the cost effectiveness of that effort.

Elements of the Promotional Mix

Advertising : Marketing must carefully select media by identifying the typical readership, viewers or listeners and matching the medium to their target audience. There are many considerations which affect choice and it is suggested that marketing must look not only at the absolute cost of advertising (time or space purchased) but also at the relative costs of advertising, 'that is, the cost of contacting each remember of the target audience' (Fill 1995: 310). A wide range of media may be used for advertising, including:

- TV
- Radio
- National and local press
- Trade and professional journals
- magazines
- Posters/bill boards
- Direct mailing.

For each method, details of advertising rates, readership and each are published and part of the research and planning process is also to determine the medium most likely to be cost effective and which the audience is most likely to identify.

Direct marketing : Direct mail, telemarketing and the Internet are all forms of communication which are increasingly used in the travel and tourism industry. Direct mail and telemarketing have the advantage of being more easily monitored and, therefore, the response more directly measurable. Direct response methods, such as promotional coupons, are also used successfully to promote holiday products. Unlike the Internet, the cost of these is more directly measurable.

Brochures and printed materials : The brochure is still the primary selling tool for the majority of the travel and tourism industry, including destinations, although the Internet is bringing about change on this front. The nature of the holiday product means that it is information intensive and the brochure has been the primary tool through which all information is distributed. It is, however, a costly business and marketers must consider how many brochures they need to distribute.

The real cost of brochure production and distribution can be measured by assessing the number of bookings received to the number of brochures distributed. The conversion rate for most orgnisation is, in fact, staggeringly low and the real costs of 'wastage' (brochures taken but not used as a booking medium) are high.

Direct selling : A large proportion of business to business activity is undertaken by direct sales. However, the role of selling in the travel industry is often a controversial one, especially when considering the role of the travel agent. Face-to-face selling, therefore, has less of a role than, say, telesales throughout most of the industry. In reality, the purchases of holiday products involves complex decision-making, often by groups of people, some of whom take differing roles (for example, buyers or influencers). The direct selling role can therefore be controversial. However, some organisations have attempted to use direct selling when people's responses are known to be less guarded, such as in the selling of time-share in holiday resorts.

9

Managing Supply Issues

The provision of tourist transport services by public and private sector organisations is a complex process, requiring a wide range of human resource skills and mana-gerial abilities and a sound grasp of the transport business and how it operates. In recent years, meeting the needs of consumers (travellers) has also assumed a higher priority in the supply of services. In the conceptualisation and analysis of tourist transport supply issues highlighted the significance of understanding the broader strategic and contextual issues which affect the way different forms of transport supply perform in the market place.

In this chapter, the emphasis is on a number of issues highlighted by the SIA case study, namely how successful transport providers can produce, manage and operate efficient supply systems to meet tourist needs. In particular, the chapter focuses on the mechanisms and tools used by operators to manage supply issues, together with the role of the public sector. This provides a comparison of the different objectives pursued by private sector operators, such as airlines, railway companies and cruise lines. Private sector operators, are motivated by the financial performance of the business, to ensure that an efficient operation delivers products to its customers.

In contrast, the public sector agencies directly and indirectly associated with the provision of tourist transport services are often not motivated by profit. They frequently have a more strategic view and are concerned with planning, coordination and liaison functions to ensure tourist transport provision meets public policy objectives at various spatial scales. The chapter commences with a discussion of one of the most important tools used by transport providers in the late 1990s—information technology (IT). This is followed by a review of one important strategy used by airlines to improve supply issues and competitiveness - alliances. Next, the role of the state in regulating tourist transport supply issues is discussed in relation to airline deregulation in the USA. The supply of transport services in destination areas is then reviewed.

Information technology and supply issues in tourist transport: a role for logistics and IT?

It is widely acknowledged that society has entered the 'information age' and that this has had implications for transport provision. One of the immediate impacts for tourist transport providers is that up-to-date information flows are now vital when a supply chain exists, and the transport provider is just one component of the overall tourist product.

As Christopher observes, the customer service explosion means there is a need for 'consistent provision of time and place utility. In other words, products do not have value until they are in the hands of the customer at the time and place required.' Christopher argues that logistics of service delivery are of paramount importance and enable organisations to add value and deliver a consistent product. Logistics is a vital concept to recognise, particularly when IT is also introduced, since IT and logistics enable transport providers to achieve their objectives in a competitive environment.

According to Quayle,

> *Logistics is the process which seeks to provide for the management and co-ordination of all activities within the supply chain from sourcing and acquisition, through production where appropriate, and through distribution channels to the customer.*

Logistics provides a competitive advantage by offering a strategic view of operational issues and an understanding of the links in the supply system. It also assists in the coordi-nation of the service delivery function, and transport in its own right is a vital element of logistics in moving the customer nearer to the product in a tourism context.

Logis-tics is documented in detail by Quayle (1993) and Christopher (1994) and performs a vital role in providing the link between the marketplace and operating activity of the business. Figure outlines the business functions which fall within the remit of logistics.

Within the literature on IT in tourism, the seminal study by Sheldon (1997) is fast becoming the key reference source, replacing the earlier work by Poon (1993). The tourist industry generates large volumes of information that needs to be processed and used within a logistics context. For example, Sheldon (1997) notes that each airline booking generates 25 transactions that need processing. In Sheldon's (1997) model of tourism information flows, there are three main agents involved: travellers, suppliers and travel intermediaries.

For the purpose of the discussion here, it is the supplier's use of IT to handle, utilise and manage these information flows which is of interest. From a transport supplier's perspective, information is essential to allow the organisation to function and for different departments to make decisions about corporate objectives, their consumers and competitors. It can also be harnessed in the marketing function. Sheldon (1997) cites the example of the airline industry which makes extensive use of IT in a wide range of contexts, including:

- Global Distribution Systems (see WTO 1994).
- Frequent flyer databases
- Yield management programmes.
- Distribution and marketing of their products.
- The design, operation and maintenance of aircraft and luggage handling.
- Check-in systems at airport.

Although other transport sectors involved in tourism also make use of IT (including train operators, car rental agencies and coach and cruise ship operators), it is probably most highly developed in the airline sector, due to large investment in capital and the highly competitive nature of the business. In that sense, IT is seen as integral to gaining a competitive edge, and in the case of SIA, in maintaining continuous product innovations. For example, on its Mega-top-747s, all passengers have access to an in-flight telephone to make credit card calls from air to ground, and the developments listed in the SIA case study, all enlist state-of-the-art IT.

Sheldon (1997) traces the development of IT in the airline industry, where it is primarily seen as a means of improving the efficiency of operations and of management functions. The airline sector first developed computer technology in the form of computer reservation systems (CRSs) in the 1950s. It is impossible in a book such as this to trace the rapid development of IT in the airline industry and all the other transport sectors, although it is pertinent to outline the current state of the art in IT and its organisation.

Following the rapid growth in CRSs (Knowles and Garland 1994) in the 1970s and 1980s (Archdale 1990, 1991), Sheldon (1997) outlines the typical configuration of an airline CRS; it comprises:

- A central site housing the computer systems driving the CRS (often up to 10 mainframe systems).
- The network hardware at the central site and computer staff to maintain it.
- A series of front-end communication processors to process information and on-line storage devices at the central site.

This is complemented by satellite communications to remote communication concentrators (RCCs) in key cities that relay data from the earth station. This is then relayed to reservation terminals and airports, providing rapid communications. One of the major changes in the late 1980s and 1990s has been the move from CRSs which contained only airline information for the proprietary airline to systems containing data for multiple airlines.

Sheldon (1997) traces the develop-ment of CRSs into what have now been called global distribution systems (World Tourism Organisation 1994), like the Asian GDS, Abacus, mentioned in the SIA case study (Chapter). Table outlines the principal developments contri-buting to the development of GDSs. CDSs are CRSs which are affiliated with airlines.

There has been a great deal of debate over the impact of airline affiliation on the competitiveness of air travel in North America, Sheldon (1997) argues that, following legislation, rules now exist to ensure all airlines are represented on GDS screens According to Sheldon (1997), the significance of major GDSs in 1996 was:

• Sabre	US$1,500-2,000 million
• Apollo	US$1,100 + million
• Abacus	US$650 million
• Amadeus	US$600 million
• System One	US$500 million
• Worldspan	US$500 million
• Galileo	US$400 million

***Table** : The development of GDSs*

1976	Three North American airlines began to offer their systems - Apollo (United Airlines), Sabre (American Airlines) and PARS (Trans World Airlines) as well as offering US travel agents terminals to access their systems.
1981	Eastern Airlines established System One Direct Access (SODA).
1982	Delta Airlines launched its DATAS II.
1987	In Europe, Galileo and Amadeus were formed and offered to travel agents. In Asia, Abacus was formed and also offered to travel agents.
1988	Japan Airlines formed Axess.
1990	System One was purchased by a non airlines company - EDS. The merger of PARS and DATAS II resulted in the formation of Worldspan. In Japan, All Nippon Airways and Abacus formed Infini.
1993	Galileo and Apollo were merged to establish Galileo International.
1995	System One merged with Amadeus.

Although a CRS will only show one airline's schedules, a GDS has the advantage of showing data on multiple carriers, including:

- Flight schedules and availability.
- Passenger information.
- Fare quotes and rules for travel.
- Ticketing.

Since the advent of GDSs, airlines have also established 'a presence on the Internet and (are) using that as an impor-tant distribution channel especially to consumers. By accpeting payment by credit card, airlines have harnessed a developing technology to complement GDSs and traditional distribution channels. Sheldon (1997) also discusses other airline IT applica-tions which include:

- Baggage and cargo handling systems.
- Cabin automation (e.g., entertainment systems, visual route systems on in-flight screens using Geographical Positioning System equipment).
- Safety systems.
- Decision support systems.
- Flight scheduling and planning.
- Crew scheduling and management.
- Gate management and control.

In the the case of SIA, Sheldon (1997) discusses the current development of Krismax, a yield management system to assist with revenue and inventory control. The underlying principle behind Krismax is that the amount of space available on any flight segment can be controlled in relation to different classes of seats (as discussed in Chapter).

The information is then fed into the CRS to control the availability of seats by segment. Sheldon (1997) observes that SIA's 'reservations from travel agents are taken care of with its major investment and involvement with Abacus, the Asian GDS, which has over 12,500 terminals in 5,000 travel agencies'.

Sheldon (1997) also examines the developments in IT which have been introduced into land transport operations to help the logistics of fleet management in relation to car rental and other innovations which improve the tourists' travel experience.

Having examined the significance of logistics and IT in managing tourist transport in a supply context, attention now turns to the way in which one part of the transport sector—airlines—has pursued strategies to improve supply issues through strategic alliances.

Simulation Model in Hospitality Transportation

Tourism industry development has its greatest impacts at the community level. These impacts reach far beyond jobs, wages, and revenues. Social and environmental consequences such as crime, congestion, and water pollution also can have serious impacts on the quality of life of residents as well as on the quality of vacations for tourists. Community leaders and planners have indicated a need for information about these impacts.

Since 1980, researchers at a number of universities in the Northeast and elsewhere have worked toward developing a framework and a database with which any locality could make "ball-park" estimates of the impacts of typical types of tourism development. A major research finding has been that it is not easy to define typical communities, typical developments, or average impacts.

Another finding has been that the complex interactions between residents, tourists, industry, and government make it difficult to justify a simple framework for analysis. On the other hand it is difficult to present the correct framework (assuming one exists) in a simple manner. In order to test our preliminary research hypotheses, a tourism-planning computer game has been developed which pits the player against the development pressures of a hypothetical small New England community.

In addition to meeting our objective of illustrating our long-term research goals in a palatable format the game has been used successfully in the classroom and, in fact, has taken on a project status of its own.

Project Background: A Game?

The Tourism Development Simulation Model (TDSM) is a computer program developed in conjunction with a series of projects on the impacts of tourism development.

The emphasis in the earliest project was on the development of a methodology that could be used by individual municipalities and state agencies to estimate and project impacts caused by alternative tourism product mixes at the local level. A follow-up project focused on the fiscal impact portion of the model.

In the early stages of design and development of this model, it became readily apparent that the scope of the work was very broad-too broad to produce the quick and comprehensive results users wanted. It was, in fact, difficult to describe the goals of the project or its potential value to targeted users. It was decided, therefore, that a simplified version of the model could provide the basis of a computer game, and that this game concerning tourism development in a hypothetical community could provide an alternative means of describing the usefulness of the major project objectives.

The production and distribution of the game has been so successful that it has taken on a project status of its own. Priced at cost, it was initially distributed as an amusing "think piece" for researchers and planners, and as an palatable introduction to related research projects. The game is loosely based on the impact assessment framework developed in a study of the impacts of tourism on thirteen coastal communities in the Northeast. A typical small New England community was characterized using some empirical results and some "best guess" approximations to relationships between major variables. The relationships were then refined to reflect the "reality" exhibited in recent community case studies.

In addition to providing the intended introduction to long-term project goals, the processes of designing and constructing the game and using it as a community behaviour simulator have taught us much about the implications of "reality" and "reasonableness" on mathematical representations of community behaviour. These lessons have had a considerable impact on our primary goal of developing a tourism development simulation model.

Designed to illustrate the principles of community budgeting and planning in the context of tourism industry development, the game has been used as an educational tool for students of tourism planning at the graduate and undergraduate level, and non-degree participants in leadership development programs in both the U.S. and Canada. For all audience types, the educational vehicle provided by the computer game is accepted enthusiastically. As with others, we have found this approach to have definite advantages over traditional seminar presentations. This paper describes the details of the game's design and describes the importance of the "reasonableness" criterion used in the development of the underlying model. It also attempts to persuade the reader that a computer game, based on a "best-guess" model, can provide a useful research and educational tool.

The Tourism Industry Focus

The tourism industry has many dimensions of concern to community researchers. It is recognized to include a wide range of business types whose activities impact a broad cross-section of the host community.

Tourists are of many types as are the residents of the affected community. In conducting community-based tourism research it is therefore important to identify and measure impact generators and recipients by their types so that policies can address specific problems and needs. In the model underlying this game, however, all tourist-related businesses are represented by an industry average, and all non-tourist-related businesses are represented by another average. In a similar way, residents are grouped and tourists are grouped. In contrast to the research \approach, the emphasis here is on the general dynamics of the tourism industry as it relates to other society components in a typical community setting.

The community is viewed as a circle whose outer ring is the natural resource base. Within that is the social system which provides the context for all community activities. Finally, in the centre are the four major components of the model: the tourism industry, "other" industry, local government, and the residents.

Outside the community are four factors that influence and are influenced by community activities: exports, nonresident capital, nonresident labourers, and tourists. The arrows that connect the components and outside factors illustrate the major linkages assumed by the model that underlies the game. Specific adjustments in behaviour of tourism businesses, "other" businesses, residents, and tourists are determined by equations relating causal factors to specific actions. This follows the basic econometric approach of meddling market systems.

By sacrificing the behavioural differences of different types of producers and consumers, the simulation-game goes beyond equations that are typically estimated in research projects and speculates about a very complex set of important interactions within the community. Of particular interest were the social and environmental impacts of development that can change the "quality of life" for residents, the "bottom line' for businesses, and the "quality of the vacation" for tourists. Such impacts are well documented in the literature. Finally, the game recognizes the political nature of the decision-making process, the budget-balancing skills required by individual community officers, and the unpredictable disturbances to the planning process caused by unforeseen events.

A Community Setting

In order to simulate tourism development in the most realistic way possible, the model centres on the decisions made by an administrative officer of a typical small town in New England in the late 1970's. At the beginning of a game there are 20,000 residents in 10,000 households, and the population is growing at 1% per year. Half the population is considered to be in the labour force. 7500 of these are employed by the tourism industry, 2250 are employed in the "other" industry of the local economy, and the unemployment rate is initially 2.5%. Wage rates are $ 10,000 per year in the tourism industry and $20,000 per year in the other industry. Although average firms in both tourism and "other" industries begin the simulation breaking even, profits earned in the subsequent years are distributed to the residents of the community as additional income.

Consequently disposable household income averages $11,255 per year in year 1. The natural resource base of the community is assumed to be a major recreation area, thus the draw for tourists and a major factor in the quality of life in the community. This resource might be a park or beach that is valued by the community and attractive enough to draw tourists to town, but fragile in the sense that increased use, in the absence of preventative investment, will result in a reduction in its aesthetic qualities. A number of works report on such impacts on recreational resources.

In the initial year of the simulation 200,000 tourists visit the community, staying an average of 7 days each, and visiting the natural resource recreation site on every day of their stay. Residents each make 10 visits per year to the recreation site. Residents and tourists pay the same price per visit to the recreational site, which is managed by the industry, however the tourists pay a visitor's fee to the town.

The town administrator has the authority to invest these and other town revenues in the protection/enhancement of the natural resource base. Year-to-year variation in weather is one example of the unpredictable nature of the community environment. The model assumes that changes in the average seasonal temperature from its norm of 75 degrees F will influence use of the recreational resource by residents as well as tourists.

Each year of the simulation, average seasonal temperature is assigned a random value from 70 to 80 degrees. When temperatures drop below 75 degrees, visits to the site decrease, and when temperatures exceed 75, they increase.

As residential and tourist populations increase they are assumed to impact the social and environmental characteristics of the community as well as its economy. These are manifested in crime and congestion rates and water quality measures known to the community, reported as social and environmental indexes and as headlines in the local press. Thus, the quality of life in the community is assumed to be reflected in indexes for three basic community qualities: economic, social, and environmental.

The environmental index is assumed to reflect the quality of the recreational resource. The geometric mean of the three indexes, weighted by the population of the community, is used as an overall measure of community well being. Such quality of life indexes have been pursued for a number of years, with varying degrees of success. This well being measure might also be thought of an indicator of the economist's social welfare function.

In addition to the raw indexes, the game player is presented news headlines that correspond to the severity of the index above or below their initial, equilibrium position. For example, when the social index drops 30% below its initial value the player is informed "Crime and Congestion at Record Levels. Police Frustrated." And when the environmental index rises 30% above its initial value the player is informed "National Task Force Adopts Local Environmental Plan as Model."

The Game Player

The game player assumes the role of an unusually potent town administrator who must guide development using tourism promotion and three other types of expenditure programs: "other" industrial development programs, social programs, and environmental projects. These expenditure categories are assumed to include all major expenditure items in a town's budget except for administration, which is ignored by the model.

In order to balance the town's budget the player must adjust tax rates for residential and business property and decide upon daily tourist fees. The player's objective is to achieve balanced economic, social, and environmental development as measured by their respective indexes. At the end of each year of office the player is presented with quantitative and qualitative assessments of performance, and given the opportunity to change any of the seven fiscal controls. The game ends after 10 years of service or when the player quits or is fired, which ever comes first.

The Tourism Development Model

Model Structure

Some 40 equations containing more than fifty parameters characterize the components of community activity and development in the small hypothetical town. Most of these (19 equations) characterize the tourism industry and "other" industry behaviour. These include basic supply and demand relationships for the tourism product and the "other" product produced in the town, as well as derived demands for labour and supplies and business relocation.

The multi-market model framework is common to macro meddling efforts. Supply and demand equations are logarithmic and contain a lagged dependent variable. This formulation characterizes behaviour as "partially" adjusting toward some distant equilibrium value. The amount of the adjustment declines each year following the initial change in the independent variable. The rate of adjustment is determined by the size of the lag coefficient. Such models are frequent in econometric research studies since their coefficients are directly interpretable, and the implied dynamics is intuitively appealing.

The logarithmic specification implies that the coefficient of each explanatory variable is a short-run elasticity (the percentage change in the dependent variable in the first year resulting from a 1% change in the independent variable). Long-run elasticities (the ultimate percentage change in the dependent variable after a 1% change in the independent variable) are computed as the ratio of the short-run elasticity to (1-lag coefficient).

Random Events

As described above, weather is an important cause of random variations in visits to the recreation site and has important implications for the tourism industry. Part of the change in export sales by the "other" industry in the community is also generated as a random event. The model assumes the percentage deviation of current from previous export sales is randomly selected in the range from-5% to +5%. Early in the administration of the town it is unlikely that any unforeseen event will alter the outcome of control decisions. By the fifth year of the administration, however, there is a 60% probability that some such unforeseen event has occurred. These events are announced as "Important News Flash(es)." Five types of random events are built into the model:

The percentages and the dollar amount indicated by the News Flashes are also determined randomly. The percentages range from 25 to 100%, and the dollar amount of the deficit can range from 0 to $250,000. The choice of the five events was meant to correspond to five of the major uncertainties facing tourism community administrators: unexpected catastrophes in tourism and the "other" industry, a direct threat to tourism attractiveness because of pollution, unforeseen (and unplanned) rapid growth in tourism, and a personal threat to the job security of the administrator.

The player is given the opportunity to respond to these events before the impact is levied on the social, environmental, and economic indexes. The successful planner will take corrective actions given this opportunity. The probability of a subsequent event is low for the immediate future after an event, but increases as the years pass. This may be an unrealistic representation of the planner who spends considerable time responding to crises. The game events may be repeated or not and the severity of the events, as measured by the percentage or dollar amount, will vary from occurrence to occurrence and game to game. It is very unlikely that any two games will be similar.

Community Impacts

Population Change

The 20,000 or so residents of the game community work either in the tourism industry or the "other" industry. There is a natural growth in the population of 1% per year as well as migration into and out of the community depending on the difference between the percentage of unemployed workers and an assumed "frictional" employment level of 3%. If the unemployment rate is above the frictional level there will be population migration out of the community; if the unemployment rate is less than 3% there will be some migration of population into the community.

Income Generation and Wealth

Residential income is the sum of wages paid to workers and profits earned by owners in the tourism and "other" industries. It is assumed that the major portion of current income is expended on necessities purchased from the "other" industry and luxuries including recreation-days purchased from the natural resource managers, the tourism industry.

The wealth of residents is characterized by the value of residential property (broadly defined). Residential property values are influenced by the number of residents; with more residents, demand for property rises and property values increase. Property taxes are the only taxes paid by residents, and they are controlled by the rate set by the game player.

Town Finances

The town derives revenues from five sources: daily tourist fees, residential property taxes, tourism industry property taxes, "other" industry property taxes, and interest income on any accumulated budget surplus from previous years (at a 10% annual rate). The town allocates its budget to five categories of expenditures: tourism promotion, "other" economic programs, social programs, environmental programs, and an automatic interest expense deducted for any accumulated deficit from previous years (also at a 10% annual rate).

The Quality of Life

Economic, Social and Environmental Impacts

In addition to the income generated for residents by the tourism and "other" industries in the communities, there are a host of other economic, social, and environmental characteristics that constitute the quality of community life. All these characteristics are assumed be represented by a set of four indexes. The economic index rises with the average wage rate and falls with unemployment. The social and environmental indexes rise with expenditures on social and environmental programs and fall with increases in the numbers of tourist-days and residential recreational visits.

A social-environmental index, which is also used as a measure of tourism attractiveness in the demand equation for tourist visits, is provided by the geometric mean of the social and environmental indexes. A quality of community life is provided by the geometric mean of the social-environmental index and the economic index. This index is assumed to be the objective function for the community and determines the annual game score.

Game Play and Use of Controls

Active Play

The first active screen of the game requests that the player provides three initials for identification. These are later used to record the player's final score for comparison with other scores. The player is asked at once whether the seven economic controls should be changed from their initial settings. As soon as the player is "Ready for the next year to begin," a community overview screen is shown such as the one in this screen provides current and past values for tourism industry revenue, "other" industry revenue, real disposable household income, the unemployment rate, and the accumulated town surplus or deficit.

This screen also presents up to five news headlines determined by the indexes described above and the player's current and cumulative score. The following sequence of screens afford the player the opportunity to view five detailed informational screens including:

- "Local Government Financial Statements,"
- "Social Environmental Statistics,"
- "Tourism Business Statistics," and
- "other Industry Statistics."

When the player is finally satisfied that enough information has been viewed and that the appropriate adjustments to the seven controls have been made, the next year begins, and the model calculates changes to the community and its industries. Overview results for the next year are presented summarizing these calculations. When a player chooses to change one or more of the economic controls, a screen is presented that indicates the current level of each of the controls and how controls can be changed When all controls have been changed to the desired values, the player begins the next year of the administration.

Player Performance

The first informational screen of each year provides the annual score for the player based on the overall wellbeing index. However, the player (administrator) also must attempt to balance the budget in order to keep from being fired. If the deficit (or surplus) exceeds more than a few percent of the total budget the planner is defamed in the press. If the deficit (or surplus) is greater than about 10% the player will be fired despite the overall wellbeing of the community. Thus, the relative size of the town's budget deficit or surplus

The Game

You have been hired as the town planner for a community with an important tourism industry, it generates 55% of local income. The town budget is currently \$11.9 million. Town revenues last year were generated from a \$1 daily tourist tax (\$1.4 Million last year), and property taxes from residents (\$8 M), tourism businesses (\$2 M),and other businesses (\$0.5 M). The last administration allocated \$5.5 M to social programs, \$1.5 M to tourism promotion, \$4.5 M to environmental programs, and \$0.4 M to other economic development programs. Your task is to adjust tax rates and expenditures to achieve:

The End of The Game and Scores

The game ends when the planner quits, is fired, or survives 10 years in office. The score consists of the average of the community well being index weighted by the residential population and summed over the number of years in office normalized so that 100 points per year reflects maintaining the initial levels of all indexes. The distribution of scores generated from 100 plays where the only criterion was to balance the budget is given in the scores underlying the illustration ranged from 402 to 1072 with only thirteen scores above the norm of 100 points per year for the entire ten-year period.

The distribution of scores obtained when following a specific decision rule has been a major aide in assessing the performance of the model. The rule that each year the tourist fee would be changed by exactly the ratio of the current deficit (or surplus) to the current number of tourist days. We have adopted this budget-balancing, status-quo type decision rule as our base line distribution of scores. In this distribution, the major cause of variation was games in which the player was fired prior to the ten-year maximum. The secondary cause of variation was the influence of random events on community well being.

As the bimodal distribution of the figure suggests, a typical game involved two events. When the first event was serious, the budget-balancing, status-quo player could not compensate and was fired between the fourth and seventh year as reflected in the cluster of scores between 400 and 700.

The second event occasionally resulted in a firing, but because of its timing late in the game most players reached the tenth year. Every game ends with the opportunity to view a listing of the ranked scores from the previous 100 games played. These results identify the players by initials, and the individual games played by the score earned, the number of years the office was held, and the nature of the "NEWS FLASH" events that occurred while in office.

These are indicated by the initial letter of the news flash (F, G, 0, U, or B) and provide a basis to evaluate the specific events that have most dramatically affected the well being of the game community. This list of scores has been useful to teachers for evaluating uses of the game and relative success of individual students in dealing with hypothetical community problems.

It is of particular interest to note that a major problem with the model was uncovered by students who figured out how to "beat the game." Property taxes, in the model, are treated as reductions in income prior to its allocation to leisure and non-leisure goods.

As such, the model predicts no social outrage following rapid property tax increases that are put back into social and environmental programs. Accordingly, students have found that extremely high scores can be earned by raising property taxes and spreading the proceeds across social programs. This result has lead to revisions in the game as well as the identification of new topics for tourism research.

In Research

As suggested by the distribution of scores shown in the game acts as a stochastic simulation model when a specific decision rule is adopted. A research version of the game offers the player the opportunity to change behavioural parameters and automatically restart with specific decision rules. This enables the study of the influence of individual parameters and identification of behavioural relationships that lead to extreme scores. This is the basis for an ongoing study of the model, its parameters, and future refinements of the model.

Summary and Conclusions

It has been the purpose of this paper to present the details of a project that started toward a research objective, later became an educational project, and is currently on going as a combined research and educational program. Based in research findings from a variety of studies, a "straw-man" computer game was constructed to help in the presentation of a difficult concept in a new research effort: the dynamic and stochastic nature of tourism community behaviour. This game was "borrowed" for use in the classroom and subsequently revised for educational purposes. We are convinced that game play is a very exciting way of teaching tourism planning. We have also found that students and others playing the game can provide us with an unexpectedly rich source of research assistance'.

In our quest for a "reasonable" characterization of tourism community behaviour. We have therefore altered our research procedures to explicitly account for the research-education interaction. It has been to our great delight that, on more than one occasion, students have identified inadequacies in the model by their ability to "beat the game." The future for this type of project is bright. The model has been used by over 50 researchers and 500 students, and feedback from its use has suggested a wide range of revisions.

These include adding more sectors of the economy toward the goal of a Leontief model of transactions, adding more types of tourists and residents, and adding more specific impacts thus far only generalized as social and environmental impacts. It has also been suggested that more of the complexities of community government be included such as the role of zoning on development. Many of these suggestions could result in major improvements to the model; however, the game's simplicity would need to be sacrificed. In the process of deciding upon such improvements, it will be our overriding concern to maintain a balance between the model's usefulness as an educational tool and as a research vehicle.

10

Risk Analysis

Probabilistic risk assessment (PRA) (or probabilistic safety assessment/analysis) is a systematic and comprehensive methodology to evaluate risks associated with a complex engineered technological entity (such as an airliner or a nuclear power plant).

Risk in a PRA is defined as a feasible detrimental outcome of an activity or action.

In a PRA, risk is characterized by two quantities:

1. the magnitude (severity) of the possible adverse consequence(s), and
2. the likelihood (probability) of occurrence of each consequence.

Consequences are expressed numerically (e.g., the number of people potentially hurt or killed) and their likelihoods of occurrence are expressed as probabilities or frequencies (i.e., the number of occurrences or the probability of occurrence per unit time). The total risk is the expected loss: the sum of the products of the consequences multiplied by their probabilities.

The spectrum of risks across classes of events are also of concern, and are usually controlled in licensing processes – it would be of concern if rare but high consequence events were found to dominate the overall risk, particularly as these risk assessment is very sensitive to assumptions (how rare is a high consequence event?). Probabilistic Risk Assessment usually answers three basic questions:

1. What can go wrong with the studied technological entity, or what are the initiators or initiating events (undesirable starting events) that lead to adverse consequence(s)?

2. What and how severe are the potential detriments, or the adverse consequences that the technological entity may be eventually subjected to as a result of the occurrence of the initiator?
3. How likely to occur are these undesirable consequences, or what are their probabilities or frequencies?

Two common methods of answering this last question are Event Tree Analysis and Fault Tree Analysis-for explanations of these. In addition to the above methods, PRA studies require special but often very important analysis tools like human reliability analysis (HRA) and common-cause-failure analysis (CCF). HRA deals with methods for modelling human error while CCF deals with methods for evaluating the effect of inter-system and intra-system dependencies which tend to cause simultaneous failures and thus significant increases in overall risk.

PRA studies have been successfully performed for complex technological systems at all phases of the life cycle from concept definition and pre-design through safe removal from operation. For example, the Nuclear Regulatory Commission required that each nuclear power plant in the US perform an Individual Plant Examination (IPE) to identify and quantify plant vulnerabilities to hardware failures and human faults in design and operation.

Although no method was specified for performing such an evaluation, the NRC requirements for the analysis could be met only by applying PRA methods.

Risk Analysis (Business)

Risk analysis is a technique to identify and assess factors that may jeopardize the success of a project or achieving a goal. This technique also helps to define preventive measures to reduce the probability of these factors from occurring and identify countermeasures to successfully deal with these constraints when they develop to avert possible negative effects on the competitiveness of the company. Reference class forecasting was developed to increase accuracy in risk analysis. One of the more popular methods to perform a risk analysis in the computer field is called facilitated risk analysis process (FRAP).

Facilitated Risk Analysis Process

FRAP analyses one system, application or segment of business processes at time.

FRAP assumes that additional efforts to develop precisely quantified risks are not cost effective because:

- such estimates are time consuming
- risk documentation becomes too voluminous for practical use
- specific loss estimates are generally not needed to determine if controls are needed.

After identifying and categorizing risks, a team identifies the controls that could mitigate the risk.

The decision for what controls are needed lies with the business manager. The team's conclusions as to what risks exists and what controls needed are documented along with a related action plan for control implementation.

Three of the most important risks a software company faces are: unexpected changes in revenue, unexpected changes in costs from those budgeted and the amount of specialization of the software planned.

Risks that affect revenues can be: unanticipated competition, privacy, intellectual property right problems, and unit sales that are less than forecast. Unexpected development costs also create risk that can be in the form of more rework than anticipated, security holes, and privacy invasions.

Narrow specialization of software with a large amount of research and development expenditures can lead to both business and technological risks since specialization does not necessarily lead to lower unit costs of software.

Table: *Top 9 of the market research sector 2009*

S. N.	*Company*	*Sales in 2009 (million USD)*	*Growth in %*
1	Nielsen Company	5,056.0	2.6
2	WPP Group-Kantar Group, TNS, Millward Brown, BMRB, IMRB International and Ziment Group	4692	2.5
3	IMS Health Inc.	1,958.6	8.9
4	GfK AG	1,397.3	5.4
5	Ipsos	1,077.0	6.5
6	Synovate	739.6	9.5
7	IRI	665.0	6.6
8	Westat	425.8	0.8
9	Arbitron	400.0	5.9

Combined with the decrease in the potential customer base, specialization risk can be significant for a software firm. After probabilities of scenarios have been calculated with risk analysis, the process of risk management can be applied to help manage the risk.

Methods like applied information economics add to and improve on risk analysis methods by introducing procedures to adjust subjective probabilities, compute the value of additional information and to use the results in part of a larger portfolio management problem.

A/B Testing

A/B testing, split testing or bucket testing is a method of marketing testing by which a baseline control sample is compared to a variety of single-variable test samples in order to improve response rates. A classic direct mail tactic, this method has been recently adopted within the interactive space to test tactics such as banner ads, emails and landing pages. Significant improvements can be seen through testing elements like copy text, layouts, images and colors. However, not all elements produce the same improvements, and by looking at the results from different tests, it is possible to identify those elements that consistently tend to produce the greatest improvements.

Employers of this A/B testing method will distribute multiple samples of a test, including the control, to see which single variable is most effective in increasing a response rate or other desired outcome. The test, in order to be effective, must reach an audience of a sufficient size that there is a reasonable chance of detecting a meaningful difference between the control and other tactics:

> *This method is different to multivariate testing which applies statistical modelling which allows a tester to try multiple variables within the samples distributed.*

Companies Well-known for Using A/B Testing

Many companies use the designed experiment approach to making marketing decisions. It is an increasingly common practice as the tools and expertise grows in this area. There are many A/B testing case studies which show that the practice of testing is increasingly becoming popular with small and medium businesses as well.

While it is widely used behind the scenes to maximize profits, the practice occasionally makes it into the spotlight.

- Amazon.com pioneered its use within the web ecommerce space. Also stirred controversy by testing into optimal price-points.

- BBC.
- Google. One of their top designers, Douglas Bowman, left and spoke out against excessive use of the practice.
- Microsoft
- Playdom (Disney Interactive)
- Zynga
- ebay.com

A/B Testing Resources

There are a handful of free and paid tools that help make A/B testing available to everyone, though some are best suited for large corporations and organizations.

- ABTests.com is a website where people upload and analyse A/ B tests that they've run on their own sites.
- Adobe Omniture-Test&Target allow clients to A/B and multivariable tests. The main difference is that managers are allowed to do tests based on customers' details (web analytics' metrics) to deliver the tests.
- Google Website Optimizer (GWO) is a free tool by Google that allows webmaster to split traffic across two or more pages using Javascript commands. It is a recommended option of users who are just getting started with A/B testing.
- Lazzia is a simple product for A/B testing images. It doesn't require Javascript and can automatically show the winning image once a trial has finished.
- LiveBall is a powerful testing platform created by ion interactive that allows marketers to A/B or multivariate test their web pages. It comes with the option to automatically redirect traffic to the winning page once it has reached statistical significance. With LiveBall there's no need to know code, and there's no need for an advanced degree in mathematics in order to test and optimize web pages.
- Optimizely is designed for powerful yet fast and easy A/B testing. Marketing and sales users can create and run experiments without writing any code by using the WYSIWYG editor, while advanced technical users can customize and fine tune experiments with Javascript.
- Performable, unlike GWO, allows you to create landing pages and do A/B testing without any code or IT help. They have a

library of custom templates and an interface to allow you to make your own. They also create a "social profile" of your visitors using information from Facebook, LinkedIn, Twitter and several other networks.

- Unbounce is a platform that lets you create new landing pages and perform A/B tests on them. The WYSIWYG editor includes a suite of marketing-focused templates, allowing you to publish pages without any HTML coding or help from IT personnel.
- Visual Website Optimizer is a paid alternative to GWO with many advanced features (such as WYSIWYG editor, heatmap reports and tagless integration) that makes it suitable for business who want flexibility while create A/B and multivariate tests.
- VITES is a platform that allows companies to test visitor conversion rates across different profiles using server-side techniques.
- SumoOptimize is a product for conducting A/B testing, providing users an easy way to manage and monitor their tests through visual editor.

Advertisement Tracking

Ad tracking, also known as post-testing or ad effectiveness tracking is in-market research that monitors a brand's performance including brand and advertising awareness, product trial and usage, and attitudes about the brand versus their competition.

Depending on the speed of the purchase cycle in the category, tracking can be done continuously (a few interviews every week) or it can be "pulsed," with interviews conducted in widely spaced waves (ex. every three or six months). Interviews can either be conducted with separate, matched samples of consumers, or with a single (longitudinal) panel that is interviewed over time.

Since the researcher has information on when the ads launched, the length of each advertising flight, the dollars spent, and when the interviews were conducted, the results of ad tracking can provide information on the effects of advertising.

Purpose of Ad Tracking

The purpose of ad tracking is generally to provide a measure of the combined effect of the media weight or spending level, the effectiveness of the media buy or targeting, and the quality of the advertising executions or creative. Advertisers use the results of ad tracking to estimate the return on investment (ROI) of advertising, and to refine advertising plans. Sometimes, tracking data are used to provide inputs to Marketing Mix Models which marketing science statisticians build to estimate the role of advertising, as compared to pricing, distribution and other marketplace variables on sales of the brand.

Methodology

Today, most ad tracking studies are conducted via the Internet. Some ad tracking studies are conducted continuously and others are conducted at specific points in time (typically before the advertising appears in market, and then again after the advertising has been running for some period of time).

The two approaches use different types of analyses, although both start by measuring advertising awareness. Typically, the respondent is either shown a brief portion of a commercial, or a few memorable still images from the TV ad. Other media typically are cued using either branded or de-branded visual of the ad. Then, respondents answer three significant questions.

1. Do you recognize this ad? (recognition measure)
2. Please type in the sponsor of this ad. (unaided awareness measure)
3. Please choose from the following list, the sponsor of this ad. (aided awareness measure).

The continuous tracking design analyses advertising awareness over time, in relation to ad spending; separately, this design tracks brand awareness, and then develops indices of effectiveness based on the strength of the correlations between ad spending and brand awareness.

The most popular alternate approach to the continuous tracking design is the Communicus System longitudinal design, in which the same people are interviewed at two points in time. Changes in brand measures (for example, brand purchasing and future purchase intentions) exhibited among those who have seen the advertising are compared to the changes in brand measures that occurred among those unaware of advertising.

By means of this method, the researchers can isolate those marketplace changes that were produced by advertising versus those that would have occurred without advertising.

Internet Tracking

There are several different tools to effectively track online ads: banner ads, ppc ads, pop-up ads, and other types. Several online advertising companies such as Google offer their own ad tracking service in order to effectively use their service to generate a positive ROI.

Third-party ad tracking services are commonly used by affiliate marketers.

Affiliate marketers are frequently unable to have access to the order page and therefore are unable to use a 3rd-party tool. Many different companies have created tools to effectively track their commissions in order to optimize their profit potential. The information provided will show the marketer which advertising methods are generating income and which are not. This information will allow the marketer to effectively allocate his budget in the best possible way.

Measures

Here is a list of some of the data a post-test might provide:

- Top of mind awareness
- Unaided brand awareness
- Aided brand awareness
- Brand fit
- Brand image ratings
- Brand trial
- Repeat purchase
- Frequency of use
- Purchase intent
- Price perceptions
- Unaided advertising awareness
- Aided advertising awareness
- Unaided advertising message recall
- Aided advertising message recall
- Aided commercial recall
- Ad wear out
- Promotion awareness and usage
- Market segment characteristics
- Media habits

- Lifestyle/Psychographics
- Demographics.

Advertising Research

Advertising research is a specialized form of marketing research conducted to improve the efficiency of advertising. According to MarketConscious.com, "It may focus on a specific ad or campaign, or may be directed at a more general understanding of how advertising works or how consumers use the information in advertising. It can entail a variety of research approaches, including psychological, sociological, economic, and other perspectives."

History

1879-N.W. Ayer conducts custom research in an attempt to win the advertising business of Nichols-Shepard Co., a manufacturer of agricultural machinery.

1895-Harlow Gale of the University of Minnesota mails questionnaires to gather opinions about advertising from the public.

1900s-George B. Waldron conducts qualitative research for Mahin's Advertising Agency

1910s-1911 can be considered the year marketing research becomes an industry. That year, J. George Frederick leaves his position as editor of Printer's Ink to begin his research company, the Business Bourse with clients such as General Electric and the Texas Co. Also in 1911, Kellogg Co.'s ad manager, R.O. Eastman creates the Association of National Advertisers which is now known as the Association of National Advertising Managers. The group's first project is a postcard questionnaire to determine magazine readership. The results introduce the concept of duplication of circulation. In 1916, R.O. Eastman starts his own company, the Eastman Research Bureau which boasts clients such as Cosmopolitan, Christian Herald, and General Electric.

1920s-In 1922, Dr. Daniel Starch tests reader recognition levels of magazine and newspaper advertisements and editorial content. In 1923, Dr. George Gallup begins measuring advertising readership.

1930s-In 1936, Dr. George Gallup validates his survey methodology by using the same tools polling voters during public elections. This allows him to successfully compare and validate his study's results against the election's results.

1940s-Post World War II, the U.S. sees a large increase in the number of market research companies.

1950s-Market researchers focus on improving methods and measures. In their search for a single-number statistic to capture the overall performance of the advertising creative, Day-After-Recall (DAR) is created.

1960s-Qualitative focus groups gain in popularity. In addition, some advertisers call for more rigorous measurement of the in-market effectiveness of advertising in order to provide better accountability for the large amounts being spent on advertising. In response, Seymour Smith and Associates, using Advertising Research Foundation data as a jumping-off point, develops the Communicus System, a comprehensive approach to isolating the in-market impact of advertising across media.

1970s-Computers emerge as business tools, allowing researchers to conduct large-scale data manipulations. (Honomichl) Multiple studies prove DAR (Recall) scores do not predict sales. The measure, persuasion, also known as motivation, is validated as a predictor of sales. The measure known as "breakthrough" is re-examined by researchers who make a distinction between the attention-getting power of the creative execution (attention) and how well "branded" the ad is (brand linkage). Herbert Krugman seeks to measure non-verbal measures biologically by tracking brain wave activities as respondents watch commercials. (Krugman) Others experiment with galvanic skin response, voice pitch analysis, and eye-tracking.

1980s-Researchers begin to view commercials as a "structured flow of experience" rather than a single unit to be rated on the whole, creating moment-by-moment systems such as the dial-a-meter.

1990s-Ameritest Research creates Picture Sorts to provide accurate non-verbal measurements in a moment-by-moment system. Picture Sorts results are graphed to visually represent commercial viewers' moment-by-moment image recognition (Flow of Attention), positive and negative feelings (Flow of Emotion), and brand values (Flow of Meaning). Trends in in-market tracking include a greater focus on the multimedia nature of entire advertising campaigns.

2000s-Global advertisers seek an integrated marketing research system that will work worldwide so they can compare results across countries. For a look at trends predicted for advertising research in the 21st century, see Seven Trends for the Future. Dr. Robert Heath publishes the seminal and controversial monograph "The Hidden Power of Advertising" which challenged the traditional models used in advertising research and shows how most advertising is processed at an emotional level (not a rational level). His monograph leads to re-examination of in-market research approaches that compare the behaviours of those who have seen advertising versus those who have not, such as the Communicus System, and the development of brand new pretesting systems such as the OTX AdCEP system.

Types of Advertising Research

There are two types of research, customized and syndicated. Customized research is conducted for a specific client to address that client's needs. Only that client has access to the results of the research. Syndicated research is a single research study conducted by a research company with its results available, for sale, to multiple companies. Pre-market research can be conducted to optimize advertisements for any medium: radio, television, print (magazine, newspaper or direct mail), outdoor billboard (highway, bus, or train), or Internet. Different methods would be applied to gather the necessary data appropriately. Post-testing is conducted after the advertising, either a single ad or an entire multimedia campaign has been run in-market. The focus is on what the advertising has done for the brand, for example increasing brand awareness, trial, frequency of purchasing.

Pre-testing

Pre-testing, also known as copy testing, is a form of customized research that predicts in-market performance of an ad, before it airs, by analysing audience levels of attention, brand linkage, motivation, entertainment, and communication, as well as breaking down the ad's Flow of Attention and Flow of Emotion. Measuring attention is very important in Pre-testing. The data tells us where customers look at and which parts of the ad they ignore. Attention can be measured with Eye tracking or AttentionTracking.

Pre-testing is also used on ads still in rough form – e.g., animatics or ripomatics. Pre-testing is also used to identify weak spots within an ad to improve performance, to more effectively edit 60's to 30's or 30's to 15's, to select images from the spot to use in an integrated campaign's print ad, to pull out the key moments for use in ad tracking, and to identify branding moments.

Campaign Pre-testing

A new area of pre-testing driven by the realization that what works on TV does not necessarily translate in other media. Greater budgets allocated to digital media in particular have driven the need for campaign pre-testing. The first to market with a product to test integrated campaigns was OTX in association with Sequent Partners with the introduction of MediaCEP. The latest generation of this product incorporates one of the leading media planning tools developed by a media modelling and software company Pointlogic. The addition of a media planning tool to this testing approach allows advertisers to test the whole campaign, creative and media, and measures the synergies expected with an integrated campaign.

Post-testing

Post-testing/Tracking studies provide either periodic or continuous in-market research monitoring a brand's performance, including brand awareness, brand preference, product usage and attitudes. Some post-testing approaches simply track changes over time, while others use various methods to quantify the specific changes produced by advertising—either the campaign as a whole or by the different media utilized.

Overall, advertisers use post-testing to plan future advertising campaigns, so the approaches that provide the most detailed information on the accomplishments of the campaign are most valued. The two types of campaign post-testing that have achieved the greatest use among major advertisers include continuous tracking, in which changes in advertising spending are correlated with changes in brand awareness, and longitudinal studies, in which the same group of respondents are tracked over time. With the longitudinal approach, it is possible to go beyond brand awareness, and to isolate the campaign's impact on specific behavioural and perceptual dimensions, and to isolate campaign impact by medium.

Terminology

- advertising
- aesthetic emotion
- attention
- awareness
- fit
- brand linkage
- branding moment
- copy sort
- copy test
- day-after recall (DAR)
- Flow of Attention

- Flow of Emotion
- Flow of Meaning
- motivation
- peak visual
- persuasion
- Picture Sorts
- Shockvertising
- stickiness
- stopping power.

Copy Testing

Copy testing is a specialized field of marketing research. It is the study of television commercials prior to airing them, and is defined as research to determine an ad's effectiveness based on consumers' responses to the ad. It covers all media including print, TV, radio, Internet etc. Although also known as copy testing, pre-testing is considered the more accurate, modern name (Young) for the prediction of how effectively an ad will perform, based on the analysis of feedback gathered from the target audience. Each test will either qualify the ad as strong enough to meet company action standards for airing or identify opportunities to improve the performance of the ad through editing. (Young)

Pre-testing is also used to identify weak spots within an ad campaign, to more effectively edit 60-second ads to 30-second ads or 30's to 15's, to select images from the spot to use in an integrated campaign's print ad, to pull out the key moments for use in ad tracking, and to identify branding moments.

Features of a Good Copy Testing System

In 1982, a consortium of 21 leading advertising agencies including N.W.Ayers, D'Arcy, Grey, McCann-Erikson, Needham Harper & Steers, Ogilvy & Mather, J.Walter Thompson, Young & Rubicam etc. released a public document where they laid out the PACT (Positioning Advertising Copy Testing) Principles on what constitutes a good copy testing system. According to PACT, a good copy testing system is one that meets the following criteria:

1. Provides measurements which are relevant to the objectives of the advertising
2. Requires agreements about how the results will be used in advance of each specific test.

3. Provides multiple measurements – because single measurements are generally inadequate to assess the performance of an advertisement/
4. Based on a model of human response to communications – the reception of a stimulus, the comprehension of the stimulus and the response to the stimulus.
5. Allows for consideration of whether the advertising stimulus should be exposed more than once.
6. Recognizes that the more finished a piece of copy is, the more soundly it can be evaluated and requires, as a minimum, that alternative executions be tested in the same degree of finish.
7. Provides controls to avoid the biasing effects of the exposure context.
8. Takes into account basic considerations of sample definition.
9. Demonstrates reliability and validity.

Four Types of Copy Testing Scores

There are four general themes woven into the last century of copy testing. To understand how the different types of measures relate to one another.

Report Card Measures

The first theme is the quest for a valid, single-number statistic to capture the overall performance of the advertising creative. This search has spawned the creation of various report card measures. These measures are used to filter commercial executions and help management make the go/no go decision about which ads to air. (Young).

The predominant copy testing measure of the 1950s and 1960s, Day-After Recall (DAR) was interpreted to measure an ad's ability to "break through" into the mind of the consumer and register a message from the brand in long-term memory. (Honomichl) Once this measure was adopted by Procter and Gamble, it became a research staple. In the 1970s and 1980s, after DAR was determined to be a poor predictor of sales, the research industry began to depend on the measure of persuasion as an accurate predictor of sales. This shift was led, in part, by researcher Horace Schwerin who pointed out, "the obvious truth is that a claim can be well remembered but completely unimportant to the prospective buyer of the product – the solution the marketer offers is addressed to the wrong need." (Honomichl).

As with DAR, it was Procter and Gamble's acceptance of the persuasion measure (also known as motivation) that made it an industry standard. Recall scores were still provided in copy testing reports with the understanding that persuasion was the measure that mattered. (Honomichl) The 1970s also saw a re-examination of the "breakthrough" measure. As a result, an important distinction was made between the attention-getting power of the creative execution and how well "branded" the ad was. Thus, the separate measures of attention and branding were born. (Young)

Obstacles

In the 70s, 80s, and 90s, tests were conducted to validate a link between the recall score and actual sales. For example, Procter and Gamble reviewed 10 year's worth of split-cable tests (100 total) and found no significant relationship between recall scores and sales. (Young) In addition, Wharton University's marketing guru Leonard Lodish conducted an even more extensive review of test market results and also failed to find a relationship between recall and sales. (Lodish) Harold Ross of Mapes & Ross found that persuasion was a better predictor of sales than recall. (Ross)

Diagnostic Measures

The second theme is the development of diagnostic copy testing, the main purpose of which is optimization. Understanding why diagnostic measures such as attention, brand linkage, and motivation are high or low can help advertisers identify creative opportunities to improve executions. (Young)

Obstacles

Different approaches have been developed by research companies to determine the report card measures of attention, brand linkage, and motivation. For example, Unilever analysed a database of commercials "triple-tested" using the three leading approaches to the measure of branding (Ameritest, ASI, and Millward Brown) which shows that each of the three is measuring something uncorrelated with, and therefore different from, the other two. (Kastenholtz, Kerr & Young). This condition has to be text via to the best of advertisment in section of division.

Non-Verbal Measures

The third theme is the development of non-verbal measures in response to the belief of many advertising professionals that much of a commercial's effects – e.g. the emotional impact – may be difficult for respondents to put into words or scale on verbal rating statements. In fact, many believe the commercial's effects may be operating below the level of consciousness. (Young) According to researcher Chuck Young, "There is something in the lovely sounds of our favourite music that we cannot verbalize – and it moves us in ways we cannot express."

Obstacles

In the 1970s, researchers, such as Herbert Krugman sought to measure these non-verbal measures biologically by tracking brain wave activities as respondents watched commercials. (Krugman) Others experimented with galvanic skin response, voice pitch analysis, and eye-tracking. (Young) These efforts were not popularly adopted, in part, because of the limitations of the technology as well as the poor cost-effectiveness of what was widely perceived as academic, not actionable research.

Solutions

In the 1990s, the Picture Sorts were created as a method of deconstructing a viewer's dynamic response to the film on multiple levels. A Flow of Attention graph, as one example of a Picture Sort, measures how the eye pre-consciously filters the visual information in an ad and serves both as a gatekeeper for human consciousness and as an interactive search engine. More mainstream than the biological measures, Picture Sorts have been used extensively for on-line ad testing and, because they are not language-dependent, have been used around the world by major advertisers as diverse as IBM and Unilever. More recently, research companies have started to use psychological tests, such as the Stroop effect, to measure the emotional impact of copy. These techniques exploit the notion that viewers do not know why they react to a product, image, or ad in a certain way (or that they reacted at all) because such reactions occur outside of awareness, through changes in networks of thoughts, ideas, and images.

Moment-by-Moment Measures

The fourth theme, which is a variation on the previous two, is the development of moment-by-moment measures to describe the internal dynamic structure of the viewer's experience of the commercial, as a diagnostic counterpoint to the various gestalt measures of commercial performance or predicted impact.

In the early 1980s the shift in analytical perspective from thinking of a commercial as the fundamental unit of measurement to be rated in its entirety, to thinking of it as a structured flow of experience, gave rise to experimentation with moment-by-moment systems. The most popular of these was the dial-a-meter response which required respondents to turn a meter, in degrees, toward one end of a scale or another to reflect their opinion of what was on screen at that moment.

Obstacles

Unless the dial-a-meter is calibrated by normalizing the data to each individual's reaction time, the aggregate sample data will be spread across many measurement intervals. Second, dial-a-meters contain an uncertainty range around which moment is actually being measured because of differences in respondent response times. Relatively little has been published to validate dial-a-meter diagnostics to traditional measures of overall ad performance such as recall and persuasion.

Solutions

In the 1990s, the Ameritest Picture Sorts shifted the frame of measurement from clock time (the dial-a-meter approach) to the "subjective time" of experience which is tied to the rate of information flow in the film, or the ad's visual complexity. Instead of providing a rating whenever the alarm rings, respondents rate a Picture Sort image only when the mood, message, or image changes significantly. The data results are clear, easy to understand, and visually appealing. (Young) Examples of an Ameritest Flow of Emotion Graph can be seen in The Advertising Research Handbook, (Young) and here in Exhibit 2.

In addition, the dial-a-meter's single-scale limitations are overcome with a set of moment-by-moment measures in three dimensions: wiktionary: Flow of Attention Flow of Attention which measures the memorability of each moment, Flow of Emotion which measures the positive or negative emotional response to each moment, and Flow of Meaning which measures how well the brand's strategic values are being communicated in each moment.

The Future: Seven Trends

Chuck Young, author of The Advertising Research Handbook, offers his views on the trends that will shape the way we do business in the future. (Young)

1. There will be an emergence of global research standards for global brands. Increasingly, multi-nationals are focusing on the need to build global brands, and for their brands to speak

with one voice around the world. This calls for global advertising campaigns that will be increasingly visual in style. Providing both a standard way to measure advertising performance from one region to another, and the tools to identify how different cultural factors affect advertising response, will become more important for managing ad spending in the global marketplace.

2. There will be more advertising measurement, not less. Advertising is becoming more expensive and the range of executional options becoming so diverse that more control over the process is being demanded by major clients today. Procurement departments, in particular, under the banner of accountability, are challenging advertising agencies and research companies to provide more proof of value to justify ad budgets. This will drive growth in this important sector of advertising research.
3. Most copy testing will move to the Internet. In an age of rapid-response marketing, the emphasis is on speed of decision-making. The Internet is the obvious choice for shortening the time involved in the research step of the creative development cycle. Many suppliers have already begun migrating their advertising research to the web (for both television and print testing). Even measuring attention can already be done online with AttentionTracking. Economic pressure will probably force the majority of testing online in the near future.
4. The new value proposition will be filtering plus optimization. For the foreseeable future, the cost of advertising executions will continue to go up. To manage that cost, managers will be increasingly interested in airing only their strongest ideas so that they don't spend a large portion of their advertising budgets on average ideas. Ad managers will be looking for every opportunity to make executions work harder and research systems will outperform this growing category if they can validate the power of their diagnostics, providing proof that they actually help make ads more effective.
5. Ad research will move beyond semantics – putting a new emphasis on "holistic" or 360-degree measurement of integrated advertising campaigns. Both the forces of globalization and the evolution of rich, multi-sensory media environments will continue to challenge execution from the print execution to the Internet ad.

6. Mathematics models of advertising ROI will begin to incorporate measures of creative quality.

Currently, researchers working with marketing-mix models to determine advertising ROI do not usually include measures of creative quality. As a result, current mix models are biased toward media weight or spend. In the future, sophisticated modelers will start to include a "quality" variable in these models, particularly as new forms of tracking research begin to provide relative performance rankings of competitive ads.

Council of American Survey Research Organizations

The Council of American Survey Research Organizations' 325+member companies and their 32,000 employees, all of whom are afforded membership benefits, represent nearly $8 billion in global annual revenue—about 85% of the U.S. research industry and 30% of the global research industry.

CASRO's member companies annually reaffirm their adherence to the CASRO Code of Standards and Ethics for Survey Research, an internationally-respected code of business and professional standards for more than 30 years.

CASRO is an advocate of the survey research industry throughout the US and the world. Founded in 1975, CASRO represents the viewpoints and agenda of companies engaged in all forms of survey research—public opinion, social, market, government and political.

Experimental Techniques

Experimental research designs are used for the controlled testing of causal processes.

The general procedure is one or more independent variables are manipulated to determine their effect on a dependent variable. These designs can be used where:

1. There is time priority in a causal relationship (cause precedes effect),
2. There is consistency in a causal relationship (a cause will always lead to the same effect), and
3. The magnitude of the correlation is great.

The most common applications of these designs in marketing research and experimental economics are test markets and purchase labs. The techniques are commonly used in other social sciences including sociology, psychology, and social work.

Controls

One of the most important requirements of experimental research designs is the necessity of eliminating the effects of spurious, intervening, and antecedent variables. In the most basic model, cause (X) leads to effect (Y). But there could be a third variable (Z) that influences (Y), and X might not be the true cause at all. Z is said to be a spurious variable and must be controlled for. The same is true for intervening variables (a variable in between the supposed cause (X) and the effect (Y)), and anteceding variables (a variable prior to the supposed cause (X) that is the true cause). When a third variable is involved and has not been controlled for, the relation is said to be a zero order relationship. In most practical applications of experimental research designs there are several causes (X1, X2, X3). In most designs, only one of these causes is manipulated at a time.

Purchase Laboratory

A true experimental design requires an artificial environment to control for all spurious, intervening, and antecedent variables. A purchase laboratory approaches this ideal. Participants are given money, script, or credit to purchase products in a simulated store. Researchers modify one variable at a time (for example; price, packaging, shelf location, size, or competitors' offerings) and determine what effect that has on sales volume. Internet-based purchase labs (called virtual purchase labs) are becoming more common.

Simplified versions of the purchase laboratory are often used for pragmatic reasons. An example of this would be to use tachistoscopes for testing packaging and shelf location.

Test Markets

Quasi-experimental designs control some, but not all, of the extraneous factors. A test market is an example of this. A new product is typically introduced in a select number of cities. These cities must be representative of the overall national (or international) population. They should also be relatively unpolluted by outside influences (for example : media from other cities). The marketer has some control over the marketing mix variables, but almost no control over the broader business environment variables. Competitors could change their prices during the test. Government could change the level of taxes. New competing products could be introduced. An advertising campaign could be initiated by competitors. Any of these spurious variables could contaminate the test market.

Experimental Research Designs

In an attempt to control for extraneous factors, several experimental research designs have been developed, including:

- Classical pretest-post test-The total population of participants is randomly divided into two samples; the control sample, and the experimental sample. Only the experimental sample is exposed to the manipulated variable. The researcher compares the pretest results with the post test results for both samples. Any divergence between the two samples is assumed to be a result of the experiment.
- Solomon four group design-The sample is randomly divided into four groups. Two of the groups are experimental samples. Two groups experience no experimental manipulation of variables. Two groups receive a pretest and a post test. Two groups receive only a post test. This is an improvement over the classical design because it controls for the effect of the pretest.
- Factorial design-this is similar to a classical design except additional samples are used. Each group is exposed to a different experimental manipulation.

Eye Tracking

Eye tracking is the process of measuring either the point of gaze ("where we are looking") or the motion of an eye relative to the head. An eye tracker is a device for measuring eye positions and eye movement. Eye trackers are used in research on the visual system, in psychology, in cognitive linguistics and in product design. There are a number of methods for measuring eye movement. The most popular variant uses video images from which the eye position is extracted. Other methods use search coils or are based on the electrooculogram.

History

In the 1800s, studies of eye movement were made using direct observations. In 1879 in Paris, Louis Emile Javal observed that reading does not involve a smooth sweeping of the eyes along the text, as previously assumed, but a series of short stops (called fixations) and quick saccades. This observation raised important questions about reading, which were explored during the 1900s: On which words do the eyes stop? For how long? When does it regress back to already seen words?

Edmund Huey built an early eye tracker, using a sort of contact lens with a hole for the pupil. The lens was connected to an aluminum pointer that moved in response to the movement of the eye. Huey studied and quantified regressions (only a small proportion of saccades are regressions), and show that some words in a sentence are not fixated.

The first non-intrusive eye trackers were built by Guy Thomas Buswell in Chicago, using beams of light that were reflected on the eye and then recording them on film. Buswell made systematic studies into reading and picture viewing. In the 1950s, Alfred L. Yarbus did important eye tracking research and his 1967 book is very highly quoted. He showed the task given to a subject has a very large influence on the subject's eye movement. He also wrote about the relation between fixations and interest:

> *"All the records... show conclusively that the character of the eye movement is either completely independent of or only very slightly dependent on the material of the picture and how it was made, provided that it is flat or nearly flat." The cyclical pattern in the examination of pictures "is dependent not only on what is shown on the picture, but also on the problem facing the observer and the information that he hopes to gain from the picture."*

This study by Yarbus (1967) is often referred to as evidence on how the task given to a person influences his or her eye movement.

> *"Records of eye movements show that the observer's attention is usually held only by certain elements of the picture.... Eye movement reflects the human thought processes; so the observer's thought may be followed to some extent from records of eye movement (the thought accompanying the examination of the particular object). It is easy to determine from these records which elements attract the observer's eye (and, consequently, his thought), in what order, and how often."*

> *"The observer's attention is frequently drawn to elements which do not give important information but which, in his opinion, may do so. Often an observer will focus his attention on elements that are unusual in the particular circumstances, unfamiliar, incomprehensible, and so on."*

> *"... when changing its points of fixation, the observer's eye repeatedly returns to the same elements of the picture. Additional time spent on perception is not used to examine the secondary elements, but to reexamine the most important elements."*

This study by Hunziker (1970) on *eye tracking in problem solving* used simple 8 mm film to track eye movement by filming the subject through a glass plate on which the visual problem was displayed.

In the 1970s, eye tracking research expanded rapidly, particularly reading research. A good overview of the research in this period is given by Rayner.

In 1980, Just and Carpenter formulated the influential *Strong eye-mind Hypothesis*, the hypothesis that "there is no appreciable lag between what is fixated and what is processed". If this hypothesis is correct, then when a subject looks at a word or object, he or she also thinks about (process cognitively), and for exactly as long as the recorded fixation. The hypothesis is often taken for granted by beginning eye tracker researchers.

During the 1980s, the eye-mind hypothesis was often questioned in light of covert attention, the attention to something that one is not looking at, which people often do. If covert attention is common during eye tracking recordings, the resulting scan path and fixation patterns would often show not where our attention has been, but only where the eye has been looking, and so eye tracking would not indicate cognitive processing. According to Hoffman, current consensus is that visual attention is always slightly (100 to 250 ms) ahead of the eye. But as soon as attention moves to a new position, the eyes will want to follow.

We still cannot infer specific cognitive processes directly from a fixation on a particular object in a scene. For instance, a fixation on a face in a picture may indicate recognition, liking, dislike, puzzlement etc. Therefore eye tracking is often coupled with other methodologies, such as introspective verbal protocols.

Tracker Types

Eye trackers measure rotations of the eye in one of several ways, but principally they fall into three categories:

One type uses an attachment to the eye, such as a special contact lens with an embedded mirror or magnetic field sensor, and the movement of the attachment is measured with the assumption that it does not slip significantly as the eye rotates. Measurements with tight fitting contact lenses have provided extremely sensitive recordings of eye movement, and magnetic search coils are the method of choice for researchers studying the dynamics and underlying physiology of eye movement.

The second broad category uses some non-contact, optical method for measuring eye motion. Light, typically infrared, is reflected from the eye and sensed by a video camera or some other specially designed optical sensor. The information is then analysed to extract eye rotation from changes in reflections.

Video based eye trackers typically use the corneal reflection (the first Purkinje image) and the center of the pupil as features to track over time. A more sensitive type of eye tracker, the dual-Purkinje eye tracker, uses reflections from the front of the cornea (first Purkinje image) and the back of the lens (fourth Purkinje image) as features to track. A still more sensitive method of tracking is to image features from inside the eye, such as the retinal blood vessels, and follow these features as the eye rotates. Optical methods, particularly those based on video recording, are widely used for gaze tracking and are favored for being non-invasive and inexpensive.

The third category uses electric potentials measured with electrodes placed around the eyes. The eyes are the origin of a steady electric potential field, which can also be detected in total darkness and if the eyes are closed. It can be modelled to be generated by a dipole with its positive pole at the cornea and its negative pole at the retina. The electric signal that can be derived using two pairs of contact electrodes placed on the skin around one eye is called Electrooculogram (EOG). If the eyes move from the centre position towards the periphery, the retina approaches one electrode while the cornea approaches the opposing one. This change in the orientation of the dipole and consequently the electric potential field results in a change in the measured EOG signal. Inversely, by analysing these changes in eye movement can be tracked. Due to the discretisation given by the common electrode setup two separate movement components – a horizontal and a vertical – can be identified. A third EOG component is the radial EOG channel, which is the average of the EOG channels referenced to some posterior scalp electrode. This radial EOG channel is sensitive to the saccadic spike potentials stemming from the extra-ocular muscles at the onset of saccades, and allows reliable detection of even miniature saccades.

Due to potential drifts and variable relations between the EOG signal amplitudes and the saccade sizes make it challenging to use EOG for measuring slow eye movement and detecting gaze direction. EOG is, however, a very robust technique for measuring saccadic eye movement associated with gaze shifts and detecting blinks. Contrary to video-based eye-trackers, EOG allows recording of eye movements even with eyes closed, and can thus be used in sleep research. It is a very light-weight approach that, in contrast to current video-based eye trackers, only requires very low computational power, works under different lighting conditions and can be implemented as an embedded, self-contained wearable system. It is thus the method of choice for measuring eye movement in mobile daily-life situations and REM phases during sleep.

Technologies and Techniques

The most widely used current designs are video-based eye trackers. A camera focuses on one or both eyes and records their movement as the viewer looks at some kind of stimulus. Most modern eye-trackers use contrast to locate the center of the pupil and use infrared and near-infrared non-collimated light to create a corneal reflection (CR). The vector between these two features can be used to compute gaze intersection with a surface after a simple calibration for an individual.

Two general types of eye tracking techniques are used: Bright Pupil and Dark Pupil. Their difference is based on the location of the illumination source with respect to the optics. If the illumination is coaxial with the optical path, then the eye acts as a retroreflector as the light reflects off the retina creating a bright pupil effect similar to red eye. If the illumination source is offset from the optical path, then the pupil appears dark because the retroreflection from the retina is directed away from the camera.

Bright Pupil tracking creates greater iris/pupil contrast allowing for more robust eye tracking with all iris pigmentation and greatly reduces interference caused by eyelashes and other obscuring features. It also allows for tracking in lighting conditions ranging from total darkness to very bright. But bright pupil techniques are not effective for tracking outdoors as extraneous IR sources interfere with monitoring.

Eye tracking setups vary greatly; some are head-mounted, some require the head to be stable (for example, with a chin rest), and some function remotely and automatically track the head during motion.

Most use a sampling rate of at least 30 Hz. Although 50/60 Hz is most common, today many video-based eye trackers run at 240, 350 or even 1000/1250 Hz, which is needed in order to capture the detail of the very rapid eye movement during reading, or during studies of neurology.

Eye movement is typically divided into fixations and saccades, when the eye gaze pauses in a certain position, and when it moves to another position, respectively.

The resulting series of fixations and saccades is called a scanpath. Most information from the eye is made available during a fixation, but not during a saccade.

The central one or two degrees of the visual angle (the fovea) provide the bulk of visual information; the input from larger eccentricities (the periphery) is less informative. Hence, the locations of fixations along a scanpath show what information loci on the stimulus were processed during an eye tracking session. On average, fixations last for around 200 ms during the reading of linguistic text, and 350 ms during the viewing of a scene. Preparing a saccade towards a new goal takes around 200 ms.

Scanpaths are useful for analysing cognitive intent, interest, and salience. Other biological factors (some as simple as gender) may affect the scanpath as well. Eye tracking in HCI typically investigates the scanpath for usability purposes, or as a method of input in gaze-contingent displays, also known as gaze-based interfaces.

Eye Tracking vs. Gaze Tracking

Eye trackers necessarily measure the rotation of the eye with respect to the measuring system. If the measuring system is head mounted, as with EOG, then eye-in-head angles are measured. If the measuring system is table mounted, as with scleral search coils or table mounted camera ("remote") systems, then gaze angles are measured. In many applications, the head position is fixed using a bite bar, a forehead support or something similar, so that eye position and gaze are the same. In other cases, the head is free to move, and head movement is measured with systems such as magnetic or video based head trackers.

For head-mounted trackers, head position and direction are added to eye-in-head direction to determine gaze direction. For table-mounted systems, such as search coils, head direction is subtracted from gaze direction to determine eye-in-head position.

Eye Tracking in Practice

A great deal of research has gone into studies of the mechanisms and dynamics of eye rotation, but the goal of eye tracking is most often to estimate gaze direction. Users may be interested in what features of an image draw the eye, for example. It is important to realize that the eye tracker does not provide absolute gaze direction, but rather can only measure changes in gaze direction.

In order to know precisely what a subject is looking at, some calibration procedure is required in which the subject looks at a point or series of points, while the eye tracker records the value that corresponds to each gaze position. (Even those techniques that track features of the retina cannot provide exact gaze direction because there is no specific anatomical feature that marks the exact point where the visual axis meets the retina, if indeed there is such a single, stable point.)

An accurate and reliable calibration is essential for obtaining valid and repeatable eye movement data, and this can be a significant challenge for non-verbal subjects or those who have unstable gaze. Each method of eye tracking has advantages and disadvantages, and the choice of an eye tracking system depends on considerations of cost and application. There are offline methods and online procedures like AttentionTracking.

There is a trade-off between cost and sensitivity, with the most sensitive systems costing many tens of thousands of dollars and requiring considerable expertise to operate properly. Advances in computer and video technology have led to the development of relatively low cost systems that are useful for many applications and fairly easy to use. Interpretation of the results still requires some level of expertise, however, because a misaligned or poorly calibrated system can produce wildly erroneous data.

Eye Tracking while Driving a Car in a Difficult Situation

The eye movement of two groups of drivers have been filmed with a special head camera by a team of the Swiss Federal Institute of Technology: Novice and experienced drivers had their eye-movement recorded while approaching a bend of a narrow road. The series of images has been condensed from the original film frames to show 2 eye fixations per image for better comprehension. Each of these stills correspond approximately to 0.5 seconds in realtime.

The series of images shows an example of eye fixations #9 to #14 of a typical novice and an experienced driver.

Comparison of the top images shows that the experienced driver checks the curve and even has Fixation No. 9 left to look aside while the novice driver needs to check the road and estimate his distance to the parked car. In the middle images the experienced driver is now fully concentrating on the location where an oncoming car could be seen. The novice driver concentrates his view on the parked car.

In the bottom image the novice is busy estimating the distance between the left wall and the parked car, while the experienced driver can use his peripheral vision for that and still concentrates his view on the dangerous point of the curve: If a car appears there he has to give way, i.e. stop to the right instead of passing the parked car.

Eye Tracking of Younger and Elderly People in Walking

Elderly subjects depend more on foveal vision than younger subjects during walking. Their walking speed is decreased by a limited visual field, probably caused by a deteriorated peripheral vision. Younger subjects make use of both their central and peripheral vision while walking. Their peripheral vision allows faster control over the process of walking.

Choosing an Eye Tracker

One difficulty in evaluating an eye tracking system is that the eye is never still, and it can be difficult to distinguish the tiny, but rapid and somewhat chaotic movement associated with fixation from noise sources in the eye tracking mechanism itself. One useful evaluation technique is to record from the two eyes simultaneously and compare the vertical rotation records.

The two eyes of a normal subject are very tightly coordinated and vertical gaze directions typically agree to within +/-2 minutes of arc (RMS of vertical position difference) during steady fixation. A properly functioning and sensitive eye tracking system will show this level of agreement between the two eyes, and any differences much larger than this can usually be attributed to measurement error.

Applications

A wide variety of disciplines use eye tracking techniques, including cognitive science, psychology (notably psycholinguistics, the visual world paradigm), human-computer interaction (HCI), marketing research and medical research (neurological diagnosis). Specific applications include the tracking eye movement in language reading, music reading, human activity recognition, the perception of advertising, and the playing of sport. Uses include:

- Cognitive Studies
- Medical Research
- Laser refractive surgery
- Human Factors
- Computer Usability
- Translation Process Research
- Vehicle Simulators
- In-vehicle Research
- Training Simulators
- Virtual Reality
- Adult Research
- Infant Research
- Adolescent Research
- Geriatric Research
- Primate Research
- Sports Training
- fMRI/MEG/EEG
- Commercial eye tracking (web usability, advertising, marketing, automotive, etc.)
- Finding good clues
- Communication systems for disabled
- Improved image and video communications
- Computer Science: Activity Recognition.

Commercial Applications

In recent years, the increased sophistication and accessibility of eye tracking technologies have generated a great deal of interest in the commercial sector. Applications include web usability, advertising, sponsorship, package design and automotive engineering. In general, commercial eye tracking studies function by presenting a target stimulus to a sample of consumers while an eye tracker is used to record the activity of the eye.

Examples of target stimuli may include websites, television programs, sporting events, films, commercials, magazines, newspapers, packages, shelf Displays, consumer systems (ATMs, checkout systems, kiosks), and software. The resulting data can be statistically analysed and graphically rendered to provide evidence of specific visual patterns.

By examining fixations, saccades, pupil dilation, blinks and a variety of other behaviours researchers can determine a great deal about the effectiveness of a given medium or product. While some companies complete this type of research internally, there are many private companies that offer eye tracking services and analysis.

The most prominent field of commercial eye tracking research is web usability. While traditional usability techniques are often quite powerful in providing information on clicking and scrolling patterns, eye tracking offers the ability to analyse user interaction between the clicks. This provides valuable insight into which features are the most eye-catching, which features cause confusion and which ones are ignored altogether.

Specifically, eye tracking can be used to assess search efficiency, branding, online advertisements, navigation usability, overall design and many other site components. Analyses may target a prototype or competitor site in addition to the main client site. Eye tracking is commonly used in a variety of different advertising media. Commercials, print ads, online ads and sponsored programs are all conducive to analysis with current eye tracking technology. Analyses focus on visibility of a target product or logo in the context of a magazine, newspaper, website, or televised event. This allows researchers to assess in great detail how often a sample of consumers fixates on the target logo, product or ad. In this way, an advertiser can quantify the success of a given campaign in terms of actual visual attention.

Eye tracking provides package designers with the opportunity to examine the visual behaviour of a consumer while interacting with a target package. This may be used to analyse distinctiveness, attractiveness and the tendency of the package to be chosen for purchase. Eye tracking is often utilized while the target product is in the prototype stage. Prototypes are tested against each other and competitors to examine which specific elements are associated with high visibility and appeal. One of the most promising applications of eye tracking research is in the field of automotive design. Research is currently underway to integrate eye tracking cameras into automobiles.

The goal of this endeavour is to provide the vehicle with the capacity to assess in real-time the visual behaviour of the driver. The National Highway Traffic Safety Administration (NHTSA) estimates that drowsiness is the primary causal factor in 100,000 police-reported accidents per year. Another NHTSA study suggests that 80% of collisions occur within three seconds of a distraction. By equipping automobiles with the ability to monitor drowsiness, inattention, and cognitive engagement driving safety could be dramatically enhanced.

Lexus claims to have equipped its LS 460 with the first driver monitor system in 2006, providing a warning if the driver takes his or her eye off the road. Since 2005, eye tracking is used in communication systems for disabled persons: allowing the user to speak, send e-mail, browse the Internet and perform other such activities, using only their eyes. Eye control works even when the user has involuntary movement as a result of Cerebral palsy or other disabilities, and for those who have glasses or other physical interference which would limit the effectiveness of older eye control systems.

Eye tracking has also seen minute use in autofocus still camera equipment, where users can focus on a subject simply by looking at it through the viewfinder.

Global Marketing

The Oxford University Press defines global marketing as "marketing on a worldwide scale reconciling or taking commercial advantage of global operational differences, similarities and opportunities in order to meet global objectives." Oxford University Press' Glossary of Marketing Terms. Here are three reasons for the shift from domestic to global marketing as given by the authors of the textbook, *Global Marketing Management—3rd Edition* by Masaaki Kotabe and Kristiaan Helsen, 2004.

Worldwide Competition

One of the product categories in which global competition has been easy to track in U.S.is automotive sales. The increasing intensity of competition in global markets is a challenge facing companies at all stages of involvement in international markets. As markets open up, and become more integrated, the pace of change accelerates, technology shrinks distances between markets and reduces the scale advantages of large firms, new sources of competition emerge, and competitive pressures mount at all levels of the organization.

Also, the threat of competition from companies in countries such as India, China, Malaysia, and Brazil is on the rise, as their own domestic markets are opening up to foreign competition, stimulating greater awareness of international market opportunities and of the need to be internationally competitive.

Companies which previously focused on protected domestic markets are entering into markets in other countries, creating new sources of competition, often targeted to price-sensitive market segments. Not only is competition intensifying for all firms regardless of their degree of global market involvement, but the basis for competition is changing. Competition continues to be market-based and ultimately relies on delivering superior value to consumers. However, success in global markets depends on knowledge accumulation and deployment. tiwana.

Evolution to Global Marketing

Global marketing is not a revolutionary shift, it is an evolutionary process. While the following does not apply to all companies, it does apply to most companies that begin as domestic-only companies.

Domestic Marketing

A marketing restricted to the political boundaries of a country, is called “Domestic Marketing”.

A company marketing only within its national boundaries only has to consider domestic competition. Even if that competition includes companies from foreign markets, it still only has to focus on the competition that exists in its home market. Products and services are developed for customers in the home market without thought of how the product or service could be used in other markets. All marketing decisions are made at headquarters.

The biggest obstacle these marketers face is being blindsided by emerging global marketers. Because domestic marketers do not generally focus on the changes in the global marketplace, they may not be aware of a potential competitor who is a market leader on three continents until they simultaneously open 20 stores in the Northeastern U.S. These marketers can be considered ethnocentric as they are most concerned with how they are perceived in their home country, exporting goods to other countries, loosener Rhett.

Bibliography

Ackerman, K.B.: *Practical Handbook of Warehousing*, Chapman & Hall, London, 1997.

Assael, H. : *Consumer Behaviour and Marketing Action*, USA: PWS-Kent, 1992.

Basu, Kaushik. *Analytical Development Economics, The Less Developed Economy Revisited,* Cambridge, Mass.: MIT Press, 1997.

Blanchard, B.S., *Logistics Engineering and Management*, Prentice Hall, New Jersey, 1998.

Commons, J. R., *Institutional Economics-Its Place in Political Economy*, The University of Wisconsin Press, Madison, Wisconsin, 1934.

Coyle, J.J., E.J. Bardi, and C.J. Langley: *The Management of Business Logistics*, West/Wadsworth, 1996.

Frank M., *Valuation and Valuation Planning for Closely Held Businesses*, Englewood Cliffs, NJ, Prentice Hall, 1981.

Glaskowsky, N.A., D.R. Hudson, and R.M. Ivie: *Business Logistics*, Wadsworth Pub, 1992.

Granger, Clive W. J.: *Empirical Marketing in Economics, Specification and Evaluation*, London, Cambridge University Press, 1999.

Handfield, R.B. and E.Z. Nichols: *Introduction to Supply Chain Management*, Prentice Hall, New Jersey, 1998.

Hausman, D. M.: *The Inexact and Separate Science of Economics*, Cambridge, Cambridge University Press, 1992.

John A, Marcell, *Handbook of Small Business Valuation Formulas and Rules of Thumb,* Valuation Press, 1993.

Jones, J.V.: *Integrated Logistics Support Handbook*, McGraw Hill, New York, 1998.

Kasilingam, R.G.: *Logistics and Transportation: Design and Planning*, Kluwer Academic Pub., 1999.

Kasper, Larry J.: *Business Valuations, Advanced Topics*, Westport, CT, Quorum Books, 1997.

Lindblom, C. E.: *A Strategy of Decision: Policy Evaluation as a Social Process*, New York, The Free Press, 1970.

March, J. G.: *A Behavioural Theory of the Firm*, Englewood-Cliffs, Prentice Hall, 1963.

Marris, R. L., and Wood, A.: *The Corporate Marketing Economy*, London: Macmillan, 1971.

Nerseian, R.L. and G.B. Swartz: *Computer Simulation in Logistics*, Quorum Books, 1996.

Plous, S.: *The Psychology of Judgement and Decision Making,* New York, McGraw-Hill, 1993

Pooler, V.H. and D. Pooler: *Purchasing and Supply Management: Creating the Vision*, Chapman & Hall, London, 1997.

Rappaport, A.: *Creating Shareholder Value, The New Standard for Business Performance*, New York, Free Press, 1986.

Ross, D.: *Economic Theory and Cognitive Science*, Cambridge, Mass., MIT Press, 2006.

Singh P.P.: *Modern Retail Management: Principles and Techniques*, Regal Pub, Delhi, 2007.

Singh S.K. : *Retail Marketing Research : Measurement and Method*, Anmol, Delhi, 2010.

Smith, V. L.: *Papers in Experimental Economics*, Cambridge, Cambridge University Press, 1991.

Stock, J.R. and D.M. Lambert: *Strategic Logistics Management*, Irwin Professional Pub., 1992.

Tietenberg, Tom, *Environmental Economics and Policy,* New York, HarperCollins, 1994

Tilanus, B.: *Information Systems in Logistics and Transformation*, 2nd Ed., Elsevier Science Ltd., 1997.

Warwick, D. P.: *A Theory of Public Bureaucracy*, Cambridge, MA: Harvard University Press, 1975.

Weber, M.: *The Theory of Social and Economic Organizations*, New York, Oxford University Press, 1947.

Weibull, J. W.: *Advances in Understanding Strategic Behaviour*, New York, Palgrave, 2004.

West, Thomas L.: and Jeffrey D. Jones: *Handbook of Business Valuation*, New York: Wiley, 1992.

Yegge, Wilbur M., *A Basic Guide for Valuing a Company*, New York, Wiley, 1996.

Index

❑❑❑